P9-ASH-936

Praise for *Making up the Mind*

"Chris Frith is well known for his extremely clear thinking on very complex psychological matters, such as agency, social intelligence, and the minds of people with autism and schizophrenia. And it is precisely such questions, along with the understanding of how we perceive, act, choose, remember, and feel, which are now being revolutionized by brain imaging. In *Making up the Mind*, he brings all this together in a most accessible and engaging way."

Oliver Sacks, MD

"*Making up the Mind* is a fascinating guided tour through the elusive interface between mind and brain written by a pioneer in the field. The author's obvious passion for the subject shines through every page."

V.S. Ramachandran, MD

"I soon made up my mind that this is an excellent, most readable and stimulating book. The author is a distinguished neuroscientist working especially on brain imaging."

R.L. Gregory, University of Bristol

"Chris Frith, one of the pioneers in applying brain imaging to study mental processes, has written a brilliant introduction to the biology of mental processes for the general reader. This superb book describes how we recreate in our brains a representation of the external world. Clearly and beautifully written, this book is for all who want to learn about how the brain gives rise to the mental phenomenon of our lives. A must read!"

Eric R. Kandel, Nobel Laureate

"Important and surprising. The brain will never seem the same again."

Lewis Wolpert, University College London

For Uta

Making up the Mind

How the Brain Creates our Mental World

Chris Frith

Blackwell
Publishing

NORTHWEST MISSOURI STATE
UNIVERSITY LIBRARY
MARYVILLE, MO 64468

© 2007 by Chris D. Frith

BLACKWELL PUBLISHING
350 Main Street, Malden, MA 02148-5020, USA
9600 Garsington Road, Oxford OX4 2DQ, UK
550 Swanston Street, Carlton, Victoria 3053, Australia

The right of Chris D. Frith to be identified as the Author of this Work
has been asserted in accordance with the UK Copyright, Designs, and Patents
Act 1988.

All rights reserved. No part of this publication may be reproduced, stored in a
retrieval system, or transmitted, in any form or by any means, electronic,
mechanical, photocopying, recording or otherwise, except as permitted by the
UK Copyright, Designs, and Patents Act 1988, without the prior permission
of the publisher.

First published 2007 by Blackwell Publishing Ltd

3   2008

Library of Congress Cataloging-in-Publication Data

Frith, Christopher D.
    Making up the mind : how the brain creates our mental world / Chris Frith.
       p. cm.
    Includes bibliographical references and index.
    ISBN 978–1–4051–3694–5 (hardcover : alk. paper)—
ISBN 978–1–4051–6022–3 (pbk. : alk. paper)   1. Brain—Popular works.
2. Human behavior—Physiological aspects.   3. Neuropsychiatry—Popular
works.   4. Neuropsychology—Popular works.   I. Title.

    QP376.F686 2007
    612.8′2—dc22

                                                              2006038336

A catalogue record for this title is available from the British Library.

Set in 10/13pt Galliard
by Graphicraft Limited, Hong Kong
Printed and bound in Great Britain by
by TJ International Ltd, Padstow, Cornwall

The publisher's policy is to use permanent paper from mills that operate a
sustainable forestry policy, and which has been manufactured from pulp
processed using acid-free and elementary chlorine-free practices. Furthermore,
the publisher ensures that the text paper and cover board used have met
acceptable environmental accreditation standards.

For further information on
Blackwell Publishing, visit our website:
www.blackwellpublishing.com

612.82
F91m

Contents

OCT 0 3 2008

Abbreviations

BOLD	blood oxygenation level dependent
CAT	computerized axial tomography
EEG	electroencephalogram
FFA	fusiform face area
fMRI	functional magnetic resonance imaging
MRI	magnetic resonance imaging
PET	positron emission tomography
PPA	parahippocampal place area
REM	rapid eye movement
TD	temporal difference

Preface

Inside my head there is an amazing labor-saving device. Better even than a dishwasher or a calculator, my brain releases me from the dull, repetitive task of recognizing the things in the world around me, and even saves me from needing to think about how to control my movements. I can concentrate on the important things in life: making friends and sharing ideas. But, of course, my brain doesn't just save me from tedious chores. My brain creates the "me" that is released into the social world. Moreover, it is my brain that enables me to share my mental life with my friends and thereby allows us to create something bigger than any of us are capable of on our own. This book describes how the brain makes this magic.

Acknowledgments

My work on the mind and the brain has been possible through funding from the Medical Research Council and the Wellcome Trust. The MRC enabled my work on the neuropsychology of schizophrenia through its support of Tim Crow's psychiatry unit in the Clinical Research Centre at Northwick Park Hospital in Harrow, Middlesex. At that time we could only make indirect inferences about relationships between the mind and the brain, but this all changed in the 1980s with the development of brain scanners. The Wellcome Trust enabled Richard Frackowiak to create the Functional Imaging Laboratory and supported my investigations there into the neural correlates of consciousness and social interactions. The study of the mind and the brain cuts across traditional disciplines, from anatomy and computational neurobiology to philosophy and anthropology. I have been fortunate that I have always worked in multidisciplinary – and multinational – groups.

I have benefited greatly from my interactions with my colleagues and friends at University College London, in particular Ray Dolan, Dick Passingham, Daniel Wolpert, Tim Shallice, Jon Driver, Paul Burgess, and Patrick Haggard. At the early stages of this book I had many fruitful discussions on the brain and the mind with my friends at Aarhus, Jakob Hohwy and Andreas Roepstorff, and at Salzburg, Josef Perner and Heinz Wimmer. Martin Frith and John Law have argued with me about many of the topics covered in this book for as long as I can remember. Eve Johnstone and Sean Spence generously gave me expert advice on psychiatric phenomena and their significance for brain science.

Perhaps the most important impetus for writing this book came from my weekly discussions with the breakfast group, past and present. Sarah-Jayne Blakemore, Davina Bristow, Thierry Chaminade, Jenny Coull,

Andrew Duggins, Chloë Farrer, Helen Gallagher, Tony Jack, James Kilner, Hakwan Lau, Emiliano Macaluso, Eleanor Maguire, Pierre Maquet, Jen Marchant, Dean Mobbs, Mathias Pessiglione, Chiara Portas, Geraint Rees, Johannes Schultz, Sukhi Shergill, and Tania Singer all have helped to shape this book. I am deeply grateful to them.

Karl Friston and Richard Gregory read sections of the book and have given me much help and useful advice. I am grateful to Paul Fletcher for his encouragement at an early stage to create the Professor of English and the other characters who argue with the narrator.

Philip Carpenter went well beyond the call of duty to provide incisive comments.

Most of all I am grateful to those who read all the chapters and provided detailed comments. Shaun Gallagher and two anonymous readers made many useful suggestions. Rosalind Ridley caused me to think more carefully about my claims and to be more precise in my terminology. Alex Frith helped me to eliminate jargon and failures of continuity.

Uta Frith was closely involved in all stages of the development of the project. Without her example and guidance this book would not exist.

Prologue: Real Scientists Don't Study the Mind

The Psychologist's Fear of the Party

Just like any other tribe, scientists have a hierarchy. Psychologists are somewhere near the bottom. I discovered this in my first year at university, where I was studying natural sciences. It was announced that, for the first time, students would be able to study psychology in part 1 of the natural sciences tripos. I went eagerly to my college tutor to ask him if he knew anything about this new possibility. "Yes," he replied. "But I didn't think any of my students would be crass enough to want to study psychology." He was a physicist.

Possibly because I was not entirely sure what "crass" meant, I was undeterred by this remark. I switched from physics to psychology. I have continued to study psychology ever since, but I have never forgotten about my place in the hierarchy. Inevitably the question will come up at academic parties, "so what do you do?" and I think twice about replying, "I'm a psychologist."

Of course, much has changed in psychology over the last 30 years. We have borrowed many skills and concepts from other disciplines. We study the brain as well as behavior. We use computers extensively to analyze our data and to provide metaphors for how the mind works.[1] My university identity badge doesn't say "Psychologist," but "Cognitive Neuroscientist."

"So what do you do?" someone asks. I think she's the new Head of Physics. Unfortunately the reply, "I'm a cognitive neuroscientist" to the

---

[1] I have to admit that there are a few diehards who deny that the study of the brain or of computers can tell us anything about how the mind works.

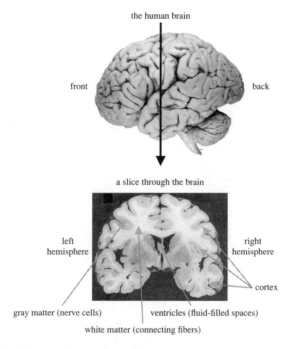

Figure p.1 Whole brain and post-mortem slice
The human brain seen from the side (top). The arrow indicates where this has been sliced to reveal the lower picture. The brain's outermost layer (the cortex) consists of gray matter and is heavily folded in order to fit a large surface area into a small volume. The cortex contains about 10 billion nerve cells.

Source: University of Wisconsin-Madison Brain Collection 69-314, *http://www.brainmuseum.org*. Images and specimens funded by the National Science Foundation, as well as by the National Institute of Health.

question simply delays matters. After I have tried to explain what I actually do, she says, "Ah, you're a psychologist!" with that characteristic look which I translate to mean, "Wouldn't you rather be doing real science?"

The Professor of English joins the conversation and starts talking about psychoanalysis. One of her new girls is "having difficulty accepting Freud." I don't want to spoil my drinking time by proposing that Freud was a story-teller whose speculations about the human mind were largely irrelevant.

A few years ago the editor of the *British Journal of Psychiatry*, no doubt in error, asked me to assess a Freudian paper. I was immediately struck by a subtle difference from the papers I usually assess. As in any scientific paper, there were lots of "references." "References" refer to papers already published on the same topic. We make these references partly to acknowledge the work of our predecessors, but mainly to support the claims we make in our own paper. "Don't just take my word for it. You will find my methods fully justified in Box & Cox (1964)."[2] But no attempt was made to support the evidence in the Freudian paper. The references were not about the evidence. They were about the ideas. Using these references you could trace the development of these ideas through the various followers of Freud back to the original words of the master himself. No evidence was presented as to whether the ideas of the master were right.

"Freud may have had a big influence on literary criticism," I say to the Professor of English, "but he was no scientist. He wasn't interested in evidence. I study psychology scientifically."

"So," she replies, "you use the monster of mechanical reason to kill off our humanity."[3]

From both sides of the cultural divide I get the same response, "Scientists can't study the mind." So what's the problem?

Hard Science and Soft Science

In the dominance hierarchy of science, the top sciences are "hard" while those at the bottom are "soft." "Hard" doesn't mean that the science is more difficult. "Hard" relates to the subject matter of the science and the sort of measurements that can be made. Hard things like diamonds have definite edges that can be measured precisely. Soft things like ice creams have edges that are ill defined and may vary from one measurement to the next. The hard sciences, such as physics and chemistry, study tangible things that can be measured very precisely. For example, the speed of light (in a vacuum) is exactly 299,792,458 meters per second. An atom of iron is 55.405 times heavier than an atom of hydrogen. These numbers are very important. From the atomic weights of the

---

[2]   Believe it or not, this is a genuine reference to an important statistical method, which you will find at the end of the book.
[3]   She is a specialist in the works of the Australian novelist Elizabeth Costello.

various elements the periodic table could be constructed providing the first clues about the sub-atomic structure of matter.

Biology used to be a rather softer science than physics and chemistry, but this changed dramatically with the discovery that genes consist of precise sequences of base pairs in DNA molecules. For example, the sheep prion gene has 960 base pairs, starting ctgcagactttaagtgattcttacgtgggc, etc., etc.

Confronted with this precision of measurement, I have to admit that psychology is very soft. The most famous number in psychology is 7, the number of items that can be held in working memory.[4] But even this number has to be qualified. The title of the original paper written by George Miller in 1956 was "The Magical Number Seven, Plus or Minus Two." So the best measurement that psychologists have come up with can vary by nearly 30%. The number of items you can hold in working memory varies from time to time and from person to person. I will remember fewer numbers if I am tired or anxious. As an English speaker I can remember more numbers than a Welsh speaker.[5] "What did you expect?" says the Professor of English. "You can't pin down the human mind like a butterfly in a display case. Each one of us is different."

This remark misses the point. Of course each one of us is different. But there are also properties of the mind that are common to us all. It is these fundamental properties that psychologists are trying to discover. Chemists had exactly the same problems with the rocks they were studying before the discovery of the chemical elements in the 18th century. Every rock was different. In comparison with the "hard" sciences, psychology has had little time to discover what to measure or how to measure it. Psychology has existed for just over 100 years as a scientific discipline. I am confident that, in time, psychologists will have discovered what to measure and will have developed the instruments that will help us to make these measurements very precisely.

---

[4]   Working memory is a form of active short-term memory. This is the kind of memory we use when we try to keep a telephone number in mind without writing it down. Psychologists and neuroscientists have studied working memory intensively, but have yet to reach agreement about precisely what it is they are studying.

[5]   This statement does not reveal some anti-Welsh prejudice, but refers to one of the many important discoveries psychologists have made about working memory. Welsh speakers remember fewer numbers because sequences of numbers in Welsh take longer to say than their English equivalents.

Hard Science – Objective;
Soft Science – Subjective

These are optimistic words justified by my belief in the inexorable progress of science.[6] The problem is that, for psychology, this optimism may not be justified. There is something fundamentally different about the things we are trying to measure.

The measurements made by the hard sciences are objective. They can be checked. "You don't believe that speed of light is 299,792,458 meters per second? Here's the equipment. Measure it yourself." Once we have used the equipment to make the measurement, the numbers come from dials and print-outs and computer screens that anyone can read. But psychologists use themselves or their volunteers as measuring instruments. These measurements are subjective. They cannot be checked.

Here is a simple psychological experiment. I program my computer to display a field of black dots that moves continuously downward from the top to the bottom of the screen. I stare at the screen for a minute or two. Then I press *escape* and the dots stop moving. Objectively the dots are no longer moving. If I place the point of my pencil on top of one of the dots, I can check that it is definitely not moving. But I have the very strong subjective impression that the dots are moving slowly upward.[7] If you came into the room at that moment, you would see the stationary dots on the screen. I would tell you that the dots seemed to be moving upward, but how can you check this? The movement is only happening in my mind.

Of course, everyone can experience this illusion of movement. If you stared at the moving dots for a minute or two, then you would also see movement in the stationary dots. But now the movement is in your mind and I can't check it. And there are many other experiences that we cannot share. For example, I could tell you that, whenever I go to a party, I find myself remembering the face of the professor with whom I argued about Freud. What sort of an experience is this? Do I really have an image of her face? Do I remember the event, or do I just remember

---

[6]   This belief is not shared by the Professor of English
[7]   This phenomenon is known as the waterfall illusion or the motion after-effect. If you stare at a waterfall for a minute or two and then look at the bushes to the side, you will get the distinct impression that the bushes are moving upward, even though you can also see that they are clearly staying in the same place.

writing about the event? Such experiences can never be checked. How can they be the basis of scientific study?

A real scientist wants to make her own, independent check on the measurements reported by someone else. "*Nullius in verba*" is the motto of the Royal Society of London: "Don't believe what people tell you, however authoritative they may be."[8] If I followed this principle, then I would have to agree that the scientific study of your mental life is impossible because I rely on your report of your mental experience.

For a while psychologists pretended to be real scientists by studying only behavior: making objective measurements of things like movements and button-presses and reaction times.[9] But studying behavior is never enough. It misses out on everything that is interesting about human experience. We all know that our mental life is just as real as our life in the physical world. Rejection by the one we love causes as much pain as a burn from a hot oven.[10] Mental practice can cause improvements in performance that can be measured objectively. For example, if you imagine playing a particular piece on the piano, then your perform- ance will improve. So why can't I accept your report that you were imagining playing the piano? Now we psychologists are back studying subjective experiences: perceptions, recollections, intentions. But the problem remains: The mental things that we study have a completely different status from the material things that other scientists study. The only way I can know about the things in your mind is because you tell me about them. You press a button to tell me when you see the red light. You tell me precisely what shade of red it is. But there is no way I can get into your mind and check the redness of your experience.

For my friend Rosalind, numbers have special positions in space and days of the week have special colors (see Figure CP1, color plate section). But aren't these just metaphors? I don't have such experiences. Why should I believe her when she says these are direct sensory experiences that she cannot control? Her experiences are examples of something in the mental world that I can never check.

---

[8]   *Nullius addictus iurarae in verba magistri*: "I am not bound to swear allegiance to the word of any master." Horace, *Epistulae*.

[9]   These were the behaviourists, of whom the most famous advocates were John Watson and B.F. Skinner. The fervor with which they promoted their approach hints at its unsatis- factory nature. One of my tutors at college was an ardent behaviorist who later became a psychoanalyst.

[10]   Indeed, brain imaging studies suggest that physical pain and the pain of social rejection involve the same brain regions.

Can Big Science Save Soft Science?

Hard science becomes big science when the measuring instruments used are very expensive. Brain sciences became big when brain scanners were developed in the last quarter of the 20th century. A brain scanner typically costs over £1000,000. By pure luck, by being in the right place at the right time, I was able to use these machines as soon as they became available in the mid-1980s.[11] The first machines were based on the long-established principle of the X-ray. The X-ray machine can show you the bones inside your body because bones are much more solid (dense) than skin and flesh. Few X-rays get through the bone, but many get through the flesh. This variation in density is also found in the brain. The bony skull around the brain is very dense; the brain tissue itself is much less dense, like flesh. In the middle of the brain are spaces (the ventricles) that are filled with liquid, so that these spaces are the least dense of all. The breakthrough came with the development of the technique of computerized axial tomography (CAT) and the construction of the CAT scanner. This machine uses X-rays to measure density and then solves a very large number of mathematical equations (needing a powerful computer) to construct a three-dimensional image of the brain (or any other part of the body) showing the variations in density. For the first time it was possible to see the internal structure of the brain in a living volunteer.

A few years later an even better technique was developed called magnetic resonance imaging (MRI). This technique does not use X-rays, but radio waves and a very strong magnetic field.[12] Unlike X-rays, this procedure poses no risk to health. The MRI scanner is far more sensitive to differences in density than the CAT scanner is. The pictures it produces distinguish between different kinds of brain tissue. These pictures of the living brain are of the same quality as a photograph of a brain after death that has been removed from the skull, preserved with chemicals, and cut into slices.

---

[11] The decision of the Medical Research Council to close down the Clinical Research Centre where I had worked for many years on the problem of schizophrenia gave me the impetus to risk a major change in my career as a psychologist. Subsequently both the MRC and the Wellcome Trust have shown great foresight in their support for the new brain imaging technology.

[12] No, I don't really understand how MRI works, but here is a physicist who does. J.P. Hornak, "The Basics of MRI," *http://www.cis.rit.edu/htbooks/mri/index.html*.

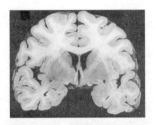

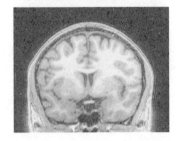

Figure p.2 Example of structural scan (MRI) alongside photo of a post-mortem brain slice
The upper picture shows a brain that has been removed from the skull after death and
sliced. The lower picture has been acquired from a living volunteer using magnetic
resonance imaging (MRI).
Source: Functional Imaging Laboratory; thanks to Chloe Hutton.

Structural brain imaging has had an enormous impact on medicine.
Brain damage, whether caused by a road accident, a stroke, or the growth
of a tumor, can have dramatic effects on behavior. There might be severe
loss of memory or a dramatic change in personality. Before brain scanners

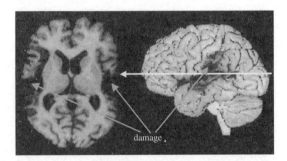

Figure p.3 Example of MRI scan revealing brain lesion
This patient had the misfortune to experience two successive strokes which destroyed his left
and right auditory cortex. The damage can clearly be seen in the magnetic resonance image.
Source: Figure 2 in: Engelien, A., Huber, W., Silbersweig, D., Stern, E., Frith, C.D., Doring, W.,
Thron, A., & Frackowiak, R.S. (2000). The neural correlates of "deaf-hearing" in man:
Conscious sensory awareness enabled by attentional modulation. *Brain*, *123*(Pt. 3), 532–545.
Used with permission.

existed the only way to discover exactly where the brain damage had occurred was to open up the skull and look. This was mainly done after death, but occasionally in life when neuro-surgery was required. Brain scanners can now precisely locate the damage. All the sufferer has to do is lie still in the scanner for about 15 minutes.

Structural brain imaging is hard science as well as big science. The measurements of brain structure based on these techniques can be very precise and objective. How are such measurements relevant to the problem with psychology?

Measuring Mental Activity

Help for the problem with psychology did not come from the *structural* brain scanners. It came from the *functional* brain scanners that were developed a few years later. These scanners detect the energy consumed by the brain. Whether we are awake or asleep, the 10 billion nerve cells (neurons) in our brain are continuously sending messages to each other. This activity uses up energy. Indeed our brain consumes about 20% of our body's energy even though the brain is only 2% of our body in terms of its weight. There is a network of blood vessels throughout the brain through which energy can be distributed in the form of oxygen carried in the blood. This energy distribution is finely tuned so that more energy is sent to the region of the brain that is currently most active. If we are using our ears, then the most active part of the brain will be two regions at the side where neurons receive messages directly from the ears (see Figure CP2, color plate section). When the neurons in this region are active, there will also be greater local supply of blood. This relationship between brain activity and local changes in blood flow was known to physiologists for more than 100 years, but it was not possible to detect the changes in blood flow until brain scanners were invented.[13] The functional brain scanners (positron emission tomography, PET and functional magnetic resonance imaging, fMRI) detect these changes in blood supply that indicate which region of the brain is currently most active.

The major disadvantage of brain scanners is the discomfort experienced by the person being scanned. You have to lie flat on your back for an hour or so, keeping as still as possible. There is very little you can

---

[13] In 1928 someone was found who had an abnormality in the blood supply to the back of his brain. It was possible to hear the change in blood flow in the visual area of his brain as he opened and closed his eyes.

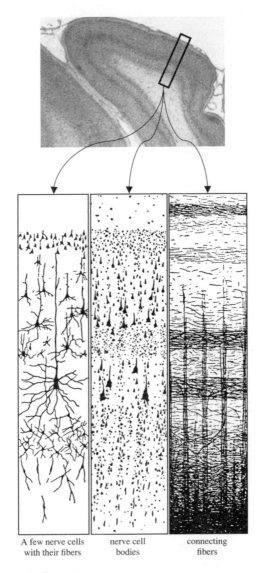

A few nerve cells
with their fibers

nerve cell
bodies

connecting
fibers

Figure p.4   Cortex and cells
The cortex under the microscope showing three different aspects of nerve cells.

Source: Figure 11.2 in: Zeki, S. (1993). A vision of the brain. Oxford: Blackwell; Figure E1-3 in:
Popper, K.R., & Eccles, J.C. (1977). *The self and its brain*. London: Routledge & Kegan Paul.

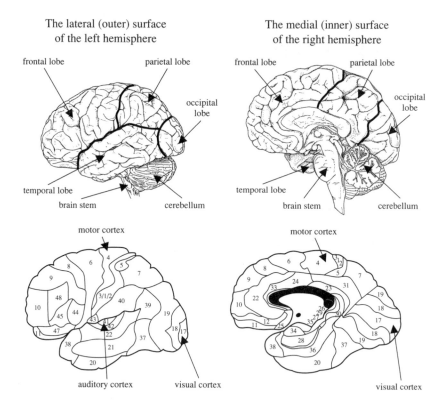

Figure p.5 Brain regions and subdivisions
The upper pictures show the major brain regions.
The lower pictures show subdivisions of the cortex according to Brodmann (cerebellum and brain stem removed). Brodmann's subdivisions are based on the appearance of the cortex under the microscope. His numbers are arbitrary.

actually do in a scanner except think, and even that is difficult with fMRI since the noise it makes is equivalent to someone operating a small pneumatic drill next to your head. In one of the very early, pioneering studies using a primitive form of PET scanner, volunteers were asked to imagine leaving their house and then to imagine turning left at every street corner they came to.[14] This purely mental activity was quite sufficient to activate many brain areas.

[14] This pioneering work occurred in Scandinavia. David Ingvar and Niels Lassen developed the earliest form of functional brain scanning for people. In the first study they injected radioactive material into each other's carotid arteries! Subsequently Per Roland used a more volunteer-friendly version of this technique to look at brain activity when people imagined walking from their house.

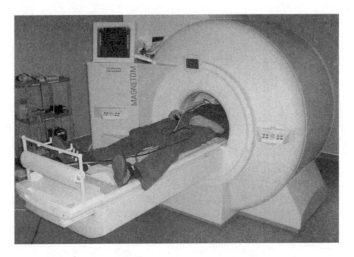

Figure p.6 A volunteer lying in a brain scanner
Source: Functional Imaging Laboratory; thanks to David Bradbury.

And this is where big science comes to the aid of soft psychology. The person in the scanner imagines he[15] is walking along the street. He is not actually moving or seeing anything. These events are only in his mind. I have no way of getting into his mind to check that he is really doing what he was asked to do. But by using the scanner I can get into his brain. And I can see that his brain shows a particular pattern of activity when he imagines walking along the street and turning left.

Of course, most brain imaging studies are much more objective. Real lights are flashed in the volunteer's eyes and the volunteer presses buttons to show that he is making real finger movements. But I (and a few others) have always been more interested in the brain activity associated with purely mental events. We have found that when a volunteer imagines that he is pressing a button, then the same brain areas become active as when he is really pressing a button. If we had no brain scanner, there would be absolutely no objective sign that our volunteer was imagining pressing a button. We check that there are no tiny finger

---

[15] Seeing the glint in the eye of the Professor of English, I must quickly state that this is not sexist. The early functional imaging studies used PET rather than fMRI. With this technique the volunteer is injected with small amounts of radioactive material. Because of the health risks, most of these studies were restricted to men, or young, right-handed male students, to be more precise.

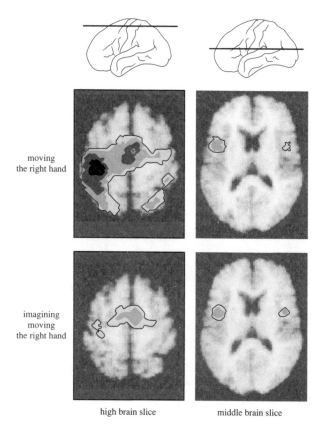

Figure p.7 Brain images of real movement and imaginary movements
Top figures show positions (high and middle) of the brain cross-sections made to reveal activity. Upper cross-sections show the activity when you move your right hand; lower ones show the activity when you imagine moving it.

Source: Redrawn from Figures 1 and 3 in: Stephan, K.M., Fink, G.R., Passingham, R.E., Silbersweig, D., Ceballos-Baumann, A.O., Frith, C.D., Frackowiak, R.S. (1995). Functional anatomy of the mental representation of upper extremity movements in healthy subjects. *Journal of Neurophysiology*, *73*(1), 373–386. Used with permission.

movements or twitches of the muscles. We assume that he is following our instructions to imagine that he is pressing the button every time he hears the signal. By measuring brain activity, we have an objective confirmation of these mental events. By using a brain scanner, I could probably tell whether you were imagining moving your finger or your foot. But, as yet, I probably could not tell which finger you were thinking about.

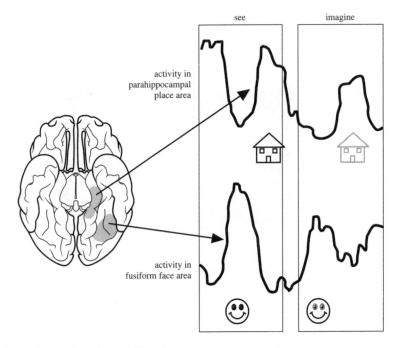

Figure p.8 Imagining faces and houses
The brain is seen from underneath showing areas that respond differentially to faces and places. The drawing on the right shows that activity in the face area increases when you see a face or when you imagine a face. The same effect is also seen for the place area.

Source: Redrawn from Figure 3 in: O'Craven, K.M., & Kanwisher, N. (2000). Mental imagery of faces and places activates corresponding stimulus-specific brain regions. *Journal of Cognitive Neuroscience*, *12*(6), 1013–1023.

I could do even better by studying vision. Nancy Kanwisher and her group at MIT have shown that when you look at a face (any face) a particular region of the brain consistently becomes active, whereas when you look at a house (any house) another nearby brain region becomes active.[16] If you ask people to imagine the face or the house they have seen a few seconds before, the same brain regions become active. The location of the brain activity indicates whether the person is thinking about a face or a house. If I am lying in her scanner, Dr Kanwisher can tell me what I am thinking about (as long as I only think about faces or houses).

[16]   An area of the brain that responds specifically to faces was first reported by Aina Puce and colleagues in 1995. Subsequently Nancy Kanwisher confirmed this observation, coining the term fusiform face area (FFA) and, later, parahippocampal place area (PPA).

So the problem with psychology is solved. We no longer need to worry about these soft, subjective accounts of mental life. We can make hard, objective measurements of brain activity instead. Perhaps now I can admit that I am a psychologist.

Back at the party I can't restrain myself from telling them all about the big science of brain imaging. The physicist quite likes this new development in psychology. After all without physicists it would never have happened. But the Professor of English doesn't accept that studying brain activity can tell you anything about the human mind.

"You used to think of the mind as a camera. Now you think of it as a computer. Even if you can see inside this computer, you still have the same tired metaphor. Computers are certainly cleverer than cameras. Maybe computers can recognize faces and pick up eggs with their robot arms.[17] But they will never think of new ideas and communicate them to other computers. They will never create a computer culture. This is beyond the reach of mechanical reasoning."

I move off to refill my glass. I don't argue. I am not a philosopher. I do not expect to persuade people of truth by the power of argument. The only arguments I accept come from practical experiments. I have to show how the impossible can be done.

How Can the Mental Emerge from the Physical?

Of course it is nonsense to think that we can just measure brain activity and forget about the mind. Brain activity can indicate that mental activity is occurring and, to that extent, provides an objective marker of subjective experience. But brain activity is not the same as mental experience. With the right equipment I could probably find a neuron in my brain that only responds when I experience the color blue. But, as the Professor of English would delight in telling me, the activity isn't blue. What the brain imaging experiments reveal so starkly is the seemingly unbridgeable gap between objective physical matter and subjective mental experience.

The hard sciences are concerned with material objects that can directly affect our senses. We can see light. We can feel the weight of a lump of iron. Hard sciences often involve hard physical work with the material being studied. Marie Curie is the romantic model for such a scientist, allegedly handling several tons of pitchblend in order to extract one-

---

[17]   In fact computers are not very good at recognizing faces or picking up objects.

tenth of a gram of radium. It was her hard physical work that led to the identification of radium, the medical use of X-rays, and, ultimately, the development of brain scanners. Of course, special instruments have been developed to help us make accurate measurements when we are dealing with very rare elements like radium, very small things like the base pairs in gene sequences, or very fast things like light. But these special instruments are, like magnifying glasses, simply extensions of our senses. They help us to see what is really there. No such instrument can help us see what is happening in the mind. The contents of the mind are not real.

I Can Read Your Mind

And then finally at the party comes the inevitable interaction that I fear most of all. This time the question comes from a cocky young man with no tie, probably a molecular geneticist.

"You're a psychologist? So can you can read my mind?"

He must be clever. How can he say such a stupid thing? He just says it to annoy me.

Only very recently did I come to realize that I was the stupid one. Of course I can read people's minds. And it's not just psychologists who can do this. We all read each other's minds all the time. How else are we able to exchange ideas and create culture? But how do our brains enable us to enter those private worlds hidden in the minds of others?

I can see the edges of the universe with a telescope and I can see the activity in your brain with a scanner, but I can't "see" into your mind. The mental world, we all believe, is quite distinct from physical reality. And yet in everyday life we are at least as much concerned with other minds as we are with physical reality. Most of our interactions with other people are interactions between minds, not between bodies. You are learning about my mind by reading this book. I am hoping to change the ideas in your mind by writing this book.

How the Brain Creates the World

So is this the problem for psychologists? We try to study mental life and mental events, while "real" science is concerned with the physical world? The physical world is utterly different from the mental world. We have direct contract with the physical world through our senses. But the mental world is private to each one of us. How can such a world be studied?

In this book I shall show that this distinction between the mental and the physical is false. It is an illusion created by the brain. Everything we know, whether it is about the physical or the mental world, comes to us through our brain. But our brain's connection with the physical world of objects is no more direct than our brain's connection with the mental world of ideas. By hiding from us all the unconscious inferences that it makes, our brain creates the illusion that we have direct contact with objects in the physical world. And at the same time our brain creates the illusion that our own mental world is isolated and private. Through these two illusions we experience ourselves as agents, acting independently upon the world. But, at the same time, we can share our experiences of the world. Over the millennia this ability to share experience has created human culture that has, in its turn, modified the functioning of the human brain.[18]

By seeing through these illusions created by our brain, we can begin to develop a science that explains how the brain creates the mind.

"But don't expect me just to believe what you say," says the Professor of English. "Show me the evidence."

And I promise her that, throughout this book, everything I say will be supported by rigorous experimental evidence. If you wish to check the sources for this evidence, you will find them laid out at the end of the book.

---

[18]   The letters used to write English are very ambiguous. There are 1,120 ways of representing 40 sounds in English. There are only 33 ways to represent 25 sounds in Italian. As a result, people brought up in English-speaking countries use slightly different brain areas for reading than people brought up in Italy.

Part I

Seeing through the Brain's Illusions

Chapter 1

Clues from a Damaged Brain

Sensing the Physical World

Chemistry was my worst subject at school. The only bit of science I remember from those lessons was a trick to use in practicals. You are confronted with a lot of little dishes of white powder that you are supposed to identify. Try tasting them. The one that tastes sweet is *lead acetate*. Just don't taste too much of it.

This is the ordinary person's approach to chemistry, usually applied to the contents of those jars at the back of the kitchen cupboard. If you can't tell what it is by looking at it, then try tasting it. This is how we find out about the physical world. We explore it with our senses.

It follows that, if your senses are damaged, then your ability to explore the physical world will be reduced. You are probably short-sighted.[1] If I ask you to take your glasses off and look around, you will no longer be able to identify small objects that are more than a few feet away. This observation is not very surprising. It is our sense organs, eyes, ears, tongue, etc., that provide the link between the physical world and our minds. Just like a video recorder, our eyes and ears pick up information[2] about the physical world and transmit it to our minds. If our eyes or ears are damaged, then the information can no longer be transmitted properly. It will not be so easy for us to find out about the world.

The problem becomes more interesting when we start to wonder how the information gets from the eyes to the mind. Let us for the moment

[1] About one third of the general population is short-sighted. But short-sightedness is even more frequent in people like you who do a lot of reading and are of high intelligence.
[2] The development of a method of measuring information was of major importance in the development of computers and in the understanding of brain function (see Chapter 5).

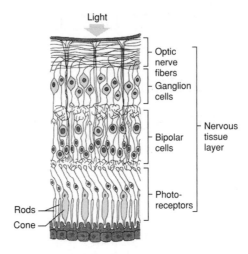

Figure 1.1   The retina, where light creates brain activity
The retina at the back of the eye contains large number of special neurons (photo-receptors) that become active when struck by light. In the middle of the retina (the fovea) are the cones. There are three kinds of cone that are activated by different wavelengths of light (corresponding to red, green, and blue). Around the fovea are the rods that respond to dim light of any color. All theses cells send signals via the optic nerve to the visual cortex.

Source: Prof. W.S. Stark, Biology, St. Louis University, Missouri.

suppress our worry about how electrical activity in a photo-receptor in the eye[3] gets turned into a mental experience of color and simply note that the information from my eye (and ear and tongue, etc.) goes to my brain. It follows that damage to my brain can also reduce my ability to find out about the physical world.

The Mind and the Brain

Before we explore how brain damage can affect our experience of the world, we need to worry a bit more about the relationship between the mind and the brain. The relationship must be close. As we discovered in the Prologue, if I decide to think about a face, then a specific "face" area

---

[3]   Light has to pass through various blood vessels before it reaches the light-sensitive cells in the retina. We are not aware of all these blood vessels that we have to look through in order to see the world outside. But they may be the origin of the "pink elephants" supposedly seen by some heavy drinkers.

in my brain will become active. In this example, knowing about the contents of my mind has enabled me to predict which brain area will be active. As we shall discover in a moment, damage to the brain can have profound effects on the mind. Indeed, knowing where the brain has been damaged enables me to predict the contents of the person's mind. But the relationship between brain and mind is not perfect. It is not one-to-one. There can be changes in the activity in my brain without any changes in my mind. On the other hand I firmly believe that there cannot be changes in my mind without there also being changes in brain activity.[4] This is because I believe that everything that happens in my mind (mental activity) is caused by, or at least depends upon, brain activity.[5]

So, if my belief is correct, the chain of events would be something like this. Light strikes the sensory receptors in my eye causing the receptors to send messages to brain. This mechanism is pretty well understood. Then the activity in the brain somehow creates the experience of color and shape in my mind. This mechanism is not understood at all. But, whatever the mechanism, we can conclude that my mind can have no knowledge about the physical world that isn't somehow represented in the brain.[6] I can only know about that world through my brain. So perhaps the question we should be asking is not, "How do I (or how does my mind) know about the physical world?" Instead we should ask "How does my brain know about the physical world?"[7] By asking the question about the brain, rather than the mind, I can put off for a moment the problem of how knowledge about the physical world gets into my mind. Unfortunately this trick doesn't really work. The first

[4]   I am not a dualist.

[5]   I am a materialist. But I admit that I sometimes sound like a dualist. I talk of the brain "not telling me everything it knows" or "deceiving me." I use such phrases because this is what the experience is like. Most of what my brain does never reaches my consciousness. This is the stuff that my brain knows about, but I don't. On the other hand I am firmly convinced that I am a product of my brain, as is the awareness that accompanies me.

[6]   Neurophysiologists often talk of activity in neurons "representing" something outside in the physical world. For example, neurons can be found that only become active when the eye is stimulated by red light. Activity in such a neuron is said to represent the color red. It has even been claimed that activity in certain neurons at the front of the brain "represents to-be-attended information."

[7]   The Professor of English doesn't like this formulation. "Does the brain 'know' things? Only minds can know things. An encyclopedia contains information about the world, but we would not say that the encyclopedia knows about the world. Is the brain like an encyclopedia with activity in neurons replacing letters on a page? If so, who reads it?"

thing I would do if I wanted to find out what your brain knew about the outside would be to ask *you*, "What can you see?" I am using your mind to find out what's represented in your brain. As we shall see, this method doesn't always work.

When the Brain Doesn't Know

Of all the sensory systems in the brain, we know most about the visual system.[8] The visual world is first represented in the neurons at the back of the retina. Just as in a camera, the image is upside-down and mirror-reversed, so that neurons at the top left of the retina represent the bottom right of the visual scene. The retina sends signals to the primary visual cortex (V1) at the back of the brain via the thalamus, a sensory relay station in the middle of the brain. The neurons conveying the signal partially cross over, so that the left side of each eye is represented in the right half of the brain, and vice versa. The "photographic" image is retained in the primary visual cortex,[9] so that neurons at the top left of the cortical area represent the bottom right of the visual scene.

The effect of damage to the primary visual cortex depends upon where the damage occurs. If the top left region of the visual cortex is damaged, then the sufferer will experience a blank area in the bottom right of the visual scene. In this part of the visual field they are blind.

Some people who suffer from migraines experience brief periods in which part of the visual field goes blank due to a temporary reduction of blood supply to the visual cortex. The experience often starts with a small blank area that gradually gets larger and larger. The blank area is often edged by flashing zig-zag lines described as fortifications.

Before information in the primary visual cortex is passed on to the next processing stage in the brain, the visual scene is deconstructed into different features such as shape, color, and motion. These different features are passed on to different brain areas. In rare cases damage can occur to brain regions concerned with just one of these specific features while all other areas remain intact. If the color area (V4) is damaged, then the sufferer sees the world drained of color (achromatopsia). Since we have

[8]   If you want to learn more about the visual system of the brain, read Semir Zeki's book *A Vision of the Brain*.
[9]   This is called a retinotopic representation since activity in particular neurons represents light hitting a particular part of the retina. This means that whenever I move my eyes, the pattern of activity in the primary visual cortex will change dramatically. But I don't see the world changing.

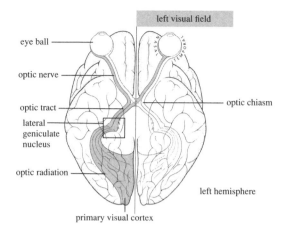

Figure 1.2   How neural activity gets from the retina to the visual cortex
Light from the left side of the visual field goes to the right hemisphere. The brain is seen
from underneath.

Source: Figure 3.3 in: Zeki, S. (1993). *A vision of the brain*. Oxford, Boston: Blackwell
Scientific Publications.

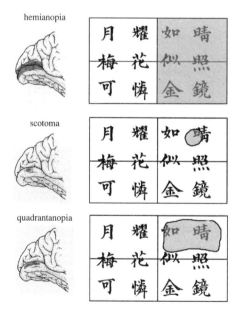

Figure 1.3   How damage to the visual cortex affects experience
Damage to the visual cortex causes blindness in specific regions of the visual field. Loss of
the whole of the right visual cortex causes blindness in the left visual field (hemianopia).
Loss of a small area in the lower right visual cortex causes a spot of blindness in the upper
left visual field (scotoma). Loss of the whole of the lower right visual cortex cause blindness
in the upper right visual field (quadrantanopia).

Source: From figure 3.7 in: Zeki, S. (1993). *A vision of the brain*. Oxford, Boston: Blackwell
Scientific Publications.

0 minutes   3 minutes

7 minutes   10 minutes

Figure 1.4 The development of a migraine, described by Karl Lashley
At the beginning of his migraine an area of blindness appeared near the middle of his visual field and then slowly increased in size.
Source: Lashley, K. (1941). Patterns of cerebral integration indicated by scotomas of migraine. *Archives of Neurological Psychiatry, 46*, 331–339.

all seen black and white films and photographs, this experience is not too difficult to imagine. It is more difficult to imagine the world of someone with damage to the visual movement area (V5). From one moment to the next, objects, such as cars, will appear in different positions – but they don't appear to move (akinetopsia). This experience must be something like the opposite of the waterfall illusion that I mentioned in the Prologue. In that illusion, which we can all experience, objects stay in the same place from one moment to the next, but we still see movement.

At the next stage of visual processing, information from features such as shape and color is recombined in order to recognize the objects in the visual scene. The brain regions where this occurs can sometimes be damaged while the earlier visual processing regions remain intact. Some people with this condition have a general problem recognizing objects. They can see and describe the various features of the object, but they don't know what the object is. This problem is referred to as "agnosia" or loss of knowledge.[10] The basic sensory information is available, but it can no longer be understood. Sometimes these people have a specific problem with faces (prosopagnosia). They know it's a face, but they have no idea whose face it is. These people have damage to the face area that I described in the Prologue.

---

[10]   The term "agnosia" was introduced by Freud before he got distracted by psychoanalysis.

These observations all seem straightforward. Damage to the brain interferes with the transmission of information picked up by our senses from the physical world. The effect upon what our mind can know about the world is determined by the stage in transmission at which the damage occurs. But sometimes the brain plays tricks on us.

When the Brain Knows, But Doesn't Tell

It is the dream of every neuropsychologist[11] to discover someone who has such an unusual view of the world that we are forced to reconsider our ideas about how the brain works. Two things are necessary to discover such a person. First, we have to be lucky enough to meet him or her. Second, we have to be clever enough to recognize the importance of what we are observing.

"I'm sure you're both lucky and clever," says the Professor of English.

Not so. I was lucky once, but not clever. As a young research worker at the Institute of Psychiatry in south London, I was studying how people learn. I was introduced to someone with severe loss of memory. For a week he visited my lab[12] every day in order to learn a simple motor skill. His performance improved in a fairly normal manner and even after a gap of a week he retained the new skill he had learned. But, at the same time, his memory loss was so severe that each day he would claim that he had never met me before and had never performed the task before. "How strange!" I thought. But I was interested in problems of motor skill learning. This man learned the skill I taught him normally and so I wasn't interested in him. Many others have, of course, recognized the importance of people like this. Such people can remember nothing that has happened to them even if it happened only yesterday. We assumed that this was because the events that happened were not recorded in the brain. But, in the person I studied, the experiences he had yesterday clearly had a long-term effect on his brain since he was able to perform the motor task better today than yesterday. But this long-term change in the brain had no effect on his conscious mind. He could not remember anything that happened yesterday. Such people show that our brain can know things about the world that our mind does not know.

[11]   Neuropsychologists study, and sometimes try to help, people who have suffered brain damage.

[12]   In the 1960s this was a small bathroom that had been converted into a "laboratory" by putting a sheet of hardboard over the bath.

Mel Goodale and David Milner made no mistake when they met the person known as DF. They immediately recognized the importance of what they were observing. DF had the misfortune to suffer from carbon monoxide poisoning as the result of a faulty water heater. The poisoning damaged part of the visual system of her brain concerned with the recognition of shape. She has a vague impression of light, shade, and color, but cannot recognize anything because she can't see what shape it is. Goodale and Milner noticed that she seemed to be able to walk around and pick things up far better than would be expected given that she was nearly blind. Over the years they have performed a whole series of experiments with her. These confirm that there is a big discrepancy between what she can see and what she can do.

One of Goodale and Milner's experiments works like this. You hold up a rod and ask DF about its orientation. She cannot say whether it is horizontal or vertical or at an angle. It is as if she cannot see the rod and is just guessing. Then you ask her to reach out and grasp the rod. She does this normally. She rotates her hand so that her fingers have the same orientation as the rod. She grasps the rod smoothly whatever its angle. This observation shows that DF's brain "knows" about the angle of the rod and can use this information to control the movements of her hand. But DF can't use this information to see the orientation of the rod. Her brain knows something about the physical world, while her conscious mind does not.

Very few people have been found with precisely the same problem as DF. But there are many people with brain damage where the brain plays similar tricks. Probably the most spectacular dissociation is seen in people with "blindsight," a problem associated with damage to the primary visual cortex. As we already discovered, this damage causes the person to become blind for part of the visual field. Larry Weiskrantz was the first to show that, in a few people, this blind area is not truly blind after all.[13] In one experiment a spot of light is moved slowly across the part of the visual field that is blind and the participant is asked to report what he sees. As far as this participant is concerned, this is an extremely stupid task. He can't see anything. So instead he is asked to guess, "Was the spot moving right or left?" This also seems a fairly stupid task, but the participant assumes that this eminent Oxford professor knows what he is doing. Professor Weiskrantz discovered that some people could guess

---

[13] A handful of people with blindsight have now been identified. They have been intensively investigated by a considerably larger number of neuropsychologists.

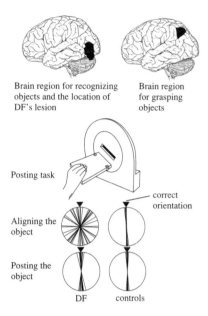

Brain region for recognizing objects and the location of DF's lesion

Brain region for grasping objects

Posting task

correct orientation

Aligning the object

Posting the object

DF   controls

Figure 1.5   Action without awareness
DF has a lesion in the part of her brain necessary for recognizing objects, while the part of her brain necessary for grasping is intact. She can't see whether or not the "letter" is lined up with the slot. But she can orient the "letter" when she posts it through the slot.

Source: Lesion location: Plate 7; posting data: Figure 2.2 in Goodale, M.A. & Milner, A.D. (2004). *Sight unseen*. Oxford: Oxford University Press.

much better than chance. In one experiment a participant was correct more than 80% of the time, while still claiming to see nothing. So, if I suffered from blindsight, my mind could have absolutely no visual content and yet my brain would know things about the visual world and could somehow enable me to make accurate "guesses" about that visual world. What sort of knowledge is this that I don't know I have?

When the Brain Tells Lies

At least the unknown knowledge of the person with blindsight is correct. Sometimes brain damage can cause the mind to have information about the physical world that is completely false. A deaf old lady was woken up in the middle of the night by loud music. She searched her flat for the source of the music, but could not find it. Eventually she realized that the music was only in her mind. Hearing this non-existent music became a nearly

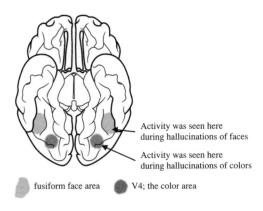

Activity was seen here
during hallucinations of faces

Activity was seen here
during hallucinations of colors

fusiform face area   V4; the color area

Figure 1.6 Spontaneous brain activity associated with blindness (Charles Bonnet syndrome) causes visual experiences. The nature of the experience depends upon the location of the activity. The brain is seen from underneath.

Source: Redrawn from data given in: ffytche, D.H., Howard, R.J., Brammer, M.J., David, A., Woodruff, P., & Williams, S. (1998). The anatomy of conscious vision: An fMRI study of visual hallucinations. *Natural Neuroscience, 1*(8), 738–742.

constant experience for her. Sometimes she heard a baritone voice accompanied by a guitar, sometimes a choir accompanied by a full orchestra.

Vivid auditory and visual hallucinations are experienced by about 10% of elderly people who suffer from severe hearing or visual loss. The visual hallucinations, associated with Charles Bonnet syndrome,[14] are often just colored patches or patterns. Sufferers describe very fine golden wire netting, oval shapes full of brickwork patterns, or fireworks exploding in vivid colors. Faces and figures are also seen. Faces are usually distorted and ugly with prominent eyes and teeth. When figures are reported, they are typically small and wearing hats or period costumes.

> There's heads of 17th-century men and women, with nice heads of hair. Wigs, I should think. Very disapproving all of them. They never smile.

Dominic ffytche and his colleagues at the Institute of Psychiatry scanned people with Charles Bonnet syndrome while these hallucinations were occurring. Just before faces were seen, activity started to increase in the face area. Likewise activity in the color area started to increase just before the participant reported seeing a colored patch.

---

[14]   The Swiss philosopher Charles Bonnet first described visual hallucinations associated with visual impairment. He reported his grandfather's visual experiences and, later, developed the disorder himself.

How Brain Activity Creates False Knowledge

There are now many studies demonstrating that activity in the brain can create a false experience of something happening in the outside world. On example is found with epilepsy. Epilepsy affects about 1 person in every 200. It is a disorder of the brain in which the electrical activity in large numbers of neurons sometimes runs out of control, causing a seizure or "fit." In many cases the seizure is triggered by activity in a particular brain region where a small area of damage can sometimes be located. Uncontrolled electrical activity starts in this region and then spreads to the rest of the brain.

Just before a seizure occurs, many sufferers start to have a strange experience known as an "aura." Sufferers rapidly learn exactly what their own aura is like and, when it starts, they know that a seizure is about to occur. The exact nature of the experience differs from one person to the next. For one person it might be the smell of burning rubber. For another it might be a buzzing noise. The sensation experienced is related to the location in the brain where the seizure begins.

In about 5% of people with epilepsy the seizure starts in the visual cortex. Just before the seizure, simple colored shapes are seen, which sometimes spin or flash. We can get some idea of what the experience is like from drawings made by sufferers after the seizure (see Figure CP3, color plate section).

One, sufferer, Kathryn Mize, wrote a vivid account of the complex visual hallucinations she experienced in association with seizures brought on a by an attack of flu. These experiences occurred for several weeks after the seizures had ceased.

> Upon closing my eyes while seated during a lecture, red shimmering geo-metric forms appeared in the blackness.[15] They startled me, but the shapes were captivating so I watched them in absolute wonder. What I saw with my eyes closed was fantastic. Vague circles and rectangles would coalesce into beautiful symmetric geometric forms. There was a constant expansion, reabsorption and expansion again about these forms. I remember what seemed like an explosion of black dots in my right field of vision. The dots gracefully floated outward from their origin and were superimposed upon a red scintillating backdrop. Two red rectangular planes appeared and

---

[15]   A useful trick that anyone can use during boring lectures is to press your knuckles hard into your eyes. This pressure causes activity in the neurons in the retina, creating shimmer-ing and moving shapes and vivid colors.

moved in opposite directions. A red ball on a stick moved in a circular fashion beside these planes. Then a red shimmering rippling wave appeared in the lower field of my vision.

In a few sufferers the seizure starts in auditory cortex and the sufferer will hear sounds and voices.

Singing, music, voices – maybe voices that I heard in the past – for a while there I thought it was a specific singer – maybe Buddy Holly . . . it gets louder and louder and then I just black out.

An aura can sometimes involve complex experiences in which past events are relived:

[A] girl began to have seizures at the age of 11. [At the beginning of an attack she would] see herself as a little girl of 7 walking through a field of grass. Suddenly she felt as though someone from behind was going to smother her or hit her on the head and she became terrified. The scene was almost exactly the same on each attack and was clearly based on a real incident [that had happened to her at the age of 7].

These observations suggest that abnormal neural activity that is associated with an epileptic seizure can cause the sufferer to acquire false knowledge about the physical world. But to be sure about this conclusion we need to perform a proper experiment in which we control the neural activity in the brain by direct stimulation.

In some severe cases of epilepsy the seizures can be controlled only by cutting out the damaged area of the brain. Before cutting out the damaged area, the neurosurgeon must be sure that removal of this area will not interfere with some vital function such as speech. The great Canadian neurosurgeon Wilder Penfield pioneered the technique in which the sufferer's brain is stimulated electrically in order to get some idea of the function of a particular area. This is done by placing the tip of an electrode on the surface of the exposed brain and passing a very small current through the brain. The current causes the neurons close to the electrode to become more active. There is no pain associated with this technique, and it can be carried out while the participant is fully conscious.

When the brain is stimulated in this way, people report experiences very similar to those associated with epileptic seizures. The experience depends upon where the brain is stimulated

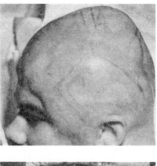

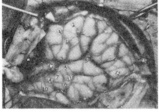

Figure 1.7   Direct stimulation of the brain causes sensory experiences
The upper figure shows the patient prepared for operation with the line of the incision marked over the left ear.
The lower figure shows the brain surface with numbered tickets indicating the sites of positive responses to stimulation.
Source: Case 2 (p. 613) from Penfield W., & Perot, P. (1963). The brain's record of auditory and visual experience. *Brain*, *86*(Pt. 4), 595–696. By permission of Oxford University Press.

Case 21: He said "Just a minute. Like a figure, on the left side. Seems like a man or a woman. I think it was a woman. She seemed to have nothing on. She seemed to be pulling or running after a wagon."

Case 13: He said, "They are saying something, but I cannot make it out." Stimulated at an adjacent site he said, "Yes, it is coming again. It is water, It sounds like a toilet flushing or a dog barking. The toilet flushed first and then the dog started to bark." Stimulated at a third adjacent site he said, "In my ears there seems to be music. It is a girl or a woman singing, but I don't know the tune. It came from a record player or a radio."

Case 15: When the electrode was applied she said, "I imagine I hear a lot of people shouting at me." After stimulation of an adjacent site she said, "Oh, everybody is shouting at me, make them stop!" She explained, "They are yelling at me for doing something wrong, everybody is yelling."

These observations confirm that we can create false knowledge about the physical world by stimulating the brain directly in the appropriate region. But in all these cases it was a damaged brain that was being stimulated. Would the same thing happen with an undamaged brain?

How to Make Your Brain Lie to You

You can't stick electrodes into people's brains except in very special circumstances. But, in all periods and in all cultures, many people have felt the need to stimulate their brains with various substances. During such stimulation the brain no longer tells us about the "real" physical world, but about another place that some believe is better. Like every one else who was a student in the 1960s, I read Aldous Huxley's essay on hallucinogenic drugs, *The Doors of Perception*. Perhaps my fascination with that book led to my devoting so much of my subsequent career to the study of hallucinations?[16]

Describing the effects of mescalin,[17] Huxley said, "This is how one ought to see, how things really are." When he closed his eyes he saw "brightly coloured, constantly changing structures." Huxley also quotes from the more detailed account of the effects of mescalin given by Weir Mitchell.

> He saw a host of "star points" and what looked like "fragments of stained glass". Then came "delicate floating films of colour". These were displaced by an "abrupt rush of countless points of white light," sweeping across the field of vision. Next there were zigzag lines of very bright colours, which somehow turned into swelling clouds of still more brilliant hues. Buildings now made their appearance, and then landscapes. There were Gothic towers of elaborate design with worn statues in the doorways or on stone brackets. "As I gazed, every projecting angle, cornice and even the faces of the stones at their joinings were by degrees covered or hung with clusters

---

[16] There is a striking similarity between the visual hallucinations associated with blindness in the elderly, epilepsy with a focus in the visual cortex, and drugs such as mescalin and LSD. How is the same final effect on brain activity achieved by these very different routes?

[17] The Mexican cactus *Anhalonium Lewini* was first introduced to Western science in 1886. The root of this cactus, known as peyotl, had a major role in the religious ceremonies of the early inhabitants of Mexico and the American Southwest. Western psychologists discovered that mescalin, the active principle of this root, had profound effects upon consciousness. In the 1950s interest in these effects was heightened by the synthesis of the closely related substance LSD and an increased understanding of how these substances acted upon the brain. It was widely believed that study of the effects of mescalin and LSD would lead to an explanation of the symptoms of schizophrenia. It didn't.

Figure 1.8 The effects drugs can have on visual experiences
Source: By permission of Comité Jean Cocteau.

of what seemed to be huge precious stones, but uncut stones, some being more like masses of transparent fruit."

LSD can have very similar effects.

Now, little by little I could begin to enjoy the unprecedented colours and plays of shapes that persisted behind my closed eyes. Kaleidoscopic, fantastic images surged in on me, alternating, variegated, opening and then closing themselves in circles and spirals, exploding in coloured fountains, rearranging and hybridizing themselves in constant flux.

When the eyes are opened, the appearance of the "real" physical world can seem strangely altered.

My surroundings had now transformed themselves in more terrifying ways. Everything in the room spun around, and the familiar objects and pieces of furniture assumed grotesque, threatening forms. They were in continuous motion, animated, as if driven by an inner restlessness.[18]

---

[18] The psychological effects of LSD were discovered by accident in 1943. A small amount of the drug soaked through the fingers of research chemist Albert Hoffman during a routine synthesis. During the following weeks he explored the effects of the drug and kept detailed notes, such as those cited here and in the previous extract.

I noticed that the various creases and ripples in my blanket were moving all over its surface, as if snakes were crawling around underneath it. I couldn't keep track of the individual "ripples" but I could quite clearly see them moving all over. Suddenly, the ripples began to gather themselves in a single area of my blanket's surface.[19]

Checking the Reality of Our Experiences

I have to conclude that if my brain was damaged or its function was interfered with by electrical stimulation or drugs I would have to be very cautious about the knowledge I acquired about the physical world. Some kinds of knowledge would no longer be available. Some kinds of knowledge might be represented in my brain, but I would not know about it. Worst of all, some of kinds of knowledge might be false and bear no relationship to the real physical world.[20]

Given this problem, my main concern must be to discover how to distinguish the false experiences from the true ones. Sometimes this is easy. If I see things when my eyes are closed, then these are visions and not part of the real physical world. If I hear voices when I am alone in a soundproof room, then they must be in my mind. I can dismiss these experiences because I know that my senses must be in contact with the world in order to acquire any information about it.

Sometimes I can dismiss an experience as being too bizarre to be real. If I see a person a few inches high dressed in 17th-century costume and pushing a perambulator, she is unlikely to be real. If I see hedgehogs and small brown rodents crawling over the ceiling above me,[21] I know that these are unlikely to be real. I can dismiss these cases because I know such things don't happen in the real world.

But if the false experience I am having is perfectly plausible, then how can I tell that it is false? When she first heard the music the deaf old lady assumed it was real and searched her apartment for the source of the

---

[19]   LSD experience described in the Erowid experience vaults. *Erowid.org* is an online library of information about psychoactive plants, chemicals, and related topics.

[20]   I believe that there is a real physical world.

[21]   A 54-year-old company director complained of excruciating headaches. A brain scan showed damage to the left side of his brain in the region of the visual cortex. Over the next few days he had visual hallucinations, lasting hours at a time, consisting of hedgehogs and small brown rodents crawling over the ceiling above him. These recurred particularly when he was drowsy. He found them curious and amusing.

sound. Only when she could find no source did she conclude that the music was in her mind. If she had lived in a flat with thin walls and suffered from noisy neighbors, she might have concluded, quite reasonably, that they had the radio on too loud again.[22]

How Do We Know What's Real?

Sometimes we can be absolutely convinced of the reality of what we are experiencing, even though it is false.

> I was haunted with a great many terrifying and disquieting *Visions and Voices*, which tho' (I believe) they had *no Reality* in themselves, yet they *seem'd* to be *such* to me, and had the *same Effect* upon me, as if they had *been really* what they *appear'd* to be.

This passage comes from "The Life of the Reverend Mr. George Trosse." This work was written by George Trosse himself and published by his order in 1714 shortly after his death. The experiences he describes occurred many years earlier when he was in his early 20s. With hindsight Mr. Trosse knew that the voices were not real, but at the time of his illness he believed completely in their reality.

> I heard a Voice, as I fancy'd, as it were just behind me, saying, *Yet more humble; Yet more humble;* with some continuance. . . . In Compliance with it I proceeded to pluck down my *Stockings*, and then my *Hose*, and my *Doublet*; and as I was thus uncloathing my self, I had a strong internal Impression, that all was well done, and a full Compliance with the design of the *Voice*.

Today, reports of such experiences would lead to a diagnosis of schizophrenia. We still don't understand the cause of this disorder. But the striking feature is that these people have false experiences that they firmly believe are real. They put much intellectual effort into explaining how such apparently impossible things can be real.

In the 1940s L. Percy King believed that he was pursued by a group of young people through the streets of New York.

---

[22] Ideas of persecution have been found to be more frequent in deaf, elderly people.

I could see them nowhere. I heard one of them, a woman, say, "You can't get away from us: we'll lay for you, and get you after a while!" To add to the mystery, one of these "pursuers" repeated my thoughts aloud, verbatim. I tried to elude these pursuers as before, but this time, I tried to escape from them by means of subway trains, darting up and down subway exits, and entrances, jumping on, and off trains until after midnight. But, at every station where I got off a train, I heard the voices of these pursuers as close as ever. The question occurred to me: How could as many of these pursuers follow me as quickly unseen?

Not believing in Gods or Devils, Mr. King uses modern technology to explain his persecution.

Were they ghosts? Or was I in the process of developing into a spiritual medium? No! Among these pursuers, I was later to gradually discover by deduction, were evidently some brothers, and sisters, who had inherited from one of their parents, some astounding, unheard of, utterly unbelievable occult powers. Believe-it-or-not, some of them, besides being able to tell a person's thoughts, are also able to project their magnetic voices – commonly called "radio voices" around here – a distance of a few miles without talking loud, and without apparent effort, their voices sounding from that distance as tho heard thru a radio head-set, this being done without electrical apparatus. This unique, occult power of projecting their "radio voices" for such long distances, apparently seems to be due to their natural, bodily electricity, of which they have a supernormal amount. Maybe the iron contained in their red blood corpuscles is magnetised. The vibration of their vocal chords [sic] evidently generates wireless waves, and these vocal radio waves are caught by human ears without rectification. Thus, in conjunction with their mind-reading ability, they are able to carry on a conversation with a person's unspoken thoughts, and then by means of their so-called "radio voices", answer these thoughts aloud audibly to the person. . . . These pursuers are also able to project their magnetic voices along a water pipe, which acts as an electrical conductor by talking against it so that their voices seem to issue from the water running from the faucet connected to the pipe. One of them is able to make his voice roar along the large water mains for miles, truly a startling phenomenon. Most persons do not dare mention such things to their associates for fear of being judged insane.

Unfortunately Mr. King did not heed his own advice. He knew that "people who have hallucinations of hearing imagine that they hear things." But he was convinced the voices he heard were real and so he was not hallucinating. He believed he had discovered "the greatest psychological phenomena extant" and he told people about it. In spite of his ingenuity in explaining the reality of the voices, the psychiatrists were not convinced. Mr. King was held in a mental hospital.

Mr. King and many other people like him are convinced that their experiences are real. If their experiences seem unlikely or impossible, then they will change their ideas about how the world works rather than deny the reality of their experiences.[23] But there is a very interesting feature of the hallucinations associated with schizophrenia. These experiences are not about the physical world. These people do not just see colors and hear noises. Their hallucinations are about the mental world. They hear voices commenting on their actions, making suggestions and commands. Our brain can also create a false mental world.[24]

So, if my brain has been interfered with, I can no longer take my experience of the world at face value. My brain can create a vivid experience that has no basis in reality. This reality is clearly false, but many sufferers are convinced it is true.

"But there is nothing wrong with my brain," says the Professor of English. "I know what's real."

In this chapter I have shown that a damaged brain doesn't just prevent us from finding out about the world. It can also create in our minds an experience of the world that is entirely false. But there is no reason to feel smug. I shall show in the next chapter that, even if your brain is intact and functioning perfectly normally, what it tells you about the world may still be false.

---

[23] Peter Chadwick is a psychologist who has written about his experience of a schizophrenic breakdown. At one point during this period of his life "I had to make sense, any sense, out of all these uncanny coincidences. I did it by radically changing my conception of reality."

[24] For as long as I can remember I have been fascinated with these false perceptions and false beliefs about the world. Are they really false? Or is there another, parallel world out there that I can't quite reach? I would like this book to be like a Sherlock Holmes story: What at first appears to be supernatural is shown in the end to have a rational, physical explanation.

Chapter 2

What a Normal Brain Tells Us about the World

Even if all our senses are intact and our brain is functioning normally, we do not have direct access to the physical world. It may feel as if we have direct access, but this is an illusion created by our brain.

Illusions of Awareness

I could blindfold you and lead you into a strange room. Then I take the blindfold off and you look around. Even with the unlikely combination of an elephant in one corner and a sewing machine in the other, you would instantly become aware of the contents of the room. You would experience no need for thought or effort in achieving this awareness.

In the early 19th century this experience of effortless and immediate perception of the physical world was entirely consistent with what was then known about brain function. The nervous system was known to consist of nerve fibers that functioned using electricity.[1] Electrical energy was known to flow extremely fast (at the speed of light) and so our perception of the world through the nerve fibers leading from our eyes could well be almost instantaneous. As a young research student, Hermann Helmholtz was told by his professor that it would be impossible to measure the speed of nerve conduction. It would be too fast. But, like all good students, he ignored this advice. In 1852 he was able to measure

---

[1] Galvani had revealed the electrical nature of nerve-muscle function in 1791. In 1826, Johannes Müller proposed the theory of "specific nerve energies." This stated that different nerves (visual, auditory, etc.) carried a kind of "code," which identified their origin to the brain.

the speed of nerve conduction and showed that it was rather slow. In sensory neurons it takes about 20 msec for the nerve impulse to travel 1 meter. Helmholtz also measured "perception time" by asking people to press a button as soon as they felt a touch on various parts of the body. These reactions times turned out to be even longer, being more than 100 msec. These observations show that our perception of objects in the outside world is not immediate. Helmholtz realized that various processes must be occurring in the brain before a representation of an object in the outside world appears in the mind. He proposed that perception of the world was not direct, but depended on "unconscious inferences."[2] In other words before we can perceive an object the brain has to infer what the object might be on the basis of the information reaching the senses.

Not only do we seem to perceive the world instantly and without effort, we also seem to perceive the whole visual scene in vivid detail. This too is an illusion. Only the middle of the visual scene that strikes the center of our eye can be seen in detail and in color. This is because only the middle of our retina (the fovea) has closely packed, color-sensitive neurons (cones). Beyond about 10 degrees from the middle the neurons are further apart and detect only light and shade (rods). The edge of our view of the world is blurred and has no color.

We are not normally aware of this blurring at the edges of our vision. Our eyes are in constant motion so that any part of the scene can be become the center of vision where perception of detail is possible. But even when we think we have looked at everything in the scene, we are still deluding ourselves. In 1997 Ron Rensink and his colleagues described "change blindness," and, ever since, this has been every cognitive psychologist's favorite demonstration at the department's open day.

The problem for psychologists is that everyone knows about our subject from their personal experience. I wouldn't dream of telling a molecular geneticist or a nuclear physicist how to interpret their data, but they have no qualms in telling me how to interpret mine. Change

---

[2]   The notion of unconscious inferences was unpopular. This was seen as an attack on the basis of morality since no blame could be attached when inferences were made unconsciously. Helmholtz later stopped using the term "unconscious inferences" "in order to avoid confusion with what seems to me a completely obscure and unjustified idea which Schopenhauer and his followers have designated by the same name" (e.g. Freud). Hermann Helmholtz (1821–1894) was one the great scientists of the 19th century, making major contributions to physics, physiology, and medicine. In 1882 he was made von Helmholtz.

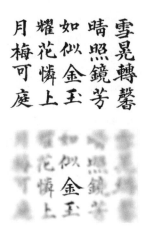

Figure 2.1 Our vision is blurred, with only the center of the visual field clearly in focus
(Upper) What you think you see.
(Lower) What you really see.

blindness is exciting for us psychologists because we can use it to show people that their personal experience is wrong. Here is something that we know about their minds that they don't know themselves.

The Professor of English has come to the open day and is making an heroic effort not to look bored. I show her the change blindness demonstration.

This consists of two versions of a complex scene that differ in one respect. In my example the picture consists of a military transport plane standing on an airport runway. In one of the two versions one of the engines is missing. This is right in the middle of the picture, taking up a large space. I show these two pictures repeatedly one after another on a computer screen (but critically with a uniform gray screen in between presentations). The Professor of English can see no difference. After a minute I point to the difference on the screen and it becomes embarrassingly obvious.[3]

"It's quite fun. But where's the science?"

What this demonstration shows is that you rapidly perceive the gist of the scene: *a military transport plane on a runway.* But you do not

---

[3]   Of course I have now ruined this demonstration for you. To see the effect you will have to try it on a naïve friend (or find another example). This effect is difficult to illustrate in a book, but many psychologists have examples on their website (e.g. *http://www.usd.edu/psyc301/Rensink.htm,* which demonstrates the airplane example).

Figure 2.2   Change blindness
How quickly can you find the difference between these two pictures?
Source: Ron Rensink: airplane: Department of Psychology, University of British Columbia.

actually have all the details in your mind. For you to notice the change in one of these details, I have to draw your attention to it (*"look at the engine"*). Otherwise you will not find the detail that changes until, by chance, you happen to be attending to it at the moment of change. And this is where a psychologist's trick creates change blindness. Because of the trick you don't know where to look in order to see the change.

In real life our peripheral vision, though blurred, is very sensitive to change. If my brain detects movement at the edge of my vision, my eye will immediately move so that I can look at that part of the scene in detail. But in the change blindness demonstration a blank gray screen is displayed between each scene. As a result there is a big visual change everywhere as every region on the screen goes from being multicolored to gray and back again. My brain gets no signal to indicate where the important change is occurring.

So we have to conclude that our experience of immediate and complete awareness of the visual scene in front of us is false. There is a short delay in which the brain makes the "unconscious inferences" by which we become aware of the gist of the scene. Furthermore, many parts of the scene remain blurred and lacking in detail. But the brain knows that the scene is not blurred and also knows that an eye movement can rapidly bring any part of the scene into vivid focus. So our experience of the visual world in rich detail is an experience of what is potentially available to us rather than what is already represented in our brain. Our access to the physical world is direct enough for all practical purposes. But this access depends upon our brain, and even our intact, healthy brain doesn't always tell us everything it knows.

Our Secretive Brain

Is it possible that my brain is aware of the changes in the change blindness demonstration even though my mind is not? Until recently this was a very difficult question to answer. Let's leave out the brain for a moment. I am asking if I can be affected by a stimulus that I am not aware of having seen. In the 1960s this was called subliminal perception and was very controversial. On the one hand, many people believed that advertisers could insert hidden messages into films that would cause us to buy, say, more soft drinks, without knowing that we were being manipulated.[4] On the other hand, many psychologists believed that there was no such thing as subliminal perception. If the experiments were done properly, they claimed, effects would be found only when people were aware of what they had seen. Since then, many experiments have been performed, and there is no evidence that subliminal messages hidden in films cause us to buy more soft drinks. Nevertheless, some subtle effects

---

[4]   In 1957 James Vicary claimed to have inserted two advertising messages, *Eat Popcorn* and *Drink Coca-Cola*, in the film *Picnic*. The messages were shown repeatedly, but their duration was so short that they were never consciously perceived. Vicary claimed that over a six-week period the sales of popcorn rose by 58% and the sales of Coca-Cola rose by 18%. No evidence was ever brought forward to substantiate these claims, and in 1962, Vicary stated that he made up the whole story. Nevertheless many popular books were published based on this report, with titles such as *Subliminal Seduction*.

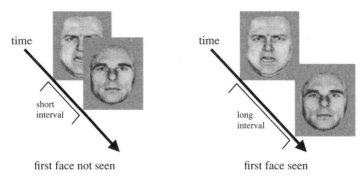

time

short
interval

first face not seen

time

long
interval

first face seen

Figure 2.3 Visual masking
Two faces are shown on the screen, one after the other. If the interval between the first face and the second face is less than about 40 msec, you are not aware of the first face.

Source: Faces from: Ekman, P., & Friesen, W.V. (1976). *Pictures of facial affect.* Palo Alto, CA: Consulting Psychologists.

can be found that are caused by objects of which we are unaware. But these effects are very difficult to demonstrate. To make sure that you are unaware of the object, I present it very briefly and "mask" it by presenting a second object immediately afterward in the same place.

Typically the objects will be words or pictures on a computer screen. If the first object is presented sufficiently briefly, you will see only the second object. But if the first object is presented too briefly, it will have no effect on you at all. The timing of the experiment has to be exactly right. And how can I measure the effects of objects that you are unaware of seeing? If I ask you to make guesses about objects you can't see, you will find this a very strange request. You will try hard to catch a glimpse of the briefly presented object. With practice you may eventually be able to see it.

The trick is to look for effects that are still present after the object has been presented.[5] Whether I can detect these effects also depends upon what question I ask you. Robert Zajonc (pronounced Zy-unce) showed people a sequence of unknown faces, each masked by a jumble of lines so that they were not aware of seeing the faces. Then he showed each face

[5] The classic studies were conducted in the 1970s by the British psychologist Anthony Marcel. Marcel showed that a word (such as *nurse*) would facilitate the perception of a subsequent word of related meaning (such as *doctor*) even when people were not aware of seeing the first word. This result has been confirmed in many subsequent studies.

again alongside a new face. If he asked you, "Guess which of these two faces I showed you just now?" your guesses would be no better than chance. But if he asked you, "Which face do you prefer?" you would be more likely select the face that you had just seen "subliminally."

When brain scanners became available, researchers could ask a slightly different question about subliminal stimuli. "Does an object produce a change in brain activity even when you are not aware of it?" This is much easier to answer since I don't need to ask you to respond in any other way to the unseen object. I just look at your brain. Paul Whalen and his colleagues used a fearful face as the unseen object.

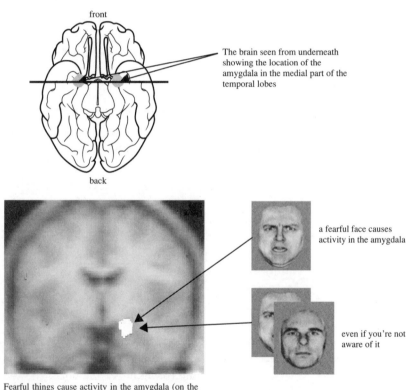

front

The brain seen from underneath showing the location of the amygdala in the medial part of the temporal lobes

back

a fearful face causes activity in the amygdala

even if you're not aware of it

Fearful things cause activity in the amygdala (on the right), even when we are not aware of seeing them.

Figure 2.4 Our brain responds to fearful things we are not aware of seeing

Sources: Whalen, P.J., Rauch, S.L., Etcoff, N.L., McInerney, S.C., Lee, M.B., & Jenike, M.A. (1998). Masked presentations of emotional facial expressions modulate amygdala activity without explicit knowledge. Journal of Neuroscience, 18(1), 411–418 (Figure 2). Faces from: Ekman, P., & Friesen, W.V. (1976). Pictures of facial affect. Palo Alto, CA: Consulting Psychologists Press. Society for Neuroscience with the assistance of Stanford University's Highwire Press.

John Morris and his colleagues had previously found that when people are shown fearful faces (as opposed to happy or neutral faces), activity increases in the amygdala, a small part of the brain that seems to be concerned with detecting dangerous situations. Whalen and his colleagues repeated the experiment, but this time the fearful faces were presented subliminally. Sometimes a fearful face was presented followed immediately by a neutral face. At other times a happy face was presented followed by a neutral face. On both these occasions you would say, "I saw a neutral face." But when the fearful faces were present, activity would occur in the amygdala even though you were unaware of the fearful face.

Diane Beck and her colleagues also used faces as objects, but they put them into the change blindness demonstration. On some occasions the face changed from one person into another. On other occasions no change occurred. The experiment was carefully designed so that you would only detect the change on about half of the occasions on which it actually occurred. For you, there would be no difference between the occasions on which no change occurred and the occasions on which a change occurred and you did not detect it. But your brain notices the difference. On the occasions on which there is change in the face, there is also an increase in activity in the face area of the brain.

So our brain doesn't tell us everything it knows. And sometimes it goes further and actively misleads us . . .

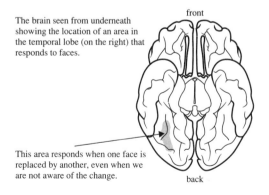

The brain seen from underneath showing the location of an area in the temporal lobe (on the right) that responds to faces.

front

This area responds when one face is replaced by another, even when we are not aware of the change.

back

Figure 2.5 Our brain responds to changes we are not aware of seeing

Sources: Redrawing of data in: Beck, D.M., Rees, G., Frith, C.D., & Lavie, N. (2001). Neural correlates of change detection and change blindness. *Nature Neuroscience*, *4*(6), 645–656.

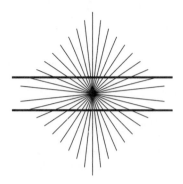

Figure 2.6 The Hering illusion
Even though we know the two horizontal lines are straight, we still see them as bowed.
Edwald Hering, 1861.

Our Distorting Brain

Before the discovery of change blindness, visual illusions were the psy-chologists' favorite trick. Here again we have simple demonstrations that what we see is not always what is really there. Most of these illusions have been know to psychologists for more than 100 years, and to artists and architects for much longer.

Here is a simple example: the Hering illusion.

The horizontal lines clearly appear bent. But if you hold a ruler against them you will find that they are absolutely straight. There are many other illusions like this in which straight lines appear to be bent or objects of the same size appear to have different sizes. Somehow the background on which the lines or objects appear prevents you from seeing them as they really are. These distorted perceptions are not just found on the pages of psychology textbooks. They are also found in objects in the real world. The most famous example is the Parthenon in Athens. The beauty of this building lies in the ideal proportions and symmetries of the lines from which it is constructed. But in reality these lines are neither straight nor parallel. The architects have built in curves and distortions precisely calculated to make the building look straight and symmetrical.[6]

---

[6] In 1846 the Society of Dilettanti sent Francis Penrose to measure the Parthenon in order to test the theory of John Pennethorne that what appears as straight and parallel in Greek architecture of the best period is generally curved or inclined, because this is the only

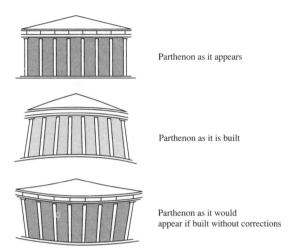

Parthenon as it appears

Parthenon as it is built

Parthenon as it would
appear if built without corrections

Figure 2.7 The perfection of the Parthenon depends upon a visual illusion
Drawings based on John Pennethorne (1844) showing much exaggerated effects.

For me, the most striking aspect of these illusions is that my brain continues to show me false information even when I know that the information is false and even when I know what the object really looks like. I cannot make myself to see the lines in the Hering illusion as straight. The "corrections" built into the Parthenon still work after more than 2,000 years.

The Ames room is an even more striking example of the lack of the effect of our knowledge on our experience of the visual world.

I know that these men are really the same size. The one on the left looks smaller because he is further away. The room is not really square. The back wall on the left is much further away than the back wall on the right. The windows in the back wall have been distorted so that they look square (as with the Parthenon). And yet my brain prefers to see this as a square room containing men of impossibly different sizes, rather than three normal-sized men in a room someone has built with a peculiar shape.

There is at least one thing in my brain's favor in this example. The Ames room is inherently ambiguous. There could be three unusual men

way to obtain the optical effect of a straight line. Immediately upon his return to England in 1847 Penrose published, as the first result of his survey, a paper entitled "Anomalies in the Construction of the Parthenon," in which he proved that the lines of the stylobate of the Parthenon are curved to the inside.

Figure 2.8   The Ames room
Invented by Adelbert Ames, Jr., in 1946, from an idea by Helmholtz.
The three men are the same size. It is the room that is distorted.

Sources: Wittreich, W.J. (1959). Visual perception and personality, *Scientific American*, *200*(4), 56–60 (58): photograph courtesy of William Vandivert.

in a square room or there could be three normal men in a weird room. My brain may be choosing an unlikely interpretation of the scene, but at least it is a possible interpretation.

"There *is* no one correct interpretation," protests the Professor of English.

I argue that, though the evidence is ambiguous, this does not mean that there is no correct interpretation. But, in addition, our brain hides from us this ambiguity and only presents us with one of the possible interpretations.

Furthermore, sometimes our brain takes no account of the evidence about the physical world at all.

Our Creative Brain

Mixing the senses

There are a few people I know who seem perfectly normal. Yet they see a world that is different from the one I see.

As a synaesthete, I inhabit a world slightly different from that of the people around me – a world of extra colours, shapes and sensations. Mine is a universe of black "1"s and pink "Wednesdays", numbers that climb skywards and a rollercoaster-shaped year.[7]

For most of us the senses are kept strictly segregated. Light waves strike our eyes and we see colors and shapes. Sound waves strike our ears and we hear words or musical notes. But for some people, the synesthetes, when sound waves strike their ears, they not only hear sounds, but experience colors as well. DS, on hearing music, also sees objects – falling gold balls, shooting lines, metallic waves like oscilloscope tracings – that float on a "screen" six inches from her nose. The commonest form of mixing is colored hearing.

Hearing a word elicits a color experience. In most cases it is the first letter that determines the color of the word. For each synesthete every letter and every digit has its own color and these colours remain constant across a lifetime (see Figure CP1, color plate section).[8]

It is disturbing for a synesthete if a letter or a number is presented in the "wrong" color. For a synesthete known as GS, 3 is bright red, while 4 is cornflower blue. Carol Mills showed GS a series of colored numbers and asked her to name the colors as quickly as possible. When GS was shown a number that was given the "wrong" color (e.g. a blue 3), then she was slowed down. The synesthetic color elicited by the number interfered with her perception of the actual color. This experiment provides objective evidence that the experiences described by synesthetes are as real as the experiences of other people. It also shows that the experience happens whether they like it or not. In extreme cases this can cause problems.

Listening to him, it was as though a flame with fibres protruding from it was advancing right towards me. I got so interested in his voice, I couldn't follow what he was saying.[9]

---

[7]   About 1 in 2,000 people experience synesthesia. This is a quote from Alison Motluk.

[8]   Synesthetes do not agree about the colors of letters. For the Russian novelist Vladimir Nabokov the letter M was pink while for his wife it was blue. A widespread family disagreement about the color of vowels was reported to Sir Francis Galton by Mrs. H, "the married sister of a well known man of science." "Of my two daughters, one sees the colours quite differently from [me]. The other is only heterodox on the A and O. My sister and I never agreed about these colours, and I doubt whether my two brothers feel the chromatic force of the vowels at all."

[9]   This is S, the synesthete studied by Luria, describing the voice of the film director Sergei Eisenstein.

But it can also be helpful.

> Occasionally, when uncertain how a word should be spelt, I have con-
> sidered what colour it ought to be, and have decided in that way. I believe
> this has often been a great help to me in spelling, both in English and
> foreign languages.[10]

The synesthete knows that the colors are not really there, but still their
brain presents them with a vivid and compelling experience.

"But why do you say the colors are not really there?" asks the Professor of English. "Are colors out there in the physical world or are they in
the mind? If colors are in the mind, then why is your version of the
world any better than that of your friend with synesthesia?"

When my friend says the colors aren't really there, I guess that what
she means is that I, and most other people, don't experience them.

The hallucinations of sleep

Synesthesia is rather rare. But every one of us has had dreams. Every
night, while we are asleep, we experience vivid sensations and strong
emotions.

> I dreamed I was coming into the room and I didn't have a key. I walked
> up to the building and Charles R was standing there. The thing was, I was
> trying to climb in the window. Anyway, Charles was standing there by the
> door and he gave me some sandwiches, two sandwiches. They were red
> – it looked like Canadian bacon and his were boiled ham. I couldn't
> understand why he gave me the worst sandwiches. Anyway, we went on
> into the room and it didn't look like the right place at all. It seemed to be
> some kind of party. I think it was at that point when I started thinking
> how fast I could get out of the place if I had to. And there was something
> about nitroglycerine, I don't quite remember. The last thing was some-
> body throwing a baseball.[11]

Though dreams are so vivid, we remember only very few of them (5%).

"How can you possibly know that I am having all these dreams when
I can't even remember them myself?" asks the Professor of English.

---

[10]   This is Miss Stones, another of the informants in Galton's study of synesthesia.
[11]   From a series of dreams collected by Richard Jones.

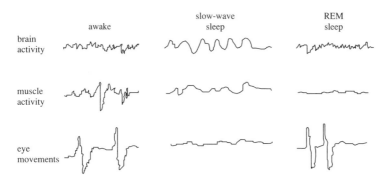

Figure 2.9 Sleep stages

Awake: rapid, desynchronized neural activity
                    muscle activity
                    eye movements

Slow-wave sleep: slow synchronized neural activity
                    some muscle activity
                    no eye movements
                    few dreams

REM sleep: rapid, desynchronized neural activity
                    paralysis, no muscle activity
                    rapid eye movements
                    many dreams

In the 1950s Aserinksy and Kleitman discovered a special stage in sleep when rapid eye movements occur. Sleep stages are associated with different patterns of brain activity that can be measured with EEG. During one stage of sleep your brain activity looks the same as when you are awake. But all your muscles are effectively paralyzed and you cannot move. The one exception is your eyes. During this stage of sleep your eyes move rapidly from side to side although the eyelids remain closed. This stage of sleep is therefore called rapid-eye-movement sleep (REM). If I wake you up during REM sleep, then most of the time (90%) you will report that you were in the middle of a vivid dream and will be able to recall many features of this dream. However, if I wake you up five minutes after the end of a period of REM sleep, you will not remember any dreams. This shows how quickly our memories of dreams fade away. Unless you happen to wake up during or just after a period of REM sleep, you will not remember your dreams. But I can know that you are having them by monitoring your eye movements and brain activity while you are sleeping.

What the brain presents to us during dreams is not a representation of the real physical world.[12] But the experience is so vivid that some people have wondered whether dreams were putting them in touch with another reality. Twenty-four centuries ago Chuang Tzu dreamt he was a butterfly. "I dreamt I was a butterfly flying through the air and knowing nothing of Chuang Tzu." When he awoke he said he did not know if he was a man who had dreamt he was a butterfly or a butterfly dreaming he was a man.[13]

Robert Frost dreams about the apples he has just been picking

. . .
And I could tell
What form my dreaming was about to take.
Magnified apples appear and disappear,
Stem end and blossom end,
And every fleck of russet showing clear.
My instep arch not only keeps the ache,
It keeps the pressure of a ladder-round.
I feel the ladder sway as the boughs bend.
. . .

(Extract from "After Apple Picking," 1914)

In most of our dreams the content is sufficiently bizarre that we would not confuse it with reality (see Figure CP4, color plate section). For example, there is often a mismatch between the identity of characters seen in dreams and their physical appearance. "I had a talk with your colleague (in my dream), but she looked different, much younger, like someone I went to school with, perhaps a 13-year-old girl."[14] Nevertheless, during

[12]   But during dreams, and especially while we are falling asleep, the brain often re-represents what we have been doing during the day. Robert Stickgold asked people to play Tetris™ for 7 hours over 3 days. On the nights after playing Tetris™ they reported seeing Tetris™ shapes floating around. This even happened in people with severe amnesia who could not remember that they had been playing Tetris™. "I see images that are turned on their side. I don't know what they are from. I wish I could remember, but they are like blocks."
[13]   It was meditating upon dreams, among other things, that led Descartes to doubt everything except his own thoughts. "I see plainly that there are never any sure signs by means of which being awake can be distinguished from being asleep."
[14]   This resembles the experience of certain people with brain damage. They recognize unknown people as familiar even though there is no obvious physical resemblance (Frégoli syndrome). Sophie Schwartz and Pierre Maquet suggest that, while dreaming, certain brain regions are under-active so that the normal brain functions as if it were damaged.

the dream we are convinced that everything that is happening to us is real. It is only at the moment of waking that we realize, usually with relief, that "It is only a dream. I can stop running away."[15]

Hallucinations in the sane

Synesthetes are unusual people. When we dream, our brain is in an unusual state. How creative is the brain of an ordinary sane, physically healthy person who is wide awake? Precisely this question was investigated at the end of the 19th century in a survey of 17,000 people conducted by the Society for Psychical Research. The principal aim of the Society for Psychical Research was to find evidence for the existence of telepathy: the communication of messages directly from one mind to another without any obvious physical means. It was believed that such messages were particularly likely to be transmitted at times of great emotional stress.

> On October 5th, 1863, I awoke at 5 a.m. I was in Minto House Normal School, Edinburgh. I heard distinctly the well-known and characteristic voice of a dear friend, repeating the words of a well-known hymn. Nothing visible. Lying quite awake in bed – in good health, and free from any special anxiety. . . . at the very same time, almost to the minute, my friend was seized suddenly with a mortal illness. He died the same day, and a telegram reached me that evening announcing that fact.

Today psychologists treat such claims with extreme suspicion. But at that time the Society for Psychical Research included a number of eminent scientists among its members.[16] The committee that oversaw the Census of Hallucinations was chaired by Professor Henry Sidgwick, the Cambridge philosopher and founder of Newnham College. The survey was conducted with great care and the report, published in 1894, includes a detailed statistical treatment. The compilers of the report tried to exclude experiences that might have been dreams or delirium associated with physical illness or hallucinations associated with mental illness. They also went to considerable trouble to distinguish between hallucinations and illusions.

---

[15]   The emotion of fear occurs more commonly in dreams than in the waking state.

[16]   The English Society for Psychical Research was organized in 1882, having as president Prof. Henry Sedgwick of Cambridge University. Among the original vice-presidents and subsequent prominent officials and investigators were Prof. Balfour Stewart, FRS, the Right Honorable Arthur J. Balfour, Prof. W.F. Barrett of Dublin University, Mr. F.W.H. Myers, Sir William Crookes, FRS, Sir Oliver Lodge, and the Bishop of Ripon. Of the value of the work, Gladstone said: "It is the most important work which is being done in the world – by far the most important."

This was the exact question that they asked their informants:

> Have you ever, when believing yourself to be completely awake, had a vivid impression of seeing or being touched by a living being or inanimate object, or of hearing a voice; which impression, so far as you could discover, was not due to any external physical cause?

The published report is nearly 400 pages long and consists mainly of the actual words of the informants describing their experiences. Ten percent of the informants had experienced hallucinations, and the majority of these hallucinations were visual (over 80%).[17] For me the most interesting are those reports that have nothing obviously to do with telepathy.

From Mrs. Girdlestone January 1891

I felt, more than I saw, many animals (principally cats) passing by me and pushing me aside, as I went downstairs in broad daylight in our house at Clifton during several months in 1886 and 1887.[18]

Mrs. G writes:

> The hallucinations consisted of hearing myself being called by name, so distinctly that I have looked around to hear whom the sound came from; though, whether from imagination or the remembrance of this having occurred before, the voice, if I may call it so, had a quite indefinable quality, which invariably startled me and separated it from any ordinary sound. This lasted for several years. I am quite unable to explain the circumstances.

Today her GP would probably suggest a neurological examination if she described experiences like these.

I also find interesting the experiences that were classified as illusions. They are classified as illusions because the experience clearly had its origin in physical events in the real world.

---

[17]   As the authors of the census point out, this figure is strikingly different from that associated with mental illness. "Among hallucinations of insane persons, there seems to be no doubt that auditory cases are much more frequent than visual, the proportions being estimated by some authorities as 3 to 1, by others as 5 to 1."

[18]   A similar experience was reported by someone with Parkinson's disease some 100 years later. "There seemed to be numerous cats in the room. They were black or brown and moved silently around the room. One jumped on my knee and I was able to stroke it."

From Dr. G.J. Stoney

Some years ago a friend and I rode – he on a bicycle, I on a tricycle – on an unusually dark night in summer from Glendalough to Rathdrum. It was drizzling rain, we had no lamps, and the road was overshadowed by trees on both sides, between which we could just see the sky-line. I was riding slowly and carefully some ten or twenty yards in advance, guiding myself by the sky-line, when my machine chanced to pass over a piece of tin or something else in the road that made a great crash. Presently my companion came up, calling to me in great concern. He had seen through the gloom my machine upset and me flung from it. The crash had excited the thought of the most likely cause for it, and this involved a visual perception in the mind, faint, but sufficient on this occasion to be seen with distinctness when not overpowered by objects seen in the ordinary way through the eyes.

In this example Dr. Stoney's friend saw something that did not actually happen. As Dr. Stoney puts it, the expectation created a visual perception in the mind sufficient to be seen as if through the eyes. In terms of my metaphor, Dr. Stoney's friend's brain created a plausible account of what had happened and this is what Dr. Stoney's friend saw as reality.

From Miss W

One evening at dusk I went into my bedroom to fetch something I wanted off the mantelpiece. A street lamp threw a slanting ray of light in at a window, just sufficient to enable me to discern the dim outline of the chief articles of furniture in the room. I was cautiously feeling for what I wanted when, partially turning round, I perceived at a short distance behind me the figure of a little old lady, sitting very sedately with her hands folded in her lap, holding a white pocket-handkerchief. I was much startled, for I had not before seen anyone in the room, and called out, "Who's that?" but received no answer, and, turning quite round to face my visitor, she immediately vanished from sight. . . .

In most reports of ghosts and visitations the story would stop here, *but* Miss W is persistent.

Being very near sighted, I began to think my eyes had played me a trick; so I resumed my search in as nearly as possible the same position as before, and having succeeded, was turning to come away when lo! and behold! there sat the little old lady as distinct as ever, with her funny little cap, dark dress, and hands folded demurely over her white handkerchief. This time I turned round quickly and marched up to the apparition. Which vanished as suddenly as before.

So the effect could be replicated. And what was the cause?

> And now being convinced that no one was playing me any trick, I deter-
> mined to find out, if possible, the why and because of the mystery. Slowly
> resuming my former position by the fireplace, and again perceiving the
> figure, I moved my head slowly from side to side, and found that it did the
> same. I then went slowly backwards, keeping my head still until I again
> reached the place, when deliberately turning round the mystery was solved.
> A small polished, mahogany stand near the window, which I used as a
> cupboard for various trifles, made the body of the figure, a piece of paper
> hanging from the partly-open door serving as the handkerchief; a vase on
> the top formed the head and head dress, and the slanting light falling upon
> it, and the white curtain of the window completed the illusion. I destroyed
> and re-made the figure several times, and was surprised to find how distinct
> it appeared when the exact relative positions were maintained.

Miss W's brain had incorrectly concluded that a chance collection of
items in a dark room was a little old lady sitting sedately in a corner. Miss
W is not convinced. But note how much hard work she has to do to
uncover the illusion. First she doubts that what she sees can correspond
to reality. She doesn't expect to find someone in that room. Her eyes
sometimes play tricks. Second she experiments with her perception by
looking at the "old lady" from different positions in the room. How easy
it would be to be fooled by such illusions. All too often there may be no
opportunity to experiment with our perception and no reason to think
that our perception is false.

Edgar Allan Poe is frightened by a sphinx

Near the close of an exceedingly warm day, I was sitting, book
in hand, at an open window, commanding, through a long
vista of the river banks, a view of a distant hill. . . . Uplifting my
eyes from the page, they fell upon the naked face of the hill, and
upon an object – upon some living monster of hideous confirmation, which was very rapidly making its way from the summit to the
bottom. . . . Estimating the size of the creature by comparison with
the diameter of the larger trees near which it passed . . . I concluded it to be far larger than any ship of the line in existence. . . . The
mouth of the animal was situated at the extremity of a proboscis

some sixty or seventy feet in length, and about as thick as the body of an ordinary elephant. Near the root of this trunk was an immense quantity of black shaggy hair – more than could have been supplied by the coats of a score of buffaloes. . . . Extending forward, parallel with the proboscis, and on each side of it, was a gigantic staff, thirty or forty feet in length, formed seemingly of pure crystal and in shape a perfect prism, – it reflected in the most gorgeous manner the rays of the declining sun. The trunk was fashioned like a wedge with the apex to the earth. From it there were outspread two pairs of wings – each wing nearly one hundred yards in length – one pair being placed above the other, and all thickly covered with metal scales. . . . I observed that the upper and lower tiers of wings were connected by a strong chain. But the chief peculiarity of this horrible thing was the representation of a Death's Head, which covered nearly the whole surface of its breast, and which was as accurately traced in glaring white, upon the dark ground of the body, as if it had been there carefully designed by an artist. While I regarded the terrific animal, . . . I perceived the huge jaws at the extremity of the proboscis suddenly expand themselves, and from them there proceeded a sound so loud and so expressive of woe, that it struck upon my nerves like a knell and as the monster disappeared at the foot of the hill, I fell at once, fainting, to the floor.

[Poe's host explains] "Let me read to you an account of the genus Sphinx, of the family Crepuscularia of the order Lepidoptera . . . : '. . . The Death's-headed Sphinx has occasioned much terror among the vulgar, at times, by the melancholy kind of cry which it utters, and the insignia of death which it wears upon its corslet.'" He here closed the book and leaned forward in the chair, placing himself accurately in the position which I had occupied at the moment of beholding "the monster."

"Ah, here it is," he presently exclaimed – "it is reascending the face of the hill, and a very remarkable looking creature I admit it to be. Still, it is by no means so large or so distant as you imagined it. . . . I find it to be about the sixteenth of an inch in its extreme length, and also about the sixteenth of an inch distant from the pupil of my eye."

(Extracts from "The Sphinx," 1850)

In this chapter I have shown that even an ordinary, healthy brain does not always give us a true picture of the world. Because we have no direct connection to the physical world around us, our brains have to make inferences about that world on the basis of the crude sensations they receive from our eyes, ears, and all the other sense organs. These inferences can be wrong. Furthermore there are all sorts of things our brains know that never reach our conscious minds.

But there is one bit of the physical world that we carry around with us everywhere we go. Surely we must have direct access to the state of our own body? Or is this too an illusion created by our brain?

Chapter 3

What the Brain Tells Us about Our Bodies

Privileged Access?

My body is an object in the physical world. But unlike other objects I have a special relationship with my body. In particular my brain is part of my body. Sensory neurons run directly into my brain from the various parts of my body. Motor neurons run the other way from my brain to all my muscles. The connections could not be more direct. I have immediate control over what my body does and I don't need to make any inferences about what state it's in. I have almost instant access to every part of my body whenever I need it.

So why do I still feel that slight shock when I see the plump elderly person in the mirror? Do I not know so much about myself after all? Or is my memory persistently distorted by vanity?

Where's the Border?

My first mistake is to think that there is such a clear-cut distinction between my body and the rest of the physical world. Here's a party trick[1] that was invented by Matthew Botvinick and Jonathan Cohen. You rest your left arm on the table and I hide it behind a screen. I put a rubber arm on the table where you can see it. Then I stroke your arm and the rubber arm simultaneously with two brushes. You can feel your own arm being stroked and you can see the rubber arm being stroked. But after some minutes the feeling of being stroked will no longer be in your own

---

[1] In this case the experiment really was first performed at a party.

Figure 3.1   The author as he appears

arm. Now the feeling is in the rubber arm. The feeling has somehow moved out of your body and into a quite separate part of the physical world.

This trick that our brain plays on us is not just good for parties. There are neurons in the parietal cortex[2] of monkeys[3] (and presumably in humans too) that become active when the monkey sees an object near its hand. It doesn't matter where the hand happens to be. The neurons will become active when anything comes near the hand. Perhaps these neurons are indicating the presence of an object that the monkey can reach. But if you give the monkey a rake to use, then after a very short time these same neurons start responding whenever the monkey sees something close to the end of the rake.[4] As far as this part of the brain is concerned, the rake has become an extension of the monkey's arm. And that is how

---

[2]   The location of the parietal lobe is shown in the Box about the brain in Figure p.5 in the Prologue (p.[9ms]). The parietal lobe controls actions of reaching and grasping.

[3]   For a long time I was confused about the terms "primate," "ape," and "monkey." Primate is the big category. We are primates. Chimpanzees are primates. Monkeys are primates. Lemurs and lorises are primates. Apes are a sub-category: gibbons, chimpanzees, humans, etc. Monkeys are another sub-category: marmosets, macaques, baboons, etc.

[4]   It was long believed that monkeys, unlike chimpanzees, do not use tools. In 1996 Atsushi Iriki demonstrated that monkeys could be taught to use a rake to get food.

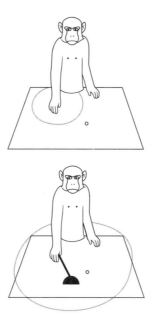

Figure 3.2 The monkey and the rake
If the monkey sees something within reach (in the circle), then neurons in the parietal cortex become more active.
Atsushi Iriki taught monkeys to use a rake to get food that was out of reach. When the monkey is using the rake, then neurons in the parietal cortex respond when the monkey sees objects inside the much larger circle.
Source: Redrawn after Figure 1c: Obayashi, S., Suhara, T., Kawabe, K., Okauchi, T., Maeda, J., Akine, Y., Onoe, H., & Iriki, A. (2001). Functional brain mapping of monkey tool use. *Neuroimage, 14*(4), 853–861.

tools feel to us. After a little practice we feel that our control over the tool is as direct as if it were part of our body. This is the case with something small like a fork or something large like a car.

So our body is extended out into the rest of the physical world whenever we use tools. But isn't there still an obvious difference? These bits of the outside world have no direct connections with our brain. I can't directly sense it if something touches the rake I am holding. I can directly feel where my arm is because of the sense organs in my muscles and joints. Yet, even though we do have these sense organs in our limbs, there are situations in which my arm or my finger might as well be a piece of wood considering how little I know about what each is doing.

We Don't Know What We Are Doing

Research in psychology changed dramatically when mini-computers became available at the end of the 1960s.[5] From then on the computer was usually all the apparatus you needed. To perform a new experiment you simply had to write another computer program. At that time I was studying how people learned to make skilled hand movements. Before computers, I had a special piece of equipment made from a gramophone turntable. People held a metal stick and tried to keep it in contact with a metal target that was glued to the edge of the turntable. This is quite difficult when the turntable is rotating 60 times a minute. All I could measure was whether the person was in contact with the target or not. After computers, the target was a box that moved around on the computer screen. People followed the target by moving a joystick that controlled the position of a pointer in the screen. I could measure the exact position of a person's hand every few milliseconds.

And do people know where their hand actually is? I could have asked this question, but the experiment was actually done many years later by Pierre Fourneret in Marc Jeannerod's lab in Lyons. People were asked to draw a vertical line on the computer screen by moving their hand forward. But they couldn't see their hand, only the line they were making on the screen. The ingenious part of this experiment was the distortion that could be created by the computer.[6] Sometimes moving your hand straight forward would not produce a vertical line on the screen, but one that deviated to the side. When this happens it is very easy to modify your hand movement (by deviating to the other side) so that you still draw a vertical line on the screen. Indeed this is so easy that, unless the distortion is very great, you don't even know that you're making this deviant movement.

So, in spite of the direct connection from my hand to my brain, I am unaware of what precisely my hand is doing. What does this observation

[5]   When I joined the Medical Research Council in 1975 I was given a PDP-11 computer for my research. It was the size of a very large filing cabinet, cost about the same as a small house, and had 16K of memory.
[6]   In fact this experiment was first done in 1965 by the Danish psychologist, T.I. Nielsen. He didn't have a computer. He built a special box with a mirror inside. The hand that people saw in the mirror was not their own but that of the experimenter's assistant. To strengthen the illusion, both the experimental subject and the experimenter's assistant wore white gloves.

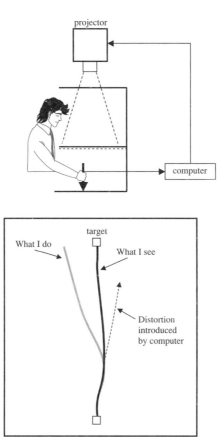

Figure 3.3 We are not aware of what we are doing
I cannot see my hand, only the cursor on the screen. I am not aware that, in order to move the cursor straight across the screen, I am actually moving to the left.

Source: Redrawing of experiment in: Fourneret, P., & Jeannerod, M. (1998). Limited conscious monitoring of motor performance in normal subjects. *Neuropsychologia, 36*(11), 1133–1140.

tell us about the border where my body ends and the outside world begins? Conventionally my body stops at the point where my hand touches the joystick. But in terms of my feeling of control, the border seems to be outside my body and stops with the pointer that I move across the screen. The joystick, the computer, and the pointer have become for me what the rake was for the monkey. And in terms of my awareness of what I am doing, the border seems to be inside my body, stopping at the point where I have the intention to draw a vertical line. My arm and hand then carry out this intention as if they had become a tool in the world outside.[7]

So how much do I really know about what my body is doing?

Who's in Control?

Most of the work that scientists do is of little interest outside a very narrow circle of other scientists in the same field. This is as true for physicists as for psychologists. It is said that the great majority of research papers are read by fewer than 10 other people. Many papers are never read at all. But occasionally an observation is made that is so startling that it is discussed widely outside the field of science. One such observation was published in 1983 by Benjamin Libet and his colleagues. The experiment is delightfully simple. All the person in the experiment had to do was lift one finger whenever he or she "felt the urge to do so." At the same time electrical activity in the brain was measured using EEG equipment. It was already well known that there is characteristic change in this activity just before someone spontaneously makes any movement like lifting a finger. This change in activity is very small, but it can be detected by combining measurements from many movements. The change in brain activity can be detected up to a second *before* the finger is actually lifted. The novel aspect of Libet's study was that he asked his volunteers to tell him *when* they "had the urge" to lift their finger. They did this by reporting the "time" that was displayed on a special clock at the moment that they "had the urge."[8] The urge to lift the finger occurred about 200 msec before the finger was actually lifted. But the key observation that caused so much fuss was that the change in brain activity occurred about *500 msec* before the finger was lifted. So brain activity indicating that the volunteer was about to lift a finger occurred about 300 msec *before* that volunteer reported having the urge to lift his or her finger.

The implication of this observation is that, by measuring your brain activity, I can know that you're going to have the urge to lift your finger before you know it yourself. This result had such a vast impact outside psychology because it seems to show that even our simplest voluntary

[7]   A very intelligent tool that can change its functioning to suit the circumstances.

[8]   Pedantic psychologists have raised many objections to this method of measuring the time at which "the urge" occurred. However, Patrick Haggard has recently repeated Libet's experiment using various different ways for measuring the time of "the urge" and confirmed Libet's results.

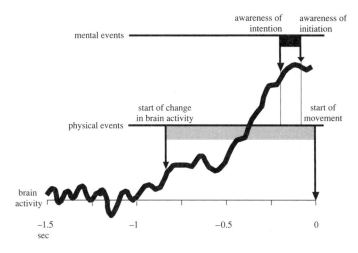

Figure 3.4 When we move, mental events don't happen at the same time as physical events
The brain activity associated with a movement starts before we are aware of our intention
to move, but the movement starts after we are aware of initiating the movement. The
intention and the initiation are closer together in mental time than in physical time (see
Chapter 6).

Source: Redrawing from data in: Libet, B., Gleason, C.A., Wright, E.W., & Pearl, D.K. (1983).
Time of conscious intention to act in relation to onset of cerebral activity (readiness-
potential): The unconscious initiation of a freely voluntary act. *Brain, 106* (Pt. 3), 623–642.

actions are predetermined. We think we are making a choice when, in
fact, our brain has already made the choice. Our experience of making a
choice at that moment is therefore an illusion. And if we are deluded in
thinking that we are making choices, then we are also deluded in thinking that we have free will.

But does this result really demonstrate that we have no free will? One
problem is that the choices involved are very trivial. It doesn't matter
what you choose. In Libet's original experiment you simply had to decide
when to lift one finger. In other experiments you might be given more
freedom and be asked to choose between the left and the right finger.
But these actions are deliberately chosen because they are trivial. With
such acts we can look at the process of choosing without interference
from social pressures or moral values. The triviality of the action does not
alter the fact that when you take part in the experiment you have to
decide for yourself precisely when to lift your finger.

So Libet's result still stands. At the moment at which we think we are
choosing an action, our brain has already made the choice. But this does

not mean that the action has not been chosen freely. It simply means that we were not *aware* of making the choice at that earlier time. As we shall discover in Chapter 6, our experience of the time at which actions occur does not bear a fixed relationship to what is happening in the physical world.

These unconscious choices are just like Helmholtz's unconscious inferences. We do not perceive the object in front of our eyes until the brain has made unconscious inferences about what that object may be. We are not aware of the action we are about to perform until the brain has made an unconscious choice about what that action should be. But this action is determined by a choice that we have previously made freely and deliberately. We have agreed to cooperate with the experiment. We may not know precisely which action we are going to perform at any one moment. But we have already selected the small set of actions from which this precise action will be chosen.

My Brain Can Act Perfectly Well without Me

In Libet's experiment we seem to lag behind what our brain is doing. But we do catch up in the end. In other experiments our brain controls our actions and we don't even know about it. This is the case in the "double-step" task developed in Lyons. Your task is to look out for a target that is a vertical rod. As soon as it appears you reach for it with your hand and grasp it. Reaching and grasping is something you can do very easily and rapidly. Here, the trick is that on some occasions, as soon as you start to move your hand, I move the target to a new position. You can easily adjust to this and will accurately grasp the target in its new position. On many of these occasions you will not notice that the target moved. But your brain notices the movement. Your hand starts moving toward the first position of the target and then, about 150 msec after the target position changes, your hand movement changes in order to reach the target in its new position. So your brain notices that the target has moved and your brain alters the movement your hand is making so that you can reach the new target position. And all this can happen without you noticing anything. You don't notice either the change in position of the target or the change in your hand movement. You will tell me that the target only moved once.[9]

[9]   This effect is seen even more clearly if you are tracking the target with your eyes rather than your hand.

Figure 3.5   The Roelofs illusion
If the frame moves to right, the observer thinks the black spot has moved to the left even though it stayed still. But if the observer reaches out to touch the remembered position of the spot, he does not make an error.

Source: Redrawn after: Bridgeman, B., Peery, S., & Anand, S. (1997). Interaction of cognitive and sensorimotor maps of visual space. *Perception and Psychophysics, 59*(3), 456–469.

In this case your brain can produce appropriate actions when you don't even know that such actions are needed. In other cases your brain can produce appropriate actions even though these are different from the actions you think should be made.

In this experiment you are sitting in the dark. I show you (briefly) a target dot inside a frame. Immediately afterwards I show you (briefly) the target inside the frame again. This time the target is still in the same place, but the frame has moved to the right. If I ask you to describe what happened, you will say, "The target moved to the left." This is a typical visual illusion in which your visual brain has wrongly decided that the frame stayed still and so the target must have moved.[10] But if I ask you to *touch* where you think the target was, then you will touch the correct point on the screen – your pointing is unaffected by any movements of the frame. So your hand "knows" that the target has not moved even though you think that it has.

These observations show that your body can interact with the world perfectly well even though you don't know what your body is doing and

[10]   An illusion originally described by Roelofs in 1935.

also when what you think you know about the world is wrong. Your brain may be directly connected to your body, but the knowledge that your brain gives you about the state of your body seems to be as indirect as the knowledge it gives you about the outside world. Your brain doesn't tell you when your body moves in a different way from what you intended. Your brain can trick you into thinking that your body is in a different place from where it really is. And these are all examples of a normal brain interacting with a normal body. When things go wrong the brain becomes really creative.

Phantoms in the Brain

If you have the misfortune to have one of your arms amputated you are very likely to experience a phantom arm. You can feel your phantom arm located in a particular position in space. In some cases you can move your phantom hand and your phantom fingers. And yet you can see that you have no arm and the sense organs in the arm are no longer there. So these phantoms are created in your brain. With time your phantom arm may disintegrate so that you experience a hand, but not a forearm. You may lose the ability to move the arm. Worst of all, you may feel a real pain in your phantom arm. Sometimes this pain seems to be the result of your phantom hand being stuck in a very awkward position from which you cannot move it. Such pains are very difficult to treat.

Up until the 1980s neuropsychologists were taught that, after about the age of 16, our brains are mature and no new brain growth can occur. If the fibers connecting neurons were damaged, then those neurons would stay disconnected. If you lost a neuron, it would never be replaced. We now know this is wrong. Our brains are very plastic, especially when we are young, and remain so throughout our lives. Connections are constantly being made and unmade in response to our changing environment.[11]

Muscles waste away if we don't use them, but our brains respond in a rather different way if parts are not used. If one of your arms is amputated, then a small part of your brain will no longer receive any stimulation from the sense organs that were in that arm. But these neurons do not die. They are used for new purposes. Immediately next to this area of the brain is the area that receives stimulation from the sense organs in the face.

[11]   In songbirds the region of the brain which is used for singing grows during the singing season and then shrinks. Not only are new connections made during the singing season, but new neurons appear only to disappear when the season is over.

Figure 3.6   A phantom hand
After a limb has been amputated, you often experience a phantom limb. In time the
phantom may shrink and change. Alexa North and Peter Halligan manipulated photographs
to give an impression of what the experience of a phantom limb is like. In this case the
experience of the hand remains, but the forearm has gone.

Source: From Wright, Halligan and Kew, Wellcome Trust Sci Art Project, 1997.

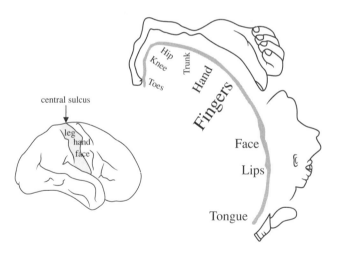

Figure 3.7   The sensory homunculus in the brain
Just behind the central sulcus there is a strip of cortex containing a "map" of different parts
of the body. The left side of the body is on the right side of the brain and vice versa. If your
leg is touched, then activity will be seen near the top of this strip, while if your face is
touched, activity will be seen further down. The amount of cortex assigned to these
different body parts depends on their sensitivity, so large areas are given to the lips and
fingers. The face and the hands are close together in this map.

Source: Modified from: McGonigle, D.J., "The body in question: Phantom phenomena and
the view from within" (*http://www.artbrain.org/phantomlimb/mcgonigle.html*).

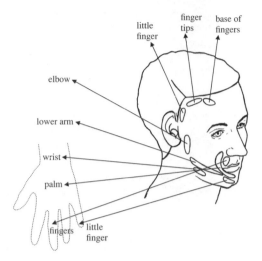

Figure 3.8 A phantom hand in the face
After her right arm was amputated, DM experienced a phantom limb. When the right side of her face was touched with a Q-tip, she would experience the stimulation of her face together with a distinct tingling sensation in specific parts of the phantom limb. There is a systematic relationship between the location in the face and the location in the phantom.

Source: Figure 2 in: Halligan, P.W., Marshall, J.C., Wade, D.T., Davey. J., & Morrison, D. (1993). Thumb in cheek? Sensory reorganization and perceptual plasticity after limb amputation. *Neuroreport, 4*(3), 233–236.

If the hand area is no longer being, used then it can be taken over by the face. The result is that when I touch your face, you will feel that touch as usual, but you will also feel that part of your phantom hand is being touched.[12] Peter Halligan and his colleagues investigated this effect systematically in a person with a phantom hand. Halligan touched each part of the person's face in turn and asked her to describe exactly where she felt the touch in her phantom hand. In this way he was able to generate a map showing the relationship between areas of the face and the phantom hand. Even though these neurons were now responding to touches to the face, this person still experienced the touch as being in a hand that no longer existed.

Most phantom limbs occur because a limb has been amputated. In such cases there is no damage in the brain of the person who is experiencing the phantom. But phantom limbs can also occur after brain

---

[12]   This phenomenon was first described by V.S. Ramachandran and his colleagues.

Figure 3.9 The woman with three arms
After damage to the front of her brain, EP sometimes experiences an extra left arm (and leg). This is her drawing of what this feels like when she is shopping.
Source: Figure 2 in: Hari, R., Hanninen, R., Makinen, T., Jousmaki, V., Forss, N., Seppa, M., & Salonen, O. (1998). Three hands: Fragmentation of human bodily awareness. *Neuroscience Letters*, *240*(3), 131–134.

damage. EP is a Finnish woman who went into hospital with a severe headache and paralysis of the left side of her body. The cause was found to be a burst blood vessel at the front of her brain, and an operation was performed to repair the damaged vessel. However, EP was left with permanent damage in a small region at the front of her brain that is concerned with the control of movements. I met EP several years after her operation. She was fully recovered apart from one very unusual feature. She frequently experiences an extra "ghost" arm on the left side of her body. This phantom arm appears in the same position that her real left arm was in a minute or two before. When the phantom is present, it feels to her as if she has three arms. The phantom left arm goes away if EP looks at her real left arm. EP knows that she hasn't really got three arms and realizes that the experience is caused by damage to her brain. However, the perception of the extra arm is so vivid that she sometimes worries that she will bump into people when shopping because she feels that she is carrying a large bag in each of her three hands.

I met EP when she flew over from Helsinki to the Functional Imaging Laboratory in Bloomsbury, London so that Dave McGonigle could scan her brain in order to discover which region became active when she was experiencing her third arm. I met up with them and we all had a very exciting Saturday in the imaging laboratory, which is not reflected at all in the paper we wrote about it afterwards.[13] EP was just about to go into the scanner when, disaster, we discovered that she had a clip in her brain that had been inserted to repair the damage to her blood vessel. Because of the powerful magnetic field involved, it is dangerous to scan people with pieces of metal in their brain.[14] What was the clip made of? EP went off to do some shopping in Oxford Street while we tried to locate the surgeon who performed the operation. Through skilled use of mobile phones he was eventually located on a golf course somewhere in Finland. The clip was titanium, non-magnetic, and therefore safe. And the result of the experiment? EP experienced her third arm whenever there was an increase in activity in a small region in the middle of her brain.[15] But this is not a region concerned with using sensation to *detect* the position of the body. It is a region concerned with sending commands that *control* the position of the body. This is an important clue for understanding how our creative brain tells us about our body.

There's Nothing Wrong with Me

EP is a very unusual woman because she is fully aware that her strange experiences are not real and are caused by the small amount of damage in her brain. A very different phenomenon is seen much more frequently in people with damage toward the back of the brain, usually on the right. The left arm of these people is often paralyzed and insensitive to touch. But such people seem to be unaware of the paralysis and deny that there is anything wrong with them (anosognosia). V.S. Ramachandran has interviewed many of these people. His reports illustrate the remarkable discrepancy between what these people believe and their actual abilities.

The left side of Mrs. F.D.'s body is completely paralyzed as the result of a stroke.

---

[13] Writing scientific papers is rather like writing poetry in an ancient verse form. Everything you want to say has to be forced into predetermined sections: introduction, method, results, discussion. You must never say "I," and the passive tense is preferred. Inevitably all the interesting things get left out.

[14] And also people with tattoos or permanent eyeliner.

[15] If you really want to know, it was located on the right medial wall in the supplementary motor area (SMA proper).

VSR:	Mrs. F.D., can you walk?
F.D.:	Yes.
VSR:	Can you move your hands?
F.D.:	Yes.
VSR:	Are both hands equally strong?
F.D.:	Yes, of course they are.

Some people seem to recognize that they are not using one arm and have to explain why.

VSR:	Mrs. L.R., why aren't you using your left arm?
L.R.:	Doctor, these medical students have been prodding me all day and I'm sick of it. I don't want to use my left arm.

Most remarkable of all are the people who believe they have moved their paralysed arm when no such movement has taken place

VSR:	Can you clap?
F.D.:	Of course I can clap.
VSR:	Will you clap for me?
	She proceeded to make clapping movements with her right hand as if clapping with an imaginary hand near the midline.
VSR:	Are you clapping?
F.D.:	Yes, I am clapping.

Mrs. F.D.'s brain seems to have created the experience of moving her left arm when no such movement actually occurred.

Who's Doing It?

In these people it is not simply their knowledge about the positions of parts of their body that is wrong. Their knowledge about whether or not they are acting on the world is also wrong. They believe they are acting on the world when, in fact, they are doing nothing. But imagine how alarming it would be if you were sitting quietly doing nothing and one of your hands started acting all by itself. This can sometimes happen in people with brain damage. The willful hand is described as "anarchic." The anarchic hand grasps doorknobs or picks up a pencil and starts to scribble with it. People with this syndrome are upset by the actions of the hand: "It will not do what I want it to do." They will often try to

Figure 3.10 The anarchic hand
In Stanley Kubrick's 1964 film *Dr. Strangelove, or How I Learned to Stop Worrying and Love the Bomb*, Dr. Strangelove (played by Peter Sellers) has a right hand with a mind of its own. In this scene he is using his left hand to stop his anarchic right hand from strangling him.
Source: Columbia Pictures, 1964.

prevent it from moving by grasping it firmly with the other hand. In one case the person's left hand would tenaciously grasp any nearby object, pull at her clothes, and even grasp her throat during sleep. She slept with the arm tied to the bed to prevent such nocturnal misbehavior.

"But these are people with damaged brains," says the Professor of English. "I don't have such problems with my body. I may be clumsy, but I know what I am trying to do. And I know when I'm doing it."

"I know it feels like that," I reply. "But this is an illusion."

Daniel Wegner has proposed that we have no direct knowledge of causing our actions.[16] All we *know* is that we have the intention to act, and then, a little later, the action occurs. We *infer* that our intention caused the action. But Wegner didn't just stop with this speculation. He did some experiments to test the idea. He predicted that, if an action occurred after you had the intention to act, then you would assume that you had caused the act even when it was actually caused by someone else. The experiment is quite tricky in all senses of the term. When you take part in this experiment you have a companion (who is really a stooge of the experimenter). You and your companion place your right forefingers

[16]   Read all about it in his excellent book *The Illusion of Conscious Will*.

on a special mouse. By moving this mouse around you move a pointer on a computer monitor.[17] There are lots of objects on the screen. Through earphones you hear someone name one of the objects. You think about moving the pointer toward the object. If your companion moves the pointer toward the object at that moment (he is also instructed through earphones), then you are very likely to think that you made the movement. Of course the timing is critical. If the mouse moves just before you had the thought, then you don't feel you caused it. If the mouse moves too long afterwards, then you don't feel you caused it either. If the interval is about 1 and 5 seconds between having the thought and the mouse moving, then you will believe you have moved your arm even when this is not actually the case.

The opposite effect can also occur. In this case you perform an action, but are firmly convinced that you did nothing. Furthermore this effect is not restricted to the psychology lab. This effect happens in "real-life" situations and can have disastrous consequences. But I am not going to tell you about it now. At the moment I am only concerned with how we know about the physical world, including your own body. The illusion that you are not performing an action occurs because you believe that someone else is performing the action. This effect involves the mental world – the world of other minds that we will not enter until Chapter 6.

Where Is the "You"?

My aim in this chapter is to convince you that you do not have privileged access to knowledge about your own body. To do this I have presented my observations from various stages in the hierarchy of knowledge through which you make your body act on the world. At the bottom level there is knowledge about the position of your body in space. This knowledge is crucial when reaching for things. You are very good at reaching. Yet you know very little about the exact position of the various parts of your body in space, and what you know can sometimes be wrong. At the next level there is knowledge about when and how to move, also crucial for reaching. You are good at making rapid reaching movements and can correct them in mid-flight. Yet you may not even know that you have made these rapid and accurate corrections. At the next level there is

---

[17] This experiment is really a version of the infamous ouija board, but you don't mention that in the grant application.

knowledge that you are the actor who is making the movements. Even on this fundamental point you may sometimes be wrong. How will this exercise end? Is there anything that you know about yourself? What is there left of "you" if you are not aware of your body or your actions?

Remember, the actions in all these examples are very simple. If someone throws a cricket ball at you, you don't think about it. You just catch it. But what about the kinds of acts that you do have to think about because you are in a novel situation and have no fixed routines to fall back on?

Elodie Varraine studies people as they walk on a treadmill. She can vary the resistance of the treadmill to make the walking more or less difficult. In one experiment she would tell you that after walking on the treadmill for a few minutes, the resistance would start to slowly increase. You had to detect when the resistance changed. In addition you had to respond to the change in resistance by altering the way you were walking. If you were instructed to keep up the same walking speed, then you would have to increase the effort you put into walking. If you were instructed to keep your effort constant, then you would have to reduce your walking speed. The important point about this experiment is that the action you have to make is not an automatic response to the change in resistance of the treadmill. The action has to be deliberately chosen on the basis of the instruction you have just received. Dr. Varraine found that people correctly changed their way of walking several seconds *before* they noticed that the resistance of the treadmill had increased. In other words your brain could detect the change in resistance and change your way of walking without you knowing that the resistance had changed or that you had changed your way of walking. Actions based on arbitrary instructions can be chosen and implemented without your awareness.

The most extreme examples of people doing things without knowing that they are doing them are associated with *hypnosis*. Here is a typical anecdote.[18]

> We sit down with the subject in the laboratory. As we are talking about the latest boxing match the operator taps three times on the table with his pencil. Instantly – and we mean instantly – the subject's eyes close and he

[18]   The following passage is taken from George H. Estabrooks's chapter on "hypnotism in warfare" in his book *Hypnotism*. Estabrooks was a Rhodes scholar, a graduate of Harvard, and a chairman of the Psychology Department of Colgate University. He was an authority on hypnosis active during World War II. He is credited with the idea of using hypnotism to create the perfect secret agent: the agent who doesn't know that he is an agent.

is sound "asleep". [The operator performs various hypnotic demonstrations of the subject in his somnambulistic state.] Then we wake him up.

He immediately starts talking about that boxing match!

A visitor to the laboratory interrupts him.

"What do you know of hypnotism?"

The subject looks surprised, *"Why, nothing."*

"When were you hypnotized last?"

"I have never been hypnotized."

"Do you realize that you were in a trance just ten minutes ago?"

"Don't be silly! No one has ever hypnotized me and no one ever can."

Psychologists are very wary of hypnosis. The technique is tainted by accusations of mysticism and fraud. Yet, at the same time, it was the investigation of hypnosis that helped to establish psychology as a scientific discipline. The problem starts with Anton Mesmer. Mesmer developed a healing technique (subsequently called mesmerism) based on his theory of animal magnetism. He achieved considerable success, first in Vienna and then in Paris. In 1784 Louis XVI appointed a Royal Commission of eminent scientists chaired by Benjamin Franklin (the American ambassador) to investigate Mesmer's claims. The commission concluded that Mesmer's cures were genuine, but that his theory was wrong. The effects were due "to imagination and to imitation" (i.e. psychological processes) rather than any physical force. Mesmer was discredited and left Paris,[19] but his technique continued to be used and, by the middle of the 19th century, mesmerism had evolved into hypnosis. Hypnosis was used to induce anesthesia before surgery and, later, to cure hysteria. By using hypnosis it seemed possible to study how ideas turn into actions. This psychological mechanism was of enormous interest, not only to clinicians such as Sigmund Freud, but also to psychologists such as William James.

During the ascendancy of behaviorism, hypnosis became a fringe topic for psychology. By just looking at them, you can't tell the difference between someone who is acting as a result of a hypnotic suggestion and someone who is simply doing what they have been told to do by a man in a white coat. For the behaviourist, hypnotism was just play-acting. Of course if you ask the person what the experience was like, then the two situations are completely different. You know when you're play-acting. You don't know when you're acting under hypnotic suggestion.

---

[19]   As a result he avoided the Revolution, unlike some members of the Royal Commission, who went to the guillotine.

Studies of hypnosis remain on the fringe of academic psychology, but important experiments are being done using this technique. Here is one described to me by John Morton.

A group of suggestible, but otherwise perfectly normal, university students were hypnotized. They were then given a word association task. The experimenter read out a list of words and the subjects responded with the first words that came into their heads (bed – *pillow*, bridge – *river*, garden – *lawn*, etc., etc.). While they were still under hypnosis the subjects were told that they could no longer remember doing this task. Then the experimenter read out the same list of words and the subjects again had to respond with the first word that came into their heads.

So this is the key question. If you had a "real" memory loss due to brain damage so that you were unable to remember having done that word association task just now, would you respond with different words or would you give the same words again?

"Obviously I would give different words next time," says the Professor of English. "Which words you give is just a matter of chance. There are so many different associations for the word *tree* that it is very unlikely that you would give the same word again."

"That's what most people think," I reply smugly. "Unless they have attended some neuropsychology lectures."

I know the Professor is wrong through studies of people with severe amnesia who really can't remember doing the task. These people tend to give the same words that they gave just before. And they may give them a little faster.[20]

The subjects in the hypnosis experiment gave different words when the word association task was repeated. Like the Professor of English, they thought that this is what happens if you can't remember doing the task before and they acted according to their belief. But they didn't know that this is what they were doing. So here's what your brain has to do in this experiment without you knowing anything about it. First, it must set up a general strategy for performing the word association task, "give a different word from last time." Second, for this strategy to be successful, it must remember which words were given last time in order to avoid giving them again. Third, it must monitor each action to overcome the strong tendency to give the same word again.

---

[20]   This is through a process of unconscious priming that is unaffected by the damage that causes their loss of memory. A temporary trace remains in our brain of every response we have just made. This makes it easier to repeat the same response again.

Figure 3.11   The author as he really is

So here we are near the top of a hierarchy for controlling action. And we find that our brain can set up and monitor a complex strategy for action with our knowing anything about it. My knowledge of my own body and how it acts on the world is not direct. There is much about me that my brain hides and much that it makes up. In which case, when I look in the mirror, why doesn't my brain show me as I truly am – young, thin, and with abundant black hair?

At the end of this first part of my book, if all has gone to plan, you should be feeling somewhat disconcerted. I have shown how our experience of an effortless interaction with the world – through our perceptions and actions – is an illusion. We have no direct contact with the world or even with our own bodies. Our brain creates this illusion by hiding from us all the complex processes that are involved in discovering about the world. We are simply not aware of all the inferences and choices our brain constantly has to make. When things go wrong, our experiences of the world can be completely false. But how can we ever be sure of what we experience? And if our contact with the physical world is so tenuous, what hope have we of entering the mental worlds of other people?

Now, having taken the brain and the mind apart, I have to try to put them back together again and reassure you that we can be confident of our experiences (most of the time).

Part II

How the Brain Does It

Chapter 4

Getting Ahead by Prediction

Everything we know about the physical world, including what we know about our own bodies, comes through our brain. In the first part of this book I have shown that our brain does not simply transmit knowledge to us like a passive TV set. Our brain actively creates pictures of the world. We know how creative the brain is because sometimes these pictures of the world can be completely false. This discovery is shocking because it makes us wonder how we can ever know whether what our brain tells us about the world is true. The surprise is that our brain ever gets things right. The brain creates its pictures of the world from the very limited and imperfect signals provided by our senses. For example, the visual image on our retina is in two dimensions only and yet our brain creates for us a vivid experience of a world of objects arranged in three-dimensional space. Thankfully, 99 times out of 100 the pictures our brain creates about the world are correct. How is this possible?

Patterns of Reward and Punishment

Learning about the world without a teacher

Our brain is continuously learning things about the world. From moment to moment it has to discover the identity of the things around it: should they be approached or avoided? It has to discover where these things are: are they nearby or far away? It has to discover how to reach for the fruit and avoid being stung by the wasp. Furthermore, this learning occurs without a teacher. We can't have someone at our side continually telling us whether we are doing the right or the wrong thing.

Travel is one of the perks of being an academic. Every month there is another conference that I could attend, often with all expenses paid. And so I find myself walking through another town that I have never visited before searching for the conference center where I shall meet many people I have never seen before and will seek out the ones I already know to talk to. Isn't that the opinionated Professor of English over there? I thought this was a scientific meeting.

I have never seen this town before and yet I walked through it without difficulty. I like to visit new places and walk about the streets on my own. I learn new things about the world, but I don't need a teacher at my side at every moment. Most learning in childhood happens without a teacher. No one can teach you how to ride a bicycle. You have to learn by doing it yourself. We learn the fundamentals of language before any teaching occurs. Nine-month-old American infants can learn to distinguish between different sounds in Chinese simply by being in the same room as someone speaking Chinese.

So how do we learn without a teacher?

Learning about the future

When scientists gain a place in popular culture, it is because people find something unusual or eccentric about them and what they do. We know that Galileo dropped things from the top of the leaning tower of Pisa, although we are not exactly sure why. We believe that Einstein made some very important discoveries about space and time, although all we actually *know* about him is that he had a funny hairstyle.

Ivan Petrovich Pavlov was another such scientist. Even though his experiments were conducted 100 years ago, everyone knows that he made dogs salivate by ringing a bell. There are all sorts of reasons why this seems an eccentric experiment. Why study dogs when most scientists study rats?[1] Why measure salivation when it would be much easier to measure an obviously visible movement? Why such an arbitrary signal as the ringing of a bell? And, the most critical question of all, what on earth is the point of such studies?

Pavlov's studies are important because they reveal something fundamental about learning that applies equally to animals and to humans.

---

[1]   Albino rats were brought into laboratories for physiological studies as early as 1828. The oldest strain of inbred rats dates from 1856, when the Jardin des Plantes reported a feeder colony of black hooded rats. That colony was still in existence 132 years later in 1988.

Figure 4.1   Ivan Petrovich Pavlov (1849–1936)
Pavlov (center) photographed with one of his dogs during a demonstration. He discovered classical conditioning, the most basic form of associative learning
Source: RIA Novosti/Science Photo Library.

The effects that Pavlov observed are not restricted to dogs, salivation, or the sound of bells.[2] Pavlov studied salivation because his original interest was in digestion. We all, like dogs, automatically start to salivate about 1 second after food is put into our mouths. This is the starting point of the process by which food is digested. This is not very surprising. There is a direct relationship between food and digestion. The food is only of any value to us if we digest it. Pavlov called the process by which food caused salivation an "unconditioned reflex."

But Pavlov also discovered, possibly by accident, that an arbitrary signal that occurred at the same time as food, for example the sound of a ticking metronome, would also cause salivation. If the sound of the metronome occurred just before the food was put in the dog's mouth, then, after this procedure had been repeated four or five times, the sound of the metronome would cause salivation without any food being given.

---

[2]   The importance of Pavlov's work was recognized almost immediately and he was awarded the Nobel Prize for Physiology in 1904. Today Pavlov's work is sometimes dismissed as part of the behaviorist school, which, during much of the 20th century, held back the progress of psychological research by denying possibility of the scientific study of mental life. In fact, Pavlov's approach differed fundamentally from behaviorism. Unlike the behaviorists, he was passionately interested in discovering the physiological mechanisms underlying psychic phenomena such as his conditioned reflex.

Pavlov called this a "conditioned reflex." Pavlov suggested that the sound of the metronome had become a signal for food. The dog didn't just salivate at the sound of the metronome. She also turned in the direction from which food usually came and began to lick her lips vigorously. When the dog heard the sound, she expected the food to arrive.[3]

Since the sound of a ticking metronome is "quite alien to food," it doesn't matter what it is. Pavlov tried many different stimuli. The smell of vanilla, the buzzing of an electric bell, the sight of a rotating object – all these stimuli could act as signals for the appearance of food.

As long as we are hungry, food is something we want. Food is rewarding. We approach it. We will shove our way through the inevitable crush around the food table at the party, ignoring all attempts at conversation until we have acquired a plateful. Pavlov showed that arbitrary stimuli could become signals of food and lead animals to approach that stimulus. That is why people at a party will automatically head for the area in the room that is most crowded. We have learned that that is where the food and drink will be.

Pavlov also showed that exactly the same kind of learning happens with punishment. If an unpleasant substance was put into the dog's mouth, she would to try to get rid of it by shaking her head violently, opening her mouth, and making tongue movements (and also salivating). Arbitrary stimuli like the beating metronome could also become signals for these punishing events that we, like dogs, will want to avoid.

Pavlov had found an experimental technique for studying a most basic kind of learning. This is a form of *associative learning* because what is learned is an association between an arbitrary stimulus and a rewarding stimulus (food in the mouth) or a punishing stimulus (electric shock). Such learning is an important mechanism for acquiring knowledge about the world. Through this mechanism we can learn which things are nice and which things are nasty. For example, color can be a signal that fruit is ripe. As a fruit ripens, it tends to become redder, or, more accurately, less green, as the chlorophyll breaks down. We prefer the nice ripe fruit over the nasty unripe fruit. So we can learn about which are the nice and nasty fruit from their color.

But the word "association" is misleading. Just putting the sound of the bell and the food close together in time is not sufficient to cause

---

[3] Strictly, the term "Pavlovian" or "Classical" conditioning applies only to the association between the sound of the metronome and salivation. The head turning and expectation involves a more complex process.

learning. In one experiment Pavlov reports that even after 374 combinations of a loud buzzer and food, no learning took place. This was because the sound of the buzzer always occurred 5 to 10 seconds *after* the food was put into the mouth. An arbitrary stimulus is only interesting if it *predicts* that something nice or nasty is going to happen in the future. If the stimulus comes after the important event, it is of no interest at all. In this case we already know about the important event. Such a stimulus tells us nothing new, so we ignore it.

The learning discovered by Pavlov is precisely the sort of learning we need in order to survive. This learning identifies all those useful stimuli in the world outside that tell us what is going to happen in the future. But, while learning which things are going to be nice and which things are going to be nasty is very helpful, it is not sufficient for survival. We must also learn what to do in order to get the nice things and avoid the nasty ones.

At around the same as Pavlov was making dogs salivate in St. Petersburg, Edward Thorndike in New York was putting cats in specially constructed puzzle boxes. These were small cages with a door that the cat could open in some way, for example by pulling a loop of string. Thorndike showed that cats could learn to pull the string, escape from the cage, and eat the fish that was just outside the cage. But the key question he wanted to answer was: how did they learn? Thorndike recognized that it was important to show how cats did *not* learn. He showed that having a teacher did not help.[4] Cats did not learn by imitation. Repeatedly watching another cat which had already learned how to get out of the box by pulling the string was of no help. Thorndike also showed that cats did not learn by demonstration. He took the cat's paw and pulled the string with it so the cat could get out and eat the fish. But, after many such demonstrations, if the cat was then left alone in the box, he did not immediately pull the string.

Thorndike concluded that the cats could learn to get out of the box only by trial and error. As soon as the cat was put into the box, he tried to escape and get at the fish. He tried to squeeze through any opening; he clawed and bit the bars; he thrust his paws out through any opening and clawed at everything within reach. By accident he eventually clawed

---

[4] Teaching often occurs without language. We learn many skills better by demonstration than through words. I foolishly spent some months trying to learn how to tie a bow-tie with the aid of a verbal description and a diagram, but with no success. But even this kind of teaching does not seem to occur in other animals. Baby chimpanzees learn to use tools by watching their mothers, but the mothers make no attempt to teach them.

Figure 4.2 One of Edward Thorndike's puzzle boxes
Thorndike discovered instrumental learning, the other basic form of associative learning.
A cat has to learn how to get out of the box and get the fish which is just outside.

Source: Robert M. Yerkes Papers. Manuscripts & Archives, Yale University Library.

the loop of string and opened the door. Each time the cat was put back in the box, he got out a little quicker. The act of pulling the string occurred sooner, until, eventually, the cat pulled the string as soon as he was put into the box.

Thorndike recognized that this also was learning by association. The cat learned to associate an action (pulling the string) with a reward (getting out of the box and getting the fish). All animals learn in this way. We humans, like cats, are more likely to perform any act that is followed by something nice. As with the learning studied by Pavlov, the reverse is also true. We are less likely to perform any act that is followed by something nasty. We can also unlearn an association (this is called extinction). If pulling the string no longer opened the door, the cat would eventual stop pulling.

By this learning mechanism we discover which of our actions influence the future.

Superstitious learning

When the cat has learned to get out of the puzzle box by pulling a string, this does not mean that he has worked out how the string opens the door. He would have learned just as well if the action had been "quite alien" to the reward, just as in the kind of learning studied by Pavlov. *Any* arbitrary action that occurs just before a reward is more likely to be repeated.

A generation after Thorndike, Burrhus F. Skinner[5] developed his eponymous box, which is essentially a refined and mechanized version of Thorndike's puzzle box. The animal in the box presses a lever (if he is rat) or pecks a key (if he is a pigeon), and rewards or punishments are automatically delivered. The times of all these events are continuously recorded.

Using his box, Skinner demonstrated the arbitrary nature of response learning in a most elegant experiment on "superstition" in the pigeon. A hungry pigeon was put into the Skinner box and food was presented at regular intervals *with no reference whatsoever to the bird's behavior*. After a short time the pigeon was seen repeatedly performing some arbitrary action. One pigeon turned counter-clockwise around the box, making two or three turns between the appearances of food. Another repeatedly thrust its head into one of the upper corners of the box. A third developed a "tossing" response, as if placing its head beneath an invisible bar and lifting it repeatedly. The pigeons had learned to repeat whatever action they happened to be performing just before the appearance of food. Skinner called this "superstitious" behavior because the pigeons acted as if they believed that their behavior caused the food to appear when this was not the case. He suggested that superstitious behavior can arise in humans in just the same way.

This may explain why so many sportsmen and their fans have lucky mascots and important pre-game rituals. A tennis player might always bounce his ball on the ground in a certain way before he makes a serve.

---

[5] B.F. Skinner was the most eminent of the behaviorist psychologists. He had an interesting life to which many stories are attached. He wanted to write a stream-of-consciousness novel, but became a behaviorist instead (True). He brought up his daughter in a Skinner box and she later committed suicide (Untrue). I had the privilege of meeting Skinner when he visited the lab where I was doing my Ph.D. He must have been utterly mystified by my attempt to explain my interest in linking behaviorism with information theory. His politely feigned interest has provided an important role model for me ever since.

Reportedly, Goran Ivanisevic avoided touching his head or facial hair throughout a tennis tournament.

This account of superstitious behavior has been eagerly taken up by psychology students. A reliable informant from the Cambridge psychology class of '68 tells me that they were able to cause an eminent neuropsychologist to lecture from the far left side of the theater by yawning and dropping their pencils whenever he moved to the right. An interesting feature of such experiments is that they work only if the target is unaware that he is learning about reward contingencies in the environment. We don't have to be aware of associations to learn them – in fact it helps if we are not aware of them.

In the first part of this book I showed how much our brain knows about the world without this knowledge ever reaching our awareness. This is especially true of what our brain knows as a result of learning by association. This is what makes perception and action seem so easy. We are not aware of all the knowledge that has been acquired to help us interact with the world. When I say below that "we learn to predict the future," you must remember that this is not normally something we do consciously or deliberately.

How does the brain learn?

Both kinds of associative learning are about the future. We learn that certain signals tell us what is going to happen in the future. We learn that certain actions will cause things to happen in the future. Of course, it is not the signals that predict what is going to happen. It is the brain that does the predicting. We can see the brain predicting in this way if we look directly at the activity in nerve cells.[6]

Nerve cells are essentially signaling devices. Information is transmitted from one end of the nerve cell to the other using electricity in much the same way as information is transmitted through a telephone line (see Chapter 5). But what happens when the signal gets to the end of the nerve? How does the signal get from one nerve to the next? There is a similar problem with a telephone. There is no electrical connection

---

[6]   Major advances in our understanding of how the brain works came from the ability to record the activity in single nerve cells. In 1958 Hubel and Wiesel were the first to show that cells in the visual cortex were tuned to respond to specific visual stimuli and received the Nobel Prize for this work in 1981. For example, some cells respond strongly to vertical lines, but not at all to horizontal lines.

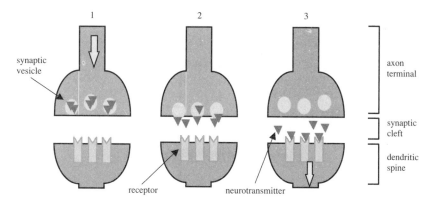

Figure 4.3 The synapse
Where one nerve cell communicates with another
1. A nerve impulse (action potential) arrives at the pre-synaptic nerve terminal.
2. This causes vesicles to move to the edge of the terminal and release the neurotransmitters they contain into the synaptic cleft.
3. The neurotransmitters float across the cleft and bind with the receptors in the post-synaptic nerve (at a dendritic spine). If the synapse is strong and excitatory, this will trigger a nerve impulse in the post-synaptic nerve cell. If the synapse is inhibitory, then the post-ynaptic nerve cell becomes less active. However, each neuron typically connects (or synapses) with many others so that what happens in the post-synaptic nerve will depend on the total effect of these many different inputs.
Subsequently the neurotransmitters are reabsorbed back into the pre-synaptic terminal and the whole process can occur again.

between the telephone and my ear. There is a gap. With telephones this problem is solved by using air molecules to transmit the signal. The receiver causes the air molecules to vibrate and this vibration is transferred across the gap and picked up by my ear. With nerve cells the mechanism for getting the signal across the gap between one nerve cell and the next is much more complex. In simple terms, when the electrical signal reaches the end of the nerve, it releases a chemical. This chemical floats across the gap and stimulates the next nerve. The gap between one nerve and the next is called the synapse (or, more accurately, the synaptic cleft). The chemicals that bridge the gap are called neurotransmitters. Many different neurotransmitters have been found in the brain, and nerve cells can be classified into different types on the basis of which of neurotransmitter they use.

One important class of nerve cells release the neurotransmitter known as dopamine. These are often called reward cells, because they become more active immediately after an animal is given food or drink. A rat will

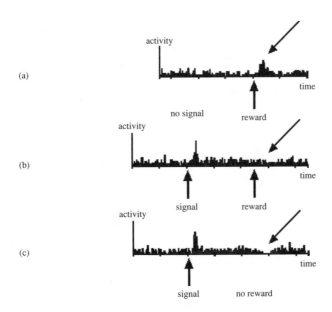

Figure 4.4 Activity in dopamine neurons represents the error in our prediction of reward
Activity was recorded from dopamine neurons (in the basal ganglia) while monkeys learned
that a light flash (the signal) would be followed after half a second by a squirt of fruit juice
in their mouth (the reward).
(a) There was no signal so the monkey doesn't know when the reward will come.
The unpredicted reward causes an increase in activity.
(b) The monkey knew when the reward would come. The reward causes no change in
activity. But the monkey doesn't know when the signal will come. The unpredicted signal of
reward causes an increase in activity.
(c) The monkey expects the reward to come, but it doesn't. The lack of the predicted reward
causes a decrease in activity.
Source: Figure 3 in: Schultz, W. (2001). Reward signaling by dopamine neurons.
Neuroscientist, 7(4), 293–302.

press a bar in order to stimulate these nerve cells and seems to find this
stimulation better even than food or sex. This is called self-stimulation.[7]

Wolfram Schultz recorded activity in these cells during a conditioning
experiment and found that they are not really reward cells. As in Pavlov's
experiments, an arbitrary signal (a light flash) was followed after one
second by a squirt of fruit juice into the monkey's mouth. At first the
dopamine nerve cells behaved like reward cells responding to the squirt
of juice, but after training they stopped responding at this time. Instead

---

[7] In Michael Crichton's novel *The Terminal Man*, a human has electrodes implanted in
his pleasure centres, with disastrous consequences.

the cells responded immediately after the monkey saw the light flash, one second before the juice arrived. The activity in the dopamine nerve cells seemed to be signaling that juice would be coming soon. Rather than responding to reward, they were predicting reward.

The importance of prediction was revealed even more clearly when the monkey saw the light and then did not receive a squirt of juice. At the time when the juice should have arrived, the dopamine nerve cells became *less* active. The monkey's brain had predicted exactly when the juice reward should arrive, and the dopamine nerve cell signaled that the reward had not arrived by reducing its activity.

How error can be our teacher

The activity in these cells does not signal reward. It does not even signal that reward will be coming soon. The activity in these cells tells us that there is an error in our prediction about reward. If the juice arrives when we expect it to arrive, then there is no error in our prediction and the dopamine nerve cells do not send out a signal. If the juice arrives unexpectedly, then the reward is better then we expected and the nerve cells send out a positive signal. If the juice fails to arrive when it should, then the reward is worse than we expected and the nerve cells send out a negative signal. These signals about the errors of our predictions enable us to learn about the world without needing a teacher. If our prediction about the world is wrong, then this is a sign to us that we need to do something in order to make our prediction better.

Even before the discovery that activity in dopamine nerve cells signals an error in our prediction, mathematicians had developed algorithms that enable machines to learn in a similar way.

An important concept in this associative learning mechanism is "value." The unconditioned stimulus in Pavlov's experiment has intrinsic value – positive value for food (reward), and negative value for an electric shock (punishment). The way this kind of associative mechanism works is that whenever we get a reward, anything that happened just before the reward becomes more valuable. Even things that happen quite a long time before the reward become very slightly more valuable. Some of these things will have occurred at this time by chance and will be irrelevant. The likelihood is that the next time such irrelevant things occur, the reward will not happen afterwards. This triggers the error signal. The anticipated reward has not appeared and the irrelevant event will be devalued. But when something occurs that correctly predicts reward, then there is no error signal and the event gains more and more value. In this way our brain learns to attach a value to all the events and objects and places around us. Many will remain neutral, but some will acquire high value and some will acquire low value.

We experience this map of values within our brain when we return from a long trip abroad – we feel a rising emotional response as the streets we are moving through become more and more familiar.

If we approached the things with high value and avoided the things with low value, we would obtain rewards and avoid punishments. But this associative learning mechanism tells us only which things are valuable. It doesn't tell us how to get these valuable things. Thorndike's cat, when first put in the puzzle box, knows that the fish is valuable, but it doesn't know what to do to get the fish.

A mechanism for learning exactly what to do to get rewards (or avoid punishments) also exists. It's called the temporal difference (TD) algorithm. This procedure allows a machine to discover the best sequence of actions to perform in order to get something of value. This procedure is also known as the Actor–Critic model. One part of the program, the Actor, chooses the next action to perform. The other part of the program, the Critic, indicates how good this action was. This critic tells the actor about any errors in the prediction. A good action is one in which the situation we are in *now* has a value that is higher than the situation we were in before performing the action. The critic is commenting on the change in value from one time to the next (hence 'temporal difference'). Value is higher after an action that gets you nearer to the reward. This is a way of discovering the pathways that lead to reward. Value is highest in the place right next to reward. As we move away from the reward, the value gets smaller. By moving toward the places with higher value, we will eventually reach the reward. Of course these values are not actually marked on the real world. They are marked only on the internal model of the world we have in our brains, the model that has been built up by learning and experience.

Wolfram Schultz and the computational scientists Peter Dayan and Reed Montague showed that the behavior of dopamine nerve cells was exactly what you would expect if the monkey's brain were using the same learning methods as a machine using the TD algorithm. The activity in the dopamine nerve cells is the prediction error that enables the monkey to learn without a teacher. This kind of learning doesn't just occur in the nerve cells of monkeys. Learning by prediction can explain the behavior of bees looking for the best flowers and the behavior of

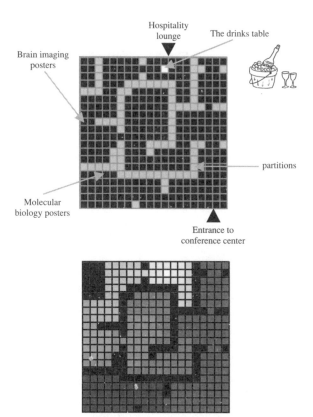

Figure 4.5 The brain represents the world as a reward space
Upper picture: A map of the conference center.
My brain's map of the conference center as a reward space.
Lower picture: I have arrived at an unknown conference center without a map. The drinks
table is hidden behind many partitions. I can find it only by trial and error.
After I have found the drinks table a few times my brain has created a map of the
conference center as a reward space. Lightness indicates value. As long as I move towards
a lighter color, I shall eventually reach the drinks table. I am not aware of this map. I just go
to the drinks table.
Source: Modified from: Bugmann, G. (1996, March 26–28). Value maps for planning and
learning implemented in cellular automata. Proceedings of the 2nd International conference
on adaptive computing in engineering design and control (ACEDC'96), Plymouth (pp. 307–309).

humans gambling for money.[8] In both cases learning by prediction creates a map of possible of actions indicating which actions are the most
likely to lead to reward.

---

[8]   A computer program using TD methodology can learn to play backgammon as well as
the best human players can.

The brain's map of the world

Through associative learning the brain constructs a map of the world. This is essentially a map of value. The map locates the objects of high value where I am likely to be rewarded and the objects of low value where I am not likely to be rewarded. The map also indicates the actions of high value that are likely to be successful and the actions of low value that are likely to fail.

Standing on the threshold of the college refectory, I instinctively go toward where the best food and drink will be found. I go to the tables where my friends will be sitting and avoid those tables frequented by molecular geneticists and Professors of English. I automatically push open the door rather than pulling it and walk without thinking to the hot food counter.[9] From time to time the administrators will decide to rearrange the tables and re-hang the doors. For a time I will persist in pushing the door rather than pulling it, but eventually the map in my brain will automatically get adjusted.

Having collected my lunch, I find myself, somewhat to my surprise, sitting next to the Professor of English and trying to convince her that these new accounts of how the brain learns about the world are interesting and important. For our brains, I tell her, this is not a buzzing blooming confusion we see around us, but a map of signs about future possibilities. And through this map of future possibilities our bodies are intimately tied to the world immediately around us. I just have to look at that mug over there and my brain starts tensing my muscles and curling my fingers in case I should want to reach for it.

This is how our minds become embedded in the physical world, I explain to the Professor. This is how our brains learn about the world without needing a teacher. In particular I want to persuade her that these ideas are not just words and hand waving. These ideas are supported by rigorous mathematical equations.

"Are you really saying," she replies, "that somewhere in my brain there is a map of every place I have ever been and instructions for picking up every object I have ever seen?"

I explain to her that this is perhaps the cleverest aspect of these learning algorithms. There is just one map, not a sequence of maps leading

---

[9]   This is an entirely fanciful example. In the competitive world of today's academic I don't discuss exciting new ideas with my colleagues over lunch, but sit alone in my office with a cup of calorie-free soup writing another grant application.

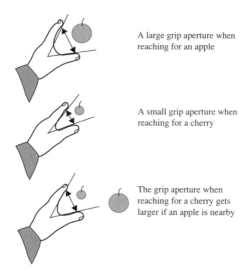

A large grip aperture when reaching for an apple

A small grip aperture when reaching for a cherry

The grip aperture when reaching for a cherry gets larger if an apple is nearby

Figure 4.6 Our brain automatically prepares action programs for the objects around us
In a series of experiments, Umberto Castiello and his colleagues have demonstrated how different objects in a visual scene automatically activate the responses needed to reach and grasp them (the action program) without any conscious intention to act. They did this by measuring very precisely the movements of the hand when people grasped objects. When we grasp an object, the distance between fingers and thumb (the grip aperture) is adjusted in advance to match the size of the object. When I reach for an apple, I open my hand more than when I reach for a cherry. But if I reach for a cherry when there is also an apple on the table, then I open my hand more than usual for a cherry. The action needed for grasping the cherry is interfering with my action of grasping the apple. This distraction arising from other objects in the visual world shows that the brain has implemented action programs for all of them in parallel.

Source: Redrawn after: Castiello, U. (2005). The neuroscience of grasping. *Nature Reviews Neuroscience*, 6(9), 726–736.

into the distant past. This map has no memory. It is like looking at the world through a kaleidoscope. As long as our predictions are correct, the pattern remains stable. A failure of prediction shakes up the pattern so that a new one can emerge to replace the old one. In this way we can adapt our behavior to an ever-changing world.

"*You* may be stuck in an eternal present," she replies. "My experience is quite different. My mind is filled past regrets and future hopes rather than present sensations. And also," she adds, "your mind may be embedded in the physical world, but my mind is embedded in the world of culture, the world created by other minds. If I am aware of the physical world at all it is precisely because it is not me. It is what hurts me when I stub my toe on the pavement." Before I can reply she goes off to give her final lecture on "The Stream of Consciousness."[10]

This interjection from the Professor of English reminds us of the dramatic discrepancy between what our brains know about the world and our conscious experience of the world. Associative learning can explain how our brains acquire knowledge about the world, but we are hardly aware of this knowledge or its acquisition. What, then, is the experience of the world that our brains create?

How the Brain Embeds Us in the World and Then Hides Us

But I realize that she is right. Whatever my *brain* may be doing, like her I do not experience myself embedded in the physical world. I experience myself *in* the physical world, but detached from it. My brain may have cleverly embedded me in the physical world, but I am not aware of this embedding.

The problem with studying dogs and cats and pigeons is that we know only about their *behavior*. We don't know about their experience. Associative learning in humans has not been so widely studied, but we do know that such learning occurs just as it does in other animals. So what is the experience of such learning? The psychology lecturer who learns to move to the left so that his students will listen to him seems to be learning to move without being aware of what is going on. There are also proper experiments showing the same effect.

In Chapter 2 I showed how secretive our brain can sometimes be. I described the experiment by Paul Whalen and his colleagues in which our brain responds to the sight of a fearful face even when we are not aware of seeing that face. John Morris and his colleagues carried out a second experiment in which they used faces as conditioned stimuli in an experiment like Pavlov's. They showed two angry faces. One was always

---

[10]   She starts with William James' attempt to describe the inner life of the baby – a blooming, buzzing confusion – leads on to William's brother Henry James' attempt to create characters through describing their thoughts and feelings, and finishes with Virginia Woolf's novel *The Waves*, in which reality is the perception of the world in individual minds. This leads to a paradox. In this novel the characters exist in subjective and lonely isolation from each other, yet the reader becomes intimately acquainted with all of them.

followed by a loud noise while the other was not. The subjects soon became conditioned to the face followed by the loud noise. The volunteer's brain now responded to this angry face as if it was a loud noise. But the volunteer himself was not aware of having seen the angry face, because it had been masked with another face. The volunteer was learning a conditioned response even though he was not aware of seeing the stimulus that elicited this conditioned response.[11]

Associative learning is vital for our survival. It embeds us in the physical world and allows us to respond quickly and efficiently to that world. Through associative learning we acquire important knowledge about the physical world. But we are hardly aware of this knowledge; our minds are on higher things. And usually these higher things are our own private wishes and desires.

The self and the world

So how do I experience myself in the world? Consider a very simple action like walking round the room as I try to think of the next sentence. There is me, and there is the world I am moving through, which is not me. The big difference is that I move and the world stays exactly where it is. And this is very odd because every time I move, this movement produces dramatic changes in what my brain senses about the world. Even just moving my eyes has a dramatic effect. On my retina, and again on my visual cortex at the back of my brain, a picture of the world is projected. But if I move my eyes this projection will change completely. As I move my eye from left to right across the fir tree in the garden, the projection of the fir tree moves from the right side to the left side of my retina. This is a dramatic change of sensation. And it raises a problem for my brain – is there a change in sensation because my eye is moving or because the fir tree is moving?

We have all experienced how ambiguous movement can be when traveling by train. I think my train has started moving again and then find it was the train on the next platform going the other way. But we rarely experience any ambiguity about whether it's the tree moving past my eye or me moving my eye past the tree. More than 100 years ago Helmholtz was worried about this problem. He showed that we can

---

[11]   After conditioning, the "unseen" face that signaled the loud noise caused increased activation in the amygdala and increased sweating – both signs of fear.

sometimes be unsure even about our own eye movements. If he moved his eye by poking it with his finger, then the world appeared to jerk from side to side.[12] So why does the world remain stable when we move our eyes in the normal way?

Helmholtz realized that our brain already has detailed information about an eye movement before the movement occurs. This is because it is our brain that sends the signals to the eye muscles that cause the movement. These signals can be used to predict exactly how our visual sensations will change when an eye movement occurs.[13] Here again the brain learns important things about the world through prediction.

Our brain can use this prediction to make us perceive the world as stable even though the image of the world is jumping around on our retina as we move our eyes. This illusion of stability is important for our survival. All animals are very sensitive to sudden changes of visual sensation. Any sudden change in sensation is likely to be caused by the movement of a small animal that we want to catch or a large animal that we want to avoid. But visual changes caused by our own movements are of no relevance at all. By predicting these unimportant changes of sensation, the brain can suppress our response to them. We can then devote all our attention to things happening in the outside world.

Why we can't tickle ourselves

There was a time when scientists were very serious people, masters of specialist knowledge that ordinary people did not expect to understand. Scientists are not like this today. We have to be publicly accountable. Our research must be relevant, understandable, and, best of all, fun.[14] So, if there are many different ways to study the process of interest, why not choose the one that is most fun. With this in mind, Sarah-Jayne

---

[12]   As long as you don't poke your eye too hard, this is an experiment that can be tried out at home. It really works.

[13]   So why can't the brain predict exactly what will happen when we poke our eye with a finger? Well, firstly, our brain has very little experience of this action and hasn't had a chance to learn how to predict. And, secondly, each time we poke our eye we are likely to put our finger in a slightly different place so the prediction will never be quite the same.

[14]   In other words, likely to be taken up by the popular press. But be warned. If it's too much fun, you may get an igNobel prize. These prizes are for (a) "research that makes you laugh and then makes you think" and (b) "research that cannot and should not be reproduced."

Blakemore, Daniel Wolpert, and I decided to study tickling. It was already well established by general experience, backed up by science, that we can't tickle ourselves. The reason lies in prediction. Our brain can predict what we are going to feel because our brain is sending the commands to the fingers that cause the tickling sensation.

There are receptors on our skin that detect when our body is being touched. These receptors send signals to areas of the cortex that are dedicated to representing touch (Figure 3.7 shows the primary somatosensory area). If I start stroking the palm of your hand while you are having your brain scanned, then I can observe a dramatic increase of neural activity in these brain regions as they respond to the touch. But if you stroked your own palm in just the same way,[15] then I will observe very little increase in activity. When you touch yourself your brain suppresses your response.

The Professor of English removes her hand just as I am trying to tickle it. "That's not very surprising," she says. "It feels much less intense when I tickle my own hand. Obviously, my brain activity will correspond to my subjective experience. You keep telling me that my experience depends upon my brain."

What the imaging study shows is the location in our brain where the suppression occurs. It occurs in the region of the cortex where the sensations of touch first arrive. For this to happen our brain must be predicting the activity so that it is ready to counteract the signal as soon as it arrives.

There is nothing special about tickling. We cause sensations whenever we move even if we are not touching ourselves or anything else. There are receptors in our muscles and joints that detect how tense our muscles are and also measure the angles of our joints. These receptors are stimulated whenever we move our limbs, but the brain's responses to this stimulation are suppressed when we move the limb ourselves. If someone else moves our limb (a passive limb movement), then the cortical responses are much greater. Our brain cannot predict what is going to happen when someone else moves our limb, and so our sensations of movement are not suppressed.

---

[15]   You rightly ask: how can I be sure that you stroke your own palm in *exactly* the same way that I stroke it? We use a combination of sensitive movement detectors and robot arms. A computer records the movements that you make and then reproduces them exactly by controlling a robot arm which tickles you.

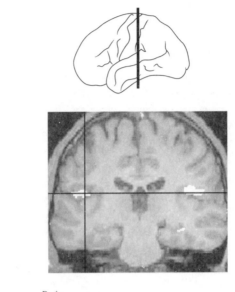

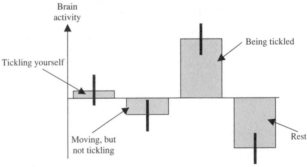

Figure 4.7   The brain's response to tickling
A slice through the middle of the brain showing an area that responds to touch: the secondary somatosensory cortex.
Activity in this region of the brain is greater when someone else tickles you than when you tickle yourself even though the touch is the same. The black vertical lines are *error bars* indicating how variable the results were. Be suspicious of a figure with no error bars.

Source: From figures supplied by Sarah-Jayne Blakemore from data in: Blakemore, S.J., Wolpert, D.M., & Frith, C.D. (1990) Central cancellation of self-produced tickle sensation. *Nature Neuroscience*, *1*(7), 635–640.

The Feeling of Being in Control

There are many reasons why prediction is a good thing. If we know what is going to happen, then we can relax. We don't have to keep making new plans about what to do. We need to change our plans only when something unexpected happens. Also if we know what is going to happen, then we feel that we are in control.

We all like the feeling of being in control. And the thing we control best is our own body. Yet, paradoxically, because our brain suppresses the bodily sensations it can predict, we feel most in control when we don't feel anything. I reach for my glass and all I experience is the look and taste of the wine as I drink it. I don't experience the various corrections made to the movements as my brain navigates my arm through the various obstacles on the table to reach the wine glass. I don't experience the change in the angles of my elbow or the feel of the glass on my fingertips as they adjust perfectly to the size of the stem. I feel in control of myself because I know what I want to do (have a drink) and I can achieve this aim without any apparent effort. As long as I stay in control, I don't have to bother with the physical world of actions and sensations. I can stay in the subjective world of desires and pleasures.

The world of the imagination

The Professor of English thinks I am talking nonsense. "You may move through the world like a zombie," she says, "but I am certainly aware of what I am doing." "No," I reply. "Most of the time you are not aware of you are doing. What you are aware of is what you *intend* to do. As long as your intentions are fulfilled, you are not aware of what movements you are actually making." Remember Pierre Fourneret's experiment from Chapter 3 (Figure 3.3)? The participants in this experiment thought they were moving their hand in a straight line when, in fact, their hand was deviating to the side. They intended to move their hand in a straight line in order to reach the target. And they did reach the target. They were not aware of the deviations their hand had to make in order to reach the target. All they were aware of was the intended movement.

We can live in this world of intentions, this imaginary world, because our brain can predict the consequences of our movements. Our brain knows in advance how long a movement will take, what our hand will look like at the end, and what the movement should feel like. And even if we do not move at all, we can imagine making movements.

Since the advent of behaviorism, psychologists have been very suspicious of the imagination. We don't quite trust subjective reports. We want some sort of objective measure in support. We are therefore pleased because we can show that when someone imagines making a movement, they take the same time to do it as when they really make that movement. We are even more pleased when we can show that when someone imagines making movements, we can see activity in the relevant motor regions of their brain. And we get really excited when we can show that imagining making movements can actually increase our skill with real, objective movements.

Yue and Cole asked one group of volunteers to train the muscle that controls the little finger (the hypothenar muscle) for four weeks, five sessions per week. Another group only imagined making these contractions, also for five sessions per week. A third group, the control group, did not do any training at all. After five weeks, the average force that could be exerted by the little finger had increased by 30% in the real training group and by 22% in the imaginary training group. The change in the control group was a trivial 2.3%. This study shows that practicing movements in the imagination can increase strength almost as much as real training can. How is this possible?

We learn by prediction. My brain predicts what is going to happen when I move and uses the error in its prediction to do better next time.[16] But if we don't move, there is no final outcome to compare with the prediction. There is no error. So how can I learn by simply imaging making a movement? Learning in the imagination is possible because my brain makes two different predictions about my movements. First, it can predict which particular sequence of commands sent to my muscles will generate the movement I want to make. This prediction is called the *inverse model* because my brain has to reason backward from the output of my motor system (my moving finger) to its input (the commands sent to my finger muscles). Second, my brain can predict which exact movements will occur if it sends a certain sequence of commands to my muscles. This prediction is called the *forward model* since my brain has to reason forward from input (the commands to the muscles) to output (the finger movements). My brain cannot test how good either of these predictions are without making movements. But we don't need to make movements to test whether or not the two predictions are consistent with one another. The prediction from the forward model, which finger movements will occur, should match the starting point of the inverse model, which fingers movements I want to make. My brain can make these two predictions and adjust them until they match without my making any actual finger movements. As a result of such purely mental practice my ability to make the real movements will improve.[17]

When the System Fails

Moving through the world and reaching for the things we want seems easy. We take it for granted. In the normal state our feeling of being in control of our actions is marked by a lack of awareness of the details of the actions we are performing. We have little awareness of our sensation when we move and we are rarely aware of having to make corrections to our movements even though we are making them all the time. But, in the background, our brain is working hard to achieve this sense of ease.

A daily marathon

IW, as the result of a viral infection, has lost all the sensations in his limbs, apart from feeling temperature and fatigue. He only knows about the positions of his limbs through his eyes. After such damage, people usually do not move even though they still have control over their muscles. This is because our brain depends upon bodily sensations to control our movements. In order to issue the right commands to the muscles our brain needs to know where our hand is before the movement begins and whether it has reached the right position after the movement has finished. For people like IW this information is no longer available, except through vision.

---

[17]   Machines can also learn to recognize objects in this way (see Chapter 5). These are sometimes called Helmholtz machines because they use the same "unconscious inferences" about which Helmholtz speculated. They use a technique called the wake–sleep algorithm, which also makes two kinds of prediction: *recognition*, predicting what object would cause these sensations (the inverse model); and *generation*, predicting what sensations this object would cause (the forward model). There is speculation that, in the brain, dreaming occurs during harmonization of the two kinds of predictions. This happens during sleep when there are no sensory inputs.

IW is very unusual. After years of effort and hard work he has learned to walk again, but falls over if the lights go out. He has learned to pick up objects as long as he can see both the object and his hand. He depends on his vision to know where his hand is before the start of a movement and he has to look to check that it has reached the right place when the movement has finished. This is not the normal way that the brain controls movements.

The control that IW has achieved does not happen automatically. He has to think carefully about his movements all the time. No automatic corrections occur. He has to think continuously about controlling his movement through the whole course of an action.

This is quite different from our normal feeling of being in control. Perhaps the nearest we can get to understanding what this might be like for IW is when we force ourselves to move in spite of extreme tiredness. Every inch of movement requires an extreme effort. This is how IW himself describes the experience. He says his life is a daily marathon.

Alien forces

PH suffers from schizophrenia. One of her most disturbing symptoms is the feeling that she is not controlling her own actions. "My fingers pick up the pen, but I don't control them. What they do is nothing to do with me." Psychiatrists call this a "delusion of control" because the person believes that her actions are being controlled by alien forces. Of course many of us might say that our actions are not under our own control. We may feel constrained by the government or our employers. There is a perfectly real sense in which many of my actions are controlled by the Wellcome Trust.[18] PH's feeling of being controlled is much more direct than this. When she moves her arm it feels to her as if she is not controlling the movement.

PH's experience is quite different from that of IW. She can control her movements without too much thought. Her brain makes all the automatic corrections that are needed when she reaches for an object. So why does she say that her movements are controlled by alien forces?

In the early part of the 20th century Karl Jaspers suggested that many of the experiences described by psychiatric patients were simply not understandable. Anxiety and depression are more extreme versions of states that all of us have experienced, but having our actions and thoughts

[18]   That wonderful medical charity which has funded my research for the last 10 years.

directly controlled by other people is beyond any experience most of us have ever had. Jaspers was critical of claims linking brain function to psychological processes. These claims were "brain mythology" that would not help us to understand the experiences of psychiatric patients.

"He's right," interjects the Professor of English. "You need psychological theories to explain psychological experiences." I take pleasure in reminding that her that Jaspers also criticized the "mythology of psychoanalysis."

I believe we can now achieve some understanding of PH's experiences because of what we have discovered about the brain. In our normal state we are hardly aware of the sensations that occur whenever we move. This is because our brain can predict these sensations and suppress our awareness of them. But what would it be like if something went wrong with the prediction and we became aware of the sensations? Normally I am aware of the sensations only when someone else moves my hand. Such a brain abnormality could explain why PH feels as if her arm is being moved by someone else. She is abnormally aware of her bodily sensations when she moves her hand. For her it really does feel as if someone else were moving her hand.

The Professor of English looks very skeptical. "Are you going to tell me that PH can tickle herself?"

"Exactly." I am delighted that she has hit on the key experiment. In the lab we found that PH and people like her could tickle themselves. It made no difference to them whether they stroked their palm themselves or the experimenter stroked it. They reported that the tickliness of the sensation felt the same. We may not yet fully understand the underlying brain abnormality, but we are beginning to understand what the experience of movement is like for these people. Their brains no longer suppress awareness of the sensations that inevitably accompany movements. For them it really does feel as if someone else is moving their limbs.

The Invisible Actor at the Center of the World

Through its ability to learn and predict, my brain ties me to the world with many strong threads. Because of these threads, the world is not a buzzing, confusing mass of sensations; instead, everything around me exerts a push or a pull because my brain has learned to attach values to them. And my brain creates more than mere pushes and pulls. It even specifies all the actions I might need to perform to reach some things and

Figure 4.8   We sometimes catch a glimpse of ourselves moving through the world

Source: M.C. Escher, *Hand with Reflecting Sphere*, 1935, lithograph. © 2006 The M.C. Escher Company–Holland. All rights reserved. *Http://www.mcescher.com.*

avoid others. But I am not aware of these strong connections – my brain creates the illusion that I am an independent being quite separate from this physical world.

Whenever I act in the world, moving my limbs and moving myself from one place to another, I cause massive changes in the signals striking my senses. The pattern of sensations on the retina at the back of my eye changes completely every few seconds. But the world outside has not really changed. And my brain manages to create for me the experience of a constant, unchanging world through which I move. I can choose to attend to the various parts of my body, and then they too become part of this external world. But most of the time I, the actor, move through the world invisibly, a shadow that one can sometimes catch a glimpse of from the corner of one's eye before it moves on.

Through associative learning our brains discover the valuable things in the world and what actions we need to take to get them.

Chapter 5

Our Perception of the World Is a Fantasy That Coincides with Reality

The kind of learning that Pavlov and Thorndike discovered may be very useful for us, but it is very crude. Everything in the world is placed in just two categories: nice or nasty. But we do not experience the physical world in terms of such crude categories. When I look out of my window onto the garden below I am instantly aware of a variety of colors and shapes so rich that it seems impossible that I could ever convey the totality of the experience to anyone else. But, at the same time as I experience all the colors and shapes, I can also see them as objects which I can recognize and name: the newly cut grass, the primroses, the old brick columns, and, at this particular moment, a magnificent green woodpecker with a bright red crown. These experiences and recognitions go far beyond the simple categories of nice and nasty. How do our brains discover what is out there in the world? How do our brains discover what is causing our sensations?

Our Brain Creates an Effortless Perception of the Physical World

The remarkable thing about our perception of the physical world in all its beauty and detail is that it seems so easy. In our experience, perception is not a problem. But this very experience that our perception of the physical world is easy and immediate is an illusion created by our brains. And we didn't know about this illusion until we tried to make machines that could "do" perception.

The only way to find out whether perception is easy or difficulty is to try to make an artificial brain that will perceive things. In order to make such a brain, we need to identify the components from which it is built and we need to know what these components do.

The Information Revolution

The components of the brain were discovered by neurophysiologists at the end of the 19th century. The fine structure of the brain was revealed by looking at thin slices of brain tissue through a microscope. These slices were stained in various ways to reveal different aspects of brain structure (see Figure p.4 in the Prologue). Studies showed that the brain contains large numbers of nerve cells[1] and a very complex network of interconnecting fibers. But the key idea about the fundamental components of the brain came from the neuro-anatomist Santiago Ramón y Cajal. Through careful observation he showed that this network of fibers grew out of the nerve cells and, most importantly, that there were gaps in this network. A fiber that grew out of one nerve cell came very close to a fiber of the next nerve cell, but did not join it. These are the gaps called synapses that I described in the previous chapter (see Figure 4.3). From his studies Cajal concluded that the basic building block of the brain was the neuron: the nerve cell with all its fibers and extensions. This proposal was widely accepted and became known as "the neuron doctrine."[2]

But what do the neurons, these building blocks of the brain, actually do? By the middle of the 19th century, Emil du Bois-Reymond had demonstrated the electrical basis of nerve impulses. And by the end of the century David Ferrier and others had shown that electrical stimulation of specific brain areas elicits specific movements and sensations. The

---

[1]   It is estimated that there are 12–15 billion neurons in the human cerebral cortex and another 70 billion in the cerebellum, giving a total of close to 100 billion (10^{11}).

[2]   The existence of these gaps was not confirmed definitively until 1954, when the electron microscope became available. Santiago Ramon y Cajal was awarded the Nobel Prize in 1906 alongside Camillo Golgi, who had invented the method of staining brain tissue to reveal its fine structure. In his acceptance speech Golgi rejected the neuron doctrine, sticking to his idea that the brain consisted of a seamless network of interconnecting fibers. Cajal was furious at Golgi for his "display of pride and self worship" for an ego "that was hermetically sealed and impermeable to the incessant changes taking place in the intellectual environment."

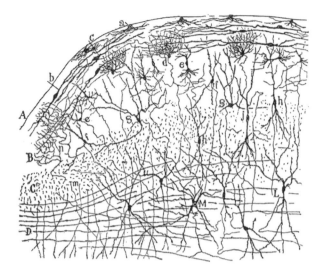

Figure 5.1 The great unraveled knot
Nerve cells are the basic building block of the brain. This drawing by Santiago Ramón y Cajal shows nerve cells in the cortex revealed by the method of staining developed by Camillo Golgi. Many different kinds of nerve cells with their associated fibers can be seen.
Source: Figure 117, Coupe tranversale du tubercule quadrijumeau antérieur; lapin âgé de 8 jours, Méthode de Golgi. In Cajal, S.R. y. (1901). *The great unraveled knot*. (From William C. Hall, (Image 2) Department of Neurobiology, Duke University Medical Center).

electrical impulses in the nerves carry energy from one brain area to another where activity in other nerve cells can be enhanced or inhibited. But how can such activity be the basis of a machine that can perceive objects?

The major advance did not come from students of brain physiology, but from telephone engineers. Telephone lines are like neurons: electrical impulses travel along both. The electrical impulses in a telephone line activate the loudspeaker at the other end, just as the electrical impulses in motor neurones can activate the muscles they are attached to. But we know that what telephone lines transmit is not energy, but messages, whether in the form of speech or as the dots and dashes that compose Morse code.

Engineers in the Bell Telephone Laboratories wanted to discover the most efficient way to transmit telephone messages. These studies led to the idea that what is being transmitted is *information*.[3] The whole

[3] Proposed by Hartley in 1928.

purpose of a message is that, when we receive it, we should know more than we did before. *Information theory*[4] provides a method for measuring how much more we know after the message has arrived.

Before the start of a cricket match we do not know who will bat first until the umpire has tossed a coin. Before this toss there are two possibilities: either England will bat first or Australia will bat first. After the coin has been tossed, these two *possibilities* have been reduced to one *certainty*: we know that England will bat. Such an increase in knowledge, when two possibilities are reduced to one, is called one bit of information. If we throw a die, which has six possibilities – rather than tossing a coin – then we gain more information because six possible messages are reduced to one. In this case the amount of information we get is 2.58 bits.[5] Using this definition we can measure how much information is being transmitted through a telephone line and the rate (described in bits per second or "baud") at which it is being transmitted. At 300 baud the line will transmit about 60 characters per second, since each character carries about 5 bits of information on average.

Of course, some characters carry less information than others. In written English, common letters like E carry much less information than uncommon letters like Z. Worst of all is the U that comes after a Q. In this position the letter U carries no information at all. This U is said to be redundant. Wouldn't communication be much more efficient if redundant letters were eliminated and letters like E were used more rarely?

In reality such efficiency is never helpful, because the real world is never perfect: handwriting is full of errors and ambiguities; typesetters make mistakes; telephone lines are noisy.[6] By the time the message reaches the other end of the line, some fragments of it will have been lost and some irrelevant sounds will have been added. For the perfect message in which no letters are redundant, this noise is disastrous. A different

---

[4]   Developed by Shannon in 1948.

[5]   Bits stand for binary digits. 2.58, which is the log of 6 to base 2, is the average number of yes/no questions we would have to ask to discover which number on the die has been thrown. I first ask, "Is it greater than 3?" If "Yes," then it must be 4, 5, or 6. I then ask, "Is it greater than 4?" If the answer is "No," then the number is 4 and I have discovered the answer in two questions. If the answer is "Yes," then the number is 5 or 6 and I need to ask one more question. I will always have to ask between two and three such questions when there are six alternatives.

[6]   One of the most fundamental laws of nature is that, however hard you try, a proportion of your effort will be wasted. The heat given out by a light bulb, the friction in a wheel bearing, the noise in a telephone line, perhaps even human error, can never be eliminated.

message would arrive at the other end of the line and there would be no way of knowing that an error had occurred.

But if messages contain bits of information that are redundant, then errors can be detected and the original message can be re-created. For example, we could send the same message twice. The second message is completely redundant, but if the two messages that arrive are different then we know that errors have occurred. Of course, we still do not know which is the correct message. If we send the same message three times, and if two of the three messages agree, then we can use this as a rule for deciding which is the correct message.

I remember the days when neither computers nor even electronic calculators were available. Complex mathematical calculations had to be done by hand, and it was almost inevitable that errors would be made. The standard procedure to guard against this was to repeat the calculation three times. If the same answer came out twice, this was probably correct since it was unlikely that exactly the same error would be made in each calculation.

Our brain has to deal with exactly the same problem. The messages about the outside world that come to us through our eyes and ears are noisy and full of errors, so our brain is not sure what is "real" and what is an "error." To avoid this, our brain takes full advantage of redundancy. When we are talking to someone face to face we are not just listening to what they say – we are also closely watching the way their lips move. By putting these two kinds of information together, our brain gets a better idea of the original message that was sent. We are not usually aware of using the lip movements in this way, but when we watch a foreign film that has been dubbed into English (or an English film that has been poorly sound edited), we are instantly aware that there is something wrong because the lip movements do not match the sounds.

By using information theory, telephone lines were made more efficient at transmitting messages.[7] But information theory had an impact far beyond the profits of telephone companies. The definition of information in terms of simple physical states (such as the ON or OFF state of an electronic switch) meant that it was now possible to store information in

---

[7]   While redundancy can be used to overcome the problem of noise and errors in a telephone line, there is always a cost since more characters have to be transmitted. Using information theory, it was possible to find optimal ways of using redundancy with minimal cost. An example would be the cyclical redundancy checking used by the modems that connect us to the internet.

a physical device: a digital memory. For a long time information had been stored in books in terms of written characters. But the new memory devices could be written and read by machines, which did not need to understand the meaning of the characters. And also, of course, the content of these new memory devices could be instantly changed.

Already by 1943 McCulloch and Pitts had proposed a new neuron doctrine, in which the neuron was seen as the fundamental unit in the brain with the function of processing information. McCulloch and Pitts also proposed that an artificial brain could be constructed from large networks of simple electronic "neurons." These artificial neural networks would store and process information. The first computers were not modeled on neural networks, but, like the artificial neural networks, they were devices that could store, transmit, and modify information according to specified rules. When these computers were first constructed in the 1940s they were immediately referred to as electronic brains. These machines were going to be able to do what brains do.

What Can Clever Machines Really Do?

In 1956 the science of making machines do clever things was named Artificial Intelligence. In this, as in any research program, the easy problems were the first to be addressed. Perception seemed easy. Since almost everyone can read handwriting and recognize faces, it should be easy to build machines that can read handwriting and recognize faces. Playing chess, on the other hand, is very difficult. Very few people can play chess at the level of a Grand Master. Building machines that could play chess would be left for later.

Fifty years have passed and a chess computer has beaten the world champion.[8] It is perception that turns out to be the hard problem. Humans are still far better than machines at recognizing faces and reading handwriting. Why is perception so hard?

Even my ability to see that the garden below my window is full of different objects turns out to be very hard for machines. There are many reasons why this problem is hard. For example, objects overlap each

---

[8]   In 1997 IBM's super-computer Deep Blue beat Garry Kasparov, considered by many to be one of the world's greatest ever chess players. The success of the computer was largely due to number crunching. It can examine 200 million moves per second. This is not the way people play chess.

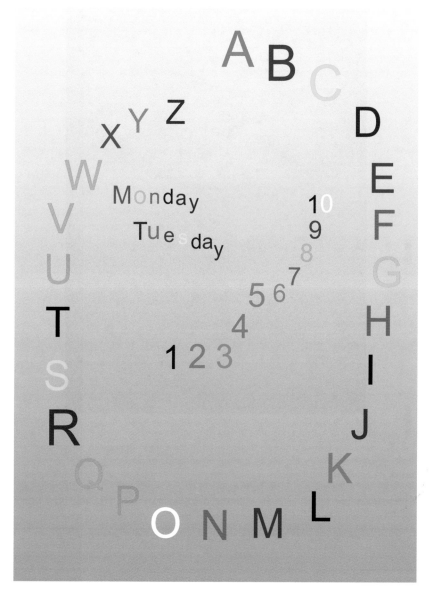

Figure CP1 The synesthetic experience

In the most common form of synesthesia, hearing a word causes an experience of color, as well as sound. Every letter and number has its own special color and often a special position in space. In this figure a synesthete shows us how she experiences the colors and positions of letters and numbers.

Source: Thanks to Rosalind Ridley.

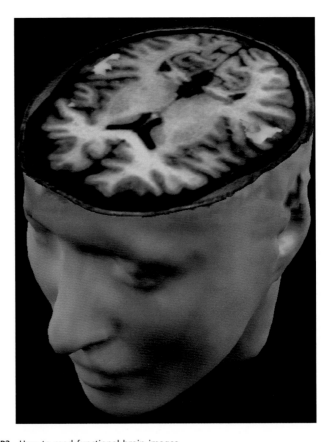

Figure CP2   How to read functional brain images

This volunteer lay in the MRI scanner listening to simple sounds. The sounds "lit up" her auditory cortex (shown by the orange patches on each side of her brain).

But all is not quite what it seems.

The black and white picture of the brain comes from a structural scan. The colored blobs are superimposed from a functional scan (fMRI) which gives a picture which is much more blurred.

All the nerves in the brain are active all the time. The colored blobs show where there was a change in activity by comparing what happened when there were no sounds (apart from the continuous loud noise made by the scanner) with what happened when the volunteer heard beeps on top of the scanner noise.

The signal measured by fMRI does not come from changes in neural activity, which happen very rapidly, but from changes in blood flow (or, more precisely changes in blood oxygenation), which happen very slowly. Neural activity requires energy, which is supplied by the blood. Studies with animals show that the changes in blood flow are a very good guide to changes in neural activity.

The colored blobs do not show the activity in a brain area, but a statistic about this activity: how likely is it that this is a real change rather than some random fluctuation. If you use a less strict statistic, then the blobs will be larger and will be seen in more brain areas.

Source: Thanks to Chiara Portas.

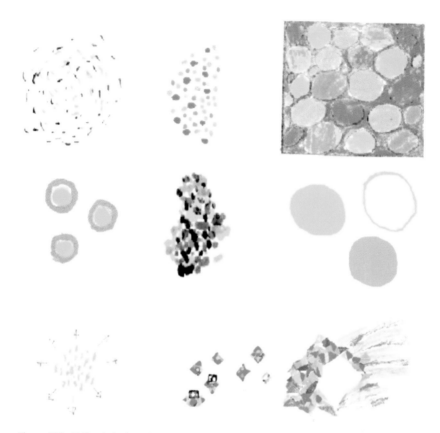

Figure CP3 Epileptic brain activity can cause visual experiences
Drawings of the experiences associated with an epileptic seizure when the origin of the seizure is in the visual cortex.

Source: Panayiotopoulos, C.P. (1999). Elementary visual hallucinations, blindness, and headache in idiopathic occipital epilepsy: Differentiation from migraine. *Journal of Neurology, Neurosurgery and Psychiatry, 66*(4), 536–540.

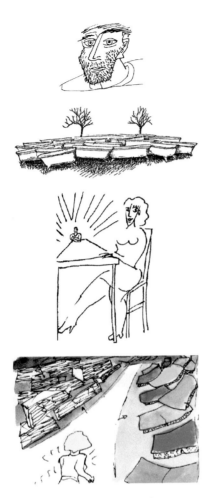

Things are not what they seem.
"I recognize A's sister . . . I am surprised by her beard . . ."

Images multiply.
Multiple images of bath tubs

Sizes are distorted.
The man at the end of the table is seen as miniscule

Color is wrong.
Color is missing from the left half of space

Figure CP4   Visual distortions in dreams

Source: Figure 3 from: Schwartz, S., & Maquet, P. (2002). Sleep imaging and the neuro-psychological assessment of dreams. *Trends in Cognitive Science*, 6(1), 23–30.

Figure CP5 A few hours work + the knowledge of a lifetime
J.M. Whistler, *Nocturne in Black and Gold: The Falling Rocket*, 1875

Source: Photo © 2004, Detroit Institute of Arts. Gift of Dexter M. Ferry, Jr. (46.309). Photo akg-images/Erich Lessing.

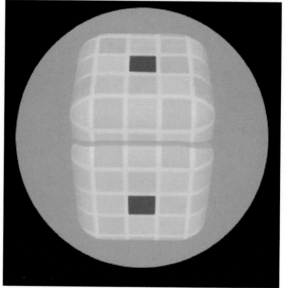

Figure CP6 Color is in the brain, not on the page

The central squares on the upper and lower surfaces of the upper object appear very different in color: green on the top and orange on the bottom. In fact they are physically identical, as shown in the lower object. If you don't believe me, cut out two holes in a piece of paper so that you can only see the two squares.

Source: Colour illusion from R. Beau Lotto, Lottolab, University College London.

Figure CP7　The experience of a storm at sea

J.M.W. Turner, *Snow Storm – Steam-Boat off a Harbour's Mouth Making Signals in Shallow Water, and Going by the Lead*, 1842.

Source: Tate Britain. Photo akg-images/Erich Lessing.

other and some of them move about. How do I know whether this patch of brown is part of a fence or a tree or a bird? My brain solves all these surprisingly hard problems and makes me think that I can perceive the world effortlessly. How does my brain do this?

The development of information theory and the digital computer revealed that perception is a hard problem to solve. But our brains have solved this problem. Does this mean that the digital computer is not a good metaphor for the brain? Or do we need to find new kinds of computations for the computers to carry out?

A Problem with Information Theory

The development of information theory was very important. It enabled us to see how a physical event, an electrical impulse, could become a mental event, a message. But there was a fundamental problem in the original formulation. The amount of information in a message or, more generally, in any stimulus was entirely determined by that stimulus. This way of defining information is all very well, but it can lead to paradoxical results.

Remember that a letter in a message carries more information when it is more surprising. So the letter Q usually carries a lot of information, while the U that comes after it carries none. We can apply the same argument to a picture. A picture is not made up of letters, but of picture elements (or pixels), which can be of different colors. Consider a simple picture of a black square on a white background. Which elements of this picture will be most informative? When we move our eye across an area of constant color there is no surprise, because there is no change. When our eye meets an edge, there is an abrupt change of color and we are "surprised." So, according to information theory, it is the edges in the picture that are most informative. This agrees with our intuition. If we replace an object by its outline, in other words leaving only the informative edges, then we can still recognize the object.

But this formulation leads to a paradox. By this definition, the most informative picture is one in which we can never predict what is going to happen next as we move our eye across it. This a picture entirely composed of random dots. These are the pictures we get when there is something wrong with our television set and all we see is "snow." As the Professor of English rightly comments when I show her my

Low spatial frequencies   Original   High spatial frequencies (edges)

Figure 5.2 We recognize an object best from its edges
The face is easy to recognize from just the edges (right panel), but the smile is easier to recognize from the blurred picture (left panel).

Source: From: Livingstone, M.S. (2000). Is it warm? Is it real? Or just low spatial frequency? *Science*, *290*(5495), 1299.

Figure 5.3 An informative display of random dots
This picture carries the maximum amount of information since you cannot predict what color each dot is going to be.

computer-constructed illustrations, these are the most boring pictures she has ever seen.

The problem with the scheme provided by information theory is that it takes no account of the viewer.[9] In this scheme all viewers are the same

---

[9] I have exaggerated the failure of information theory. The ideal Bayesian observer, whom we will meet shortly, can also be described in terms of information theory: he maximizes the mutual information between the world and himself.

Figure 5.4 *Black Square* by Kazimir Severinovich Malevich, early 1920s (c.1923). *Source:* St Petersburg, State Russian Museum/photo akg-images.

and their experience of the stimulus will be the same. But we know that all viewers are different. They have different past experiences and different expectations. These differences affect how we perceive things.

Consider the black square in Figure 5.4. For some viewers this is not just a black square. It is the *Black Square* exhibited by Kasimir Malevich in 1913, the first example of the visionary, non-objective art of the Russian suprematists. In this example, the knowledge that this is an important work of art alters your perception of the object[10] even though its information content has not changed. This is an extreme example illustrating how our prior knowledge influences our perception.

The Reverend Thomas Bayes

How, then, can we modify information theory so that it can take account of the different experience and expectations of viewers? We need to retain the insight that a message (or a picture) is informative if it is unexpected and surprising. But we must now add our new insight that the message may be more surprising to one person than to another. An objectively surprising and unexpected message may be defined as one that changes our view of the world and hence our behavior.

[10]   Or maybe not.

This evening I was looking forward to attending the seminar on neuroaesthetics, but it has been canceled. I can go and have a drink instead. In the bar I meet the Professor of English. She was unaffected by the message. She never goes to neuroscience seminars.

We can also say that a message is informative to the extent that it changes the receiver's beliefs[11] about the world. In order to know how much information the message conveyed to the receiver, we need to know about the belief of the receiver before the message arrived. We can then see how much this belief changed once the message was received. But is it possible to measure prior beliefs and changes in beliefs?

The solution to this problem comes from someone who is probably the most unlikely of all the scientific heroes in this book. The Reverend Thomas Bayes was a non-conformist minister, who never published a scientific paper in his lifetime (1702–1761), yet he became a Fellow of the Royal Society of London in 1742. It was not until two years after his death that his classic paper was finally published in the *Philosophical Transactions of the Royal Society*. It was then forgotten for more than 100 years. Only in the 1920s did his reputation begin to grow. For R.A. Fisher, then President of the Royal Statistical Society, Bayes was a great hero, and after much lobbying from statisticians he was eventually included in the British *Dictionary of National Biography*. Still he remained little known outside statistical circles. And even those who had heard of Bayesian statistics often believed that it lacked proper objectivity.

In the last 10 years Thomas Bayes has become a superstar. Multiple websites explain Bayes' theorem and tell us that "What matters is that Bayes is cool, and if you don't know Bayes, you aren't cool." And if you don't believe what they say on the internet, what about the *New York Times* for January 20, 2004? " 'In academia, the Bayesian revolution is on the verge of becoming the majority viewpoint, which would have been unthinkable 10 years ago,' says Bradley P. Carlin, a professor of public health at the University of Minnesota."

So what is all the fuss about?

Here is Bayes' theorem:

$$p(A|X) = \frac{p(X|A)^* p(A)}{p(X)}$$

[11]   This is using the word "belief" in a rather special sense: the degree to which I believe in some proposition reflects how probable I think the proposition is to be true.

Figure 5.5 The tomb of the Reverend Thomas Bayes
The Reverend Thomas Bayes is buried in Bunhill Fields in the City of London. The cemetery was used for the burial of nonconformists in the 18th century, but is now a public park. The tomb was restored in 1969, through contributions "from statisticians throughout the world."
Source: Photo taken by Professor Tony O'Hagan of Sheffield University.

Given some phenomenon (*A*) that we want to know about, and an observation (*X*) that is evidence relating to *A*, Bayes' theorem tells us how much we should *update* our knowledge of *A*, given the *new evidence* *X*. We don't need to worry about the details of this equation. The important thing is that this equation is precisely the mathematical formulation about beliefs that we are looking for. The mathematical term for belief in this case is probability. Probability provides a measure of how much I believe in something. When I am absolutely certain about something (like the sun rising every morning), the probability is 1 [this can be expressed as an equation thus: $p(\text{sun rising}) = 1$.] Or the probability is zero if I am confident that something will never happen [p(C. Frith will win the Eurovision Song Contest) = 0]. Most of my beliefs are less strongly held and lie somewhere between 0 and 1 [p(my train into work will be delayed) = 0.5]. And these intermediate beliefs will be constantly changing as I receive new evidence. Before I go to work I will check the status of London's Underground trains on the internet and this new evidence will alter my beliefs about likely delays (but not by very much . . .).

Bayes' theorem indicates by precisely how much I should change my belief about A given some new evidence X. Looking at the equation, $p(A)$ is my *prior* belief about A before the new evidence, X, arrives. $p(X|A)$ is the likelihood that evidence X will be obtained given that A is indeed true. $p(A|X)$ is my subsequent, or posterior, belief about A after taking into account the new evidence. All this will become clearer with a concrete example.

You will have been wondering why Bradley P. Carlin, a professor of public health at the University of Minnesota, is so keen on Bayes' theorem. This is because public health is one of the many areas where Bayes' theorem can be applied.

Consider the problem of breast cancer.[12] In particular consider the problem of the importance of routine screening. We know (this is the prior belief) that by the age of 40, 1% of women will have breast cancer ($p(A)$). We also have a good test (this is the new evidence) for the presence of breast cancer – mammography. Eighty percent of women with breast cancer will get positive mammographies ($p(X|A)$, correct hits), while only 9.6% of women without breast cancer will get positive mammographies ($p(X|{\sim}A)$, false positives). This is the likelihood that the evidence will be obtained given that our belief is true. From these figures it seems obvious that routine screening for breast cancer should be a good thing. So, if all women are screened, then what proportion of those with positive test results will actually have cancer: expressed mathematically as $p(A|X)$?

Given that the cancer test seems to be a good one, what would you believe about a woman who had just tested positive for breast cancer? Most people believe it is highly likely that she has cancer. Application of Bayes' theorem shows that this assumption is wrong. We can see this very easily if we forget about probabilities. Instead, let's consider a group of 10,000 women.

Before screening, the 10,000 women can be divided into two groups:

Group 1: 100 women *with* breast cancer.
Group 2: 9,900 women *without* breast cancer.

Group 1 is the 1% who have cancer: $p(A)$.

12   This example is taken from Eliezer Yudkowsky, "An Intuitive Explanation of Bayesian Reasoning," *http://yudkowsky.net/bayes/bayes.html*.

After screening, the women can be divided into four groups:

Group A: 80 women *with* breast cancer, and *positive* mammography.
Group B: 20 women *with* breast cancer, but with *negative* mammography.

Group A is the 80% correct hits: $p(X|A)$

Group C: 950 women *without* breast cancer, but with *positive* mammography.
Group D: 8,950 women *without* breast cancer, and with *negative* mammography.

Group C is the 9.6% of false positives: $p(X|{\sim}A)$.

So the screening gives a positive result in 950 women who *don't* have cancer and in only 100 women who *do* have cancer. To answer the question "What proportion of women who test positive have cancer?" we divide Group A by the sum of Group A and Group C (the total number of women who test positive). This gives an answer of 7.8%. In other words, more than 90% of the women who test positive will *not* have cancer. Even though mammography is a good test, Bayes' theorem tells us that this new evidence is not very helpful.[13] The problem arises from using the screening test blindly on *all* women over 40. For this group the prior expectation of cancer is very low. Bayes' theorem shows us that the screening test would be much more useful if we applied it to a "high-risk" group, for example women who have a history of breast cancer in their families.

By this time you probably feel you have learned more than you need about how Bayes' theorem actually works. How is the theorem relevant for solving the problem of discovering what is out there in the world?

The Ideal Bayesian Observer

The importance of Bayes' theorem is it that provides a very precise measure of how much a new piece of evidence should make us change our ideas about the world. Bayes' theorem provides a yardstick by which

---

[13] This is why although, at first sight, screening for breast cancer seems like a good idea, the whole issue has become very controversial.

Digression on the Reverend Thomas Bayes and homeland security: when the ideal observer is not ideal

As long as we don't interfere, our brain behaves like an ideal Bayesian observer. So why should this ideal system fail when we start thinking about the problem? Might it be because there are some circumstances when the "ideal observer" is not actually ideal? An example comes from a study by Jeremy Wolfe and colleagues in Boston. They used a task that was modeled on what security workers have to do when screening baggage at airports – looking for knives and explosives amongst all sorts of other objects. When the target objects were often present, the screeners did quite well, missing only 7% of objects, but when the targets were very rare the screeners did very badly. In one experiment screeners missed more than 50% of the target items when these were present in only 1% of the bags. In this experiment the screeners were behaving like "ideal observers." When a target is very rare an ideal observer needs much more evidence before he will believe that it is present. But when the target is a bomb in a suitcase, the ideal observer is no longer ideal. The consequences of missing the target are too great.

we can judge whether we are using new evidence appropriately. This leads to the concept of the *ideal Bayesian observer*: a mythical being who always uses evidence in the best possible way. As we have just seen from the example about breast cancer, we are very bad at using evidence when we think about rare events and large numbers. Psychologists have gained much pleasure and profit by inventing problems which students, even those studying statistics and logic, will always get hopelessly wrong.[14] But though we are not "ideal observers" when we think about these problems, there is now plenty of evidence that our brains are not misled by large numbers or rare events. Our brains *are* ideal observers when making use of the evidence from our senses.

For example, one problem our brain has to solve is how to combine evidence from our different senses. When we are listening to someone, our brain combines the evidence from our eyes – the sight of their lips moving – and from our ears – the sound of their voice. When we pick something up, our brain combines the evidence from our eyes – what the

---

[14]   Stuart Sutherland has written an especially entertaining account of this work.

object looks like – and from our sense of touch – what the object feels like. When combining this evidence, our brain behaves just like an ideal Bayesian observer. Weak evidence is ignored; strong evidence is emphasized. When I am speaking to the Professor of English at a very noisy party, I will find myself staring intently at her lips, because in this situation the evidence coming though my eyes is better than the evidence coming through my ears.

How a Bayesian Brain Can Make Models of the World

But there is another aspect of Bayes' theorem that is even more import-ant for our understanding of how the brain works. The theorem has two critical components: $p(A|X)$ and $p(X|A)$. $p(A|X)$ tell us how much we have to change our belief about the world (A) given the new evidence (X). $p(X|A)$ tells us what evidence (X) we should expect given our belief about the world (A). We can look at these two components as devices that make predictions and detect prediction errors. Now, on the basis of its belief about the world, my brain can predict the pattern of activity that should be detected by my eyes, ears, and other senses: $p(X|A)$. So what happens if there is an error in this prediction? These errors are very important because my brain can use them to update its belief about the world and create a better belief: $p(A|X)$. Once this update has occurred, my brain has a new belief about the world and it can repeat the process. It makes another prediction about the patterns of activity that should be detected by my senses. Each time my brain goes round this loop the prediction error will get smaller. Once the error is sufficiently small, my brain "knows" what is out there. And this all happens so rapidly that I have no awareness of this complex process. Knowing what is out there in the world may seem easy to me, but my brain never rests from this endless round of prediction and updating.

Is There a Rhinoceros in the Room?

There are various ways of talking about this belief that my brain has about the world. For example, I can talk about causes. If I believe that there is a rhinoceros in the room, then it this rhinoceros that is causing the sensations that are striking my eyes and ears. My brain has searched for the causes of my sensations and has decided that a rhinoceros is the most likely cause. I can also talk about models. My brain is able to predict what sensations a rhinoceros would cause because it has some prior ideas about what rhinoceroses are like. This prior knowledge has created a model of a rhinoceros in my mind. In my case this is a very limited model. It represents the size of the animal, its strength, its unusual horn, and very little else. It doesn't matter that my knowledge is limited, because a model is not an exhaustive list of facts about something. A model is like a map, a representation of the real world on a reduced scale.[15] Many aspects of the world are not found on a map, but distances and directions are represented very accurately. Using a map, I can predict that I shall find a turning to the left in 50 yards, and if it is a map of the zoo, it may even predict that I am likely to see another rhinoceros there. I can use a map to predict how long a journey will take without having to actually make the journey. I can run a pedometer along the route on the map, simulating the real journey and read off how may miles it will take. My brain contains many such maps and models and uses them to make predictions and simulate actions.

The English Professor is looking somewhat bemused. "There is no rhinoceros in the room," she says.

"Can't you see it?" I reply. "You simply don't have a strong enough prior belief."

In my brain, perception depends upon prior belief. It is not a linear process like that which produces an image on a photograph or on a TV screen. For my brain, perception is a loop. In a linear version of perception, energy in the form of light or sound waves would strike the senses and these clues about the outside world would somehow be translated and classified by the brain into objects in certain positions in space. It was this approach that made perception so difficult for the first generation of computers. A brain that uses prediction works in almost the opposite way. When we perceive something, we actually start on the inside: a prior belief, which is a model of the world in which there are objects in certain positions in space. Using this model, my brain can predict what signals my eyes and ears should be receiving. These predictions are compared with the actual signals and, of course, there will be errors. My brain welcomes these errors. These errors teach my brain to perceive. The

[15] Borges imagined a country where geographers became so influential that they were awarded a research grant to make a map "that was the same size as the country and coincided with it at every point." This map was completely useless.

Figure 5.6   Is there a rhinoceros in the room?
This drawing of a rhinoceros by Conrad Gesner published in 1551 was based on a previous drawing by Albrecht Dürer. Dürer himself had never seen such an animal, but had drawn it after seeing a sketch and from descriptions in a letter.
Source: Gesner, C. (1551). *Historia animalium libri I–IV. Cum iconibus. Lib. I. De quadrupedibus uiuiparis*. Zurich: C. Froschauer.

existence of the errors tells my brain that its model of the world is not good enough. The nature of the errors tells the brain how to make a better model of the world. And so we go round the loop again and again until the errors are too small to worry about. Usually only a few cycles of the loop are sufficient, which might take a brain only 100 milliseconds.

A system that constructs models of the outside world in this way will use any information it can get to help it make better models. No preference is given to vision or sound or touch as long as they are informative. And the system will make predictions about how the signals coming from all the senses will change when I act on the world. So, when I see a glass of wine, my brain is already making predictions about what the glass will feel like and what the wine will taste like. Imagine the shock and horror of picking up a glass of red wine and discovering that it is cold and sweet.

Where Does Prior Knowledge Come From?

But if perception is a loop that starts on the inside with prior knowledge, then where does this prior knowledge come from? Haven't we created a chicken and egg problem? We can't perceive something unless we already know something about it, but we can't know anything about it until we perceive it.

How does our brain acquire the prior knowledge needed for perception? Some of it is hard-wired into the brain through millions of years of evolution. For example, in certain monkeys the color sensitivity of the neurons in their eyes is ideally suited for detecting the fruit found in their environment. Evolution has built into their brain a prior hypothesis about the color of ripe fruit. Our brain is hard-wired during the first few months of life as a result of our visual experiences. There are certain facts about the world that do change very little and, therefore, become strong prior hypotheses. We can only see an object when there is light that reflects off its surface and strikes our eyes. This light also creates shadows that provide clues about the shape of the object. For millions of years there has only been one major source of light in the world – the Sun. And the light of the Sun always comes from above. This means that concave objects will be light at the top and dark at the bottom, while convex objects will be light at the bottom and dark at the top. Our brain has this simple rule built into its wiring. It uses this rule to decide whether an object is concave or convex, which you can test by looking at the figure below. The objects look unambiguous: the domino on the top has five convex spots and one concave spot. The one on the bottom has two convex spots and four concave spots. Or so it seems – in fact, the page is completely flat. We interpret the spots as concave and convex because the shading suggests there are shadows caused by light coming from above. So if you turn the page upside down, the convex spots will turn into convex spots because we assume the light is still coming from above. If you turn the page on its side, the shadows no longer make any sense and the spots start to look like holes through which we see a complex shaded sheet of material.

If the brain has the wrong prior knowledge, our perception will be false. With modern technology we can make many novel pictures that the brain has not been designed to comprehend. We cannot avoid having false perceptions of these pictures.

One object that it is almost impossible to perceive correctly is the inside of a hollow mask of a face.

When we look inside this hollow mask (bottom right picture), we cannot help but see it as a normal convex face. Our prior belief that faces are convex and not hollow is too strong to be modified. If the mask is slowly rotating, an additional illusion is caused. Because we see the mask

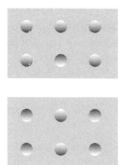

Figure 5.7 The domino illusion
The top domino has five convex spots and one concave spot. The bottom domino has two convex spots. In reality you are looking at a flat sheet of paper. The spots look concave or convex because of the shading. You expect the light to come from above so that shadow will be at the bottom of a convex spot and at the top of a concave spot. If you turn the page upside down, the concave spots become convex, and vice versa.

Figure 5.8 The hollow mask illusion
The Charlie Chaplin mask is rotated as we move from top left to bottom right. The face in the bottom right panel is concave since we are seeing the mask from the inside; we can't help but see it as convex with the nose sticking out. In this case our knowledge that faces are convex overrides our knowledge about lighting and shadows.

Source: Professor Richard Gregory, Department of Experimental Psychology, University of Bristol.

inverted, the tip of the nose appears to be the nearest part of the face, when it is in fact the part that is furthest away. As a result we misinterpret the movement of the mask and see the direction of the rotation reverse whenever we are looking into the hollow.[16]

How Action Tells Us about the World

For the brain, perception and action are intimately linked. We use our bodies to learn about the world. We do things to the world with our bodies and see what happens. This is another feature that early computers lacked. They just looked at the world. They did not do things. They had no bodies. They did not make predictions. This is another reason why perception was so difficult for them.

Even a simple movement can help us separate our perception of one object from another. When I look into my garden, I can see a fence in front of a tree. How do I know which patch of brown goes with the fence and which with the tree? If my model of the world says that the fence is in front of the tree, then I can predict that the sensations associated with the fence and the tree will change in different ways if I move my head. Because the fence is nearer to me than the tree, the bits of the fence move past my eye faster than the bits of the tree. My brain can link together all the bits of the tree because of their common motion. But it is I, the perceiver, who am moving – not the tree or the fence.

Simple movements help our perception. But movements with goals, which I shall call actions, help our perception even more. If there is a wine glass in front of me, I am aware of its shape and color. I am not aware that my brain has already worked out how to shape my hand to grasp the stem, anticipating the feel of the glass on my fingers. This preparation and anticipation happens even when I have no intention of picking up the glass (see Figure 4.6). Part of my brain represents the world around me in terms of actions: the action needed to get from here to the exit, the action needed to pick up the bottle on the table. My

[16] The ideas presented in this chapter are all prefigured in the work of Richard Gregory, whose marvelous lectures I attended in the 1960s. The hollow mask and other nice demonstrations can be found on his website: *http://www.richardgregory.org/experiments/index.htm.*

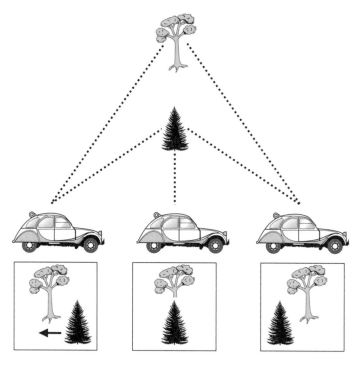

Figure 5.9 We can discover where things are by moving
When we move past the two trees, the nearby pine tree moves faster than the distant
bushy-topped tree. This is called motion parallax. Through this phenomenon we know that
the pine tree is nearer to us than the bushy-topped tree.

brain is continuously and automatically predicting the best movements
for the actions I might need to perform. Whenever I perform an action,
these predictions are tested and my model of the world is refined on the
basis of the prediction errors. Through my experience of handling the
wine glass, I have a better idea of its shape. In the future I will be better
able to "see" its shape through the imperfect and ambiguous medium of
vision.

**My brain discovers what is out there in the world by constructing
models of that world. These models are not arbitrary. They are
adjusted to give the best possible predictions of my sensations as I
act upon the world. But I am not aware of this complex mechanism.
So what is it that I am aware of?**

My Perception Is Not of the World, But of My Brain's Model of the World

What I perceive are not the crude and ambiguous cues that impinge from the outside world onto my eyes and my ears and my fingers. I perceive something much richer – a picture that combines all these crude signals with a wealth of past experience.[17] My perception is a prediction of what ought to be out there in the world. And this prediction is constantly tested by action.

Now, any system makes certain characteristic types of error when it fails. Luckily, these errors are very informative. Not only are the errors important for the system to learn, they are also important for us when we observe the system for discovering how the system works. They give us clues as to what kind of a system it is. What kind of errors will a system that works by prediction make? It will have problems whenever there is ambiguity: when two different objects in the outside world cause the same sensations.[18] This problem can usually be solved because one model is much more likely than the other. It is very unlikely that there is a rhinoceros in my room. But this means the system is fooled when the unlikely situation is, in fact, the correct one. Many of the visual illusions beloved of psychologists work because they trick the brain in this way.

In the very oddly shaped Ames room, the layout is arranged to cause the same sensations to our eye as an ordinary square room (see Figure 2.8). A model of an oddly shaped room and a model of a square room both predict the sensations at our eye equally well. But our experience with square rooms is so much more frequent that we cannot help but see the Ames room as square, while the people in it grow and shrink in an impossible manner as they move from one side to the other. The prior probability (expectation) that we will look at an Ames room is so small that our Bayesian brain takes little account of this strange evidence.

---

[17]   When Whistler exhibited his *Nocturne in Black and Gold: The Falling Rocket* (see Figure CP5, color plate section), Ruskin wrote that the artist had been impudent to ask 1,000 guineas for "flinging a pot of paint in the public's face." When Whistler sued him for libel, he stated in court that the painting had taken only a "few hours." Ruskin's lawyer said: "You asked 1,000 guineas for a few hours work?" Whistler replied: "No, I asked it for the knowledge of a lifetime."

[18]   In reality the situation is always ambiguous. There will always be more than one possible cause for the pattern of activity in our sense organs. This is the "inverse problem." This is why prior knowledge is so important.

But what happens if we have no prior reason to prefer one interpretation over another? This is the case for the Necker cube. We could see this as a rather complex two-dimensional figure, but we have much more experience with cubes. So we see a cube. The problem is that there are two possible cubes. One has the front face at the top right, while the other has the front face at the bottom left. We have no reason to prefer one version over the other, and so our perception spontaneously switches from one possible cube to the other.

Even more complex figures, like the Rubin vase figure and the wife/mother-in-law figure, show the some spontaneous reversals from one percept to another, again because both views are equally plausible. The fact that our brains make this kind of response to ambiguous figures is

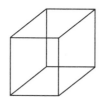

Is the front of the cube the left hand square or the right hand square?

Is this a vase or two faces looking at each other?

Is this the wife or the mother in law? (The young woman's chin becomes the old woman's nose.)

Figure 5.10 Ambiguous figures

Sources: Necker cube: Necker, L.A. (1832). Observations on some remarkable optical phenomena seen in Switzerland; and on an optical phenomenon which occurs on viewing a figure of a crystal or geometrical solid. *The London and Edinburgh Philosophical Magazine and Journal of Science, 1*(5), 329–337. Face/vase figure: Rubin, E. (1958). Figure and ground. In D. Beardslee & M. Wertheimer (Ed. and Trans.), *Readings in perception* (pp. 35–101). Princeton, NJ: Van Nostrand. (Original work published 1915.) Wife/mother-in-law figure: Boring, E.G. (1930). A new ambiguous figure. *American Journal of Psychology, 42*(3), 444–445. (Originally drawn by the well-known cartoonist W.E. Hill, and reproduced in the issue of *Puck* for the week ending November 6, 1915.)

further evidence that our brain is a Bayesian machine that discovers what is in the world by making predictions and searching for the causes of sensations.

Color Is in the Brain, Not in the World

But all these ambiguous figures have been invented by psychologists, you might say. We don't come across such objects in the real world. True. But the real world also is inherently ambiguous. Consider the problem of color. We only know about the color of objects from the light that is reflected from them. The wave-length of the light is what makes the color. Long wave-lengths give red, short wave-lengths give blue, with all the other colors in between. There are special receptors in the eye that are sensitive to these different wave-lengths of light. So does activity in these receptors tell us what color the tomato is? There is a problem here. The color isn't in the tomato. It's in the light reflected from it. When illuminated with white light, a tomato reflects red light. That is why we see it as red. But what if the tomato is illuminated with blue light? It can't reflect any red light, so does it now look blue? No. We still perceive it as red. From the colors of all the objects in the scene our brain decides that the scene is being illuminated by blue light and predicts what the "true" color of the various objects must be. What we perceive is determined by this predicted color, not by the wave-length of the light striking our eye. Because we see the predicted and not the "real" color, we can create striking illusions in which patches which are identical in terms of the wave-length of the light seem to have quite different colors (see Figure CP6, color plate section).[19]

Perception Is a Fantasy That Coincides
with Reality

Our brains build models of the world and continuously modify these models on the basis of the signals that reach our senses. So, what we actually perceive are our brain's models of the world. They are not the

[19]   Some of these illusions can be found here: *http://www.lottolab.org/*.

world itself, but, for us, they are as good as. You could say that our perceptions are fantasies that coincide with reality. Furthermore, if no sensory signals are available, then our brain fills in the missing information. There is a blind spot in our eyes where there are no light receptors. This is the point where all the nerve fibers carrying the sensory signals from the retina to the brain (the optic nerve) come together – so there is no space for light receptors. We are not aware of this blind spot because the brain makes something up to go into that part of our visual field. Our brain uses the signals from the region immediately around the blind spot to supply the missing information.

Put your finger straight in front of you and stare at it. Then close your left eye and move your finger slowly to the right, but keep staring straight ahead. There is a point where the tip of you finger will disappear and then reappear beyond the blind spot. But inside the blind spot your brain fills in the blank with the surrounding wallpaper pattern, not with the tip of your finger.

Even at the center of my vision, what I see is determined by what my brain expects to see combined with the actual sensory signals that occur. Sometimes these expectations can be so strong that I see what I expect and not what actually occurred. A striking laboratory experiment is to present people with visual stimuli, such as letters of the alphabet, so rapidly that the sensory signals can only just be detected. If you are strongly expecting to see the letter A, you may sometimes be convinced that you saw this letter when, in fact, the letter B was presented.

We Are Not the Slaves of Our Senses

You might think that this tendency to hallucinate was too high a price to pay for our brains' abilities to make models of the world. Couldn't the system be tuned so that sensory signals always dominated our experience? Then hallucinations could not occur. In fact, this is a bad idea, for many reasons. Sensory signals are simply too unreliable. But more importantly, such domination would make us slaves to our senses. Like a butterfly, our attention would continually flit from one attraction to the next. Such slavery to the senses can sometimes happen as the result of brain damage. There are some people who cannot help but act on everything they happen to see. They put a pair of spectacles upon their nose. But then they see another pair and put those on too.[20] If they see a glass, they must drink from it. If they see a pencil, they must scribble with it. They are unable to carry out a plan or follow an instruction. It turns out that these people usually have extensive damage to the front part of the brain. Their strange behavior was first described by François Lhermitte.

> The patient . . . came to see me at my apartment. . . . We returned to the bedroom. The bedspread had been taken off and the top sheet turned back in the usual way. When the patient saw this he immediately began to get undressed [including taking off his wig]. He got into bed, pulled the sheet up to his neck and prepared to go to sleep.

Through its use of controlled fantasy, our brain escapes from the tyranny of our environment. From out of the Babel of the academic cocktail party I can pick out and follow the voice of the opinionated Professor of English. I can find her face from among that sea of faces. Brain imaging studies show that when we choose to attend to faces there is an increase in neural activity in the "face area" of the brain even before the face appears in our visual field. Even when I just imagine a face, there is an increase of activity in this area (see Figure p.8). This is the power of my brain's ability to create controlled fantasies. I can anticipate the appearance of a face. I can imagine a face when there is no face there at all.

So How Do We Know What's Real?

There are two problems with fantasizing the world. First, how do we know that our brain's model of the world is true? This is not a real problem. For us to act upon the world it doesn't matter whether or not our brain's model is true. All that matters is that the model works. Does it enable us to make the appropriate actions and survive for another day? On the whole, yes it does. As we shall see in the following chapters, questions about the "truth" of the brain's models arise only when one

---

[20]   This effect of prior knowledge occurs at a much higher level than the effect of prior knowledge on the perception of objects. The Bayesian mechanism applies at all levels of brain processing.

brain communicates with another, and we discover that another person's model of the world is different from our own.

The other problem was revealed by that brain imaging study of faces. The face area in my brain becomes active when I see a face and also when I imagine a face. So how does my brain know when I am really seeing a face, and when I am just imagining one? In both cases my brain has created a face. How do we know when the model is of a real face "out there"? This problem doesn't apply just to faces, but to anything.

The solution is very simple. When we imagine a face, there are no sensory signals to compare with our predictions. There are no errors. When we see real faces, our brain's model is never quite perfect. Our brain is constantly updating the model to cope with those fleeting shifts of expression and changes in light. Thankfully, reality is always unexpected.

Imagination Is Extremely Boring

We have already seen how visual illusions reveal how the brain models reality. The Necker cube, mentioned above, is a well-known visual illusion (see Figure 5.8). We may see it as a cube with its front edge pointing to the left and down. And then our perception suddenly changes and we see it as a cube with its front edge pointing to the right and up. The explanation is simple. Our brain sees it as a cube rather than as the two-dimensional drawing it really is. But, as a cube, it is ambiguous. It has two possible three-dimensional versions. Our brain randomly switches from one to the other in its continuous attempts to find a better fit for the sensory signals

But what happens if I can find a naïve person who has never seen a Necker cube before and doesn't know about its tendency to reverse from one form to another? I show him the figure for a short time so that he does not see it reverse. Then I ask him to imagine the figure. Will it reverse as he inspects it in his imagination? I find that, in the imagination, the Necker cube never reverses. The imagination is utterly uncreative. It has no predictions to make and no errors to resolve. We don't create in our heads. We create by externalizing our thoughts with sketches and doodles and rough drafts so that we can benefit from the unexpectedness of reality. It is this continual unexpectedness that makes interacting with the real world such a joy.

In this chapter I have shown how our brains discover what is out there in the world by constructing models and making predictions. Our models are built by combining information from our senses with our prior expectations. Both sensations and expectations are essential for this process. We are not aware of all the work our brain is doing. We are only aware of the models that result from this work. This makes our experience of the world seem effortless and direct.

Chapter 6

How Brains Model Minds

"So novels bore you and you hate poetry." The Professor of English seems almost concerned about me.

"Why should you think that?"

"You just said that only the physical world was exciting and that imagination was utterly boring. You have dismissed everything creative about the human spirit, the imaginary worlds of the great writers and painters who have created our unique human culture."

"I was talking about an imaginary world created by a single brain working in isolation. You are talking about the world of other minds. I agree with you. The world of other minds is even more exciting and unpredictable than the physical world. But the world of other minds is also revealed to us by our brains."

"You can't reduce culture to brain activity," she says. "To know other minds requires understanding. All science can do is explain."

"I reject all this post-modern nonsense,[1]" interjects the new Head of Physics, who has just joined us. "But the world of other minds is a private, subjective world. You can't study such a world scientifically."

As you can imagine, we all found it too tiring to carry on our discussion at such a high level and soon reverted to academic gossip.

But, of course, I think that they are both wrong. It is our brain that enables us to enter the world of other minds, and so it is legitimate to ask: how can our brain do this?

---

[1]   She is teasing the Professor of English by referring to the spoof paper that the physicist Alan Sokal published in *Social Text*, a serious literary journal. But, as we shall see in the next chapter, we may be moving towards a hermeneutics of neuroscience.

Science can attempt to explain how we can understand other minds. This is no different from explaining how we, as individuals, understand the physical world. This is much of what the science of psychology is all about. And, as we have seen in the last chapter, our knowledge of the physical world is essentially subjective. What I know about the physical world is captured in a model of that world created by my brain. This model is created from my prior knowledge and the cues provided by my senses. My brain creates a physical world of trees and birds and people. My knowledge of the mental world, the world of other minds, can be created in exactly the same way. From the cues provided by my senses my brain creates a model of a mental world of beliefs, desires, and intentions.

But what are these signals that tell us about what is going on in the minds of others? I am not talking about speech and language. We know a lot about what is in the minds of others by simply observing the way they act upon the world, by the way they move.

Biological Motion: The Way Living Things Move

Just by looking at the way something is moving you can tell whether it is a living thing or just a leaf blowing in the wind. And you can do much better than this. You can see that it is human *and* you can see what it is doing. You don't need much information to be able to do this. In 1973 Gunnar Johansson attached small lights to the major joints of one of his students (about 14 lights on ankles, knees, elbows, etc., are sufficient) and filmed her moving in the dark. All you can see on the film is the 14 spots of light moving about in a complex way. If you view just one of these spots in isolation, nothing sensible emerges from the motion. If you see all the spots, but they are not moving, then nothing sensible emerges from this static display. But as soon as the spots start to move a figure immediately emerges. You can tell whether it's a man or a woman and whether she is walking or running or dancing. You can even tell whether she is happy or sad.[2] While I can't show you moving images in this book, Figure 6.1 shows that when we join up the spots even these simple static images give a strong impression of gender.

This ability to see biological motion is well established in the brain. Already by 4 months of age, human infants prefer to look at moving

[2]   For some nice demonstrations, see, e.g., *http://www.biomotionlab.ca/projects.php*.

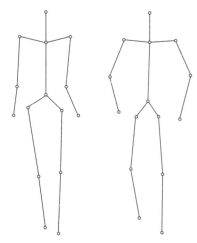

Figure 6.1 Even stick figures have a gender
For a moving version try *http://www.biomotionlab.ca/Demos/BMLgender.html* from Prof
Nikolaus Troje's Biomotion lab.

spots of light that form a moving figure rather than spots moving in the
same way, but randomly placed in relation to one another. Even cats can
easily be trained to distinguish between spots of light that form a moving
cat and the same spots of light randomly arranged.

How Movements Can Reveal Intentions

Recognizing that something is a cat from the way it moves is no different
from recognizing a cat from its shape or from the sound it makes. Our
brains will use any cues available to find out what is out there in the
world. Complex motion is one of the many cues to which our brains are
exquisitely sensitive. Recognizing that one object is a cat and another
object is a woman dancing does not give us access to the mental world of
beliefs and intentions. But perhaps recognizing that something is a cat
stalking its prey or a women feeling sad does bring us to the edges of the
mental world. In these examples the movements we see tell us something
about what the cat is intending and what the woman is feeling.

Even very simple movements can reveal something about goals and
intentions. György Gergely and colleagues showed 12-month-old infants
a movie (see *learning task* in Figure 6.2). At the beginning there is a
small gray ball and a large black ball separated by a barrier. Then the

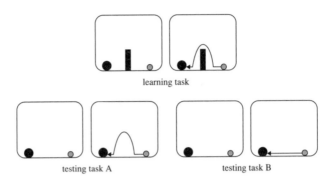

learning task

testing task A   testing task B

Figure 6.2 Twelve-month-old infants know about the goals of actions
Watching the learning task, infants infer that the gray ball jumps over the barrier to get to
the black ball. When the barrier is taken away, the infants expect that the gray ball will go
straight to the black ball (testing task B), rather than carrying on jumping (testing task A).

Source: Redrawn from Figures 1 and 3 in: Gergely, G., Nadasdy, Z., Csibra, G., & Biro, S.
(1995). Taking the intentional stance at 12 months of age. *Cognition, 56*(2), 165–193.

small gray ball jumps over the barrier and stops next to the large black
ball. The infants watch this clip several times until they are fairly bored
with it. The barrier is then removed and two new movies are shown.

The idea behind experiments like this is that the bored infant will look
more at the clip that is unexpected. The unexpected clip is more interesting. It contains more information and requires us to change our beliefs
about what was happening in the previous clip.

So which clip is more unexpected? In task A the movement of the gray
ball is exactly the same as it was in the learning task. The gray ball jumps
and then stops by the black ball. In task B the movement of the gray ball
is quite different. The gray ball moves straight to the black ball. So, in
terms of movements, task B should be more unexpected. But this is not
what the infants thought. They were much more surprised by task A,
where the gray ball jumped over the non-existent barrier. What this
experiment shows[3] is that the infants interpreted the movement of the
gray ball in terms of its goal: what the grey ball wants is to be next to the
black ball. If the barrier is in the way, then the gray ball has to jump over
it to reach the black ball. But when the barrier is gone, the gray ball will
reach the black ball by the easiest route. It doesn't need to jump any
more. So this is the behavior we (and the infants) expect when the

---

[3] To justify this interpretation, the authors used many more control tasks than I have
described here.

barrier is removed. The unexpected behavior is when the gray ball continues to jump when the barrier is not there. Now we have to change our
ideas about the goal of the gray ball. Perhaps it likes jumping?

Other people are much more interesting than small gray balls. We
watch their movements all the time and try to predict what they are
going to do next. Walking along the street, we must predict which way
the person coming toward us is going to dodge. We get this prediction
right so often that when we both dodge the same way this is a special
event marked by embarrassed smiles.

We pay particular attention to other people's eyes. When watching
someone's eyes, we can detect very small movements. We can detect an
eye movement of less than 2 millimeters when standing up to 1 meter
away from the face. This sensitivity to eye movements allows us to take
the first step into someone else's mental world. From the position of a
person's eyes we can tell very accurately where they are looking. And if
we know where people are looking, then we can discover what they are
interested in.

When we look at Figure 6.3, we know that Larry is interested in the
ball and we can't help looking at it as well.

I see the Professor of English on the other side of the crowded room.
The first thing I notice is that she is not looking at me. So who is she

Figure 6.3 We know what Larry wants by looking at his eyes
We can see that Larry is looking at the ball. We also look at the ball before we look at the
other objects.

Source: Figure 1b, the Larry story, from: Lee, K., Eskritt, M., Symons, L.A., & Muir, D. (1998).
Children's use of triadic eye gaze information for "mind reading." *Developmental
Psychology*, *34*(3), 525–539.

interested in? I cannot help but follow the direction of her gaze. Surely it cannot be that cocky young molecular biologist?

Imitation

It is not just eye movements that we follow so slavishly. Our brains have an automatic tendency to imitate any movement that we see. The most striking evidence for imitation in the brain comes from a study in which electrical activity was measured in single neurons in monkeys. Giacomo Rizzolatti and his colleagues in Parma were studying neurons involved in making grasping movements. They found that different neurons were concerned with different kinds of grasping movements. One neuron became more active when the monkey used a precision grip with finger and thumb to pick up a small object like a peanut. Another neuron became more active when the monkey used a power grip with the whole hand to pick up an object like a pencil. In the part of the brain concerned with motor control (the premotor cortex), there were neurons representing a whole vocabulary of different grasping movements.

But, to the researchers' surprise, some of these neurons didn't become active only when the monkey grasped something. They also became active when the monkey saw one of the experimenters grasping something. The neuron that responded when the monkey picked up a peanut also responded when the monkey saw the experimenter picking up a peanut. These are now called mirror neurons. The vocabulary of actions represented by these neurons applies to the observation of actions as well as to the production of actions.

The same thing happens in the human brain. Whenever we move, there is a characteristic pattern of activity in the motor areas of our brain. One of the first surprises revealed by brain imaging was that this pattern of activity is also seen when we prepare to make a movement or simply imagine making a movement (see Figure p.7). The same thing happens when we watch someone else move. Our own brain becomes active in just those regions that would be active if we made the same movement ourselves. The major difference, of course, is that we don't actually move.

Our brain responds in this way when we see someone else move, even though it will sometimes interfere with our own actions and can even be embarrassing. An uncle of mine has one stiff leg. When I was a boy and walked beside him I had to concentrate hard to stop myself from limping as well. This tendency to imitate others can take an extreme form in

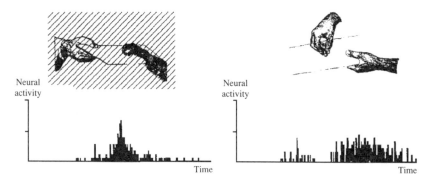

Figure 6.4 Mirror neurons
These neurons become more active when the monkey makes an action or sees someone else making the same action.
Left figure: The monkey acts (without seeing its hand).
Right figure: The monkey sees the experimenter making the same action.
Source: Part of Figure 2 from: Rizzolatti, G., Fadiga, L., Gallese, V., & Fogassi, L. (1996). Premotor cortex and the recognition of motor actions. *Cognitive Brain Research*, *3*(2), 131–141.

people with Giles de la Tourette's syndrome.[4] These people often have a compulsion to constantly imitate what others are doing: coughing, sneezing, and scratching. This makes life very difficult for them and their families.

Imitation: Perceiving the Goals of Others

Imitation is like perception. We do it automatically without having to think about it. To us it seems easy. It is only when we try to make a machine do it that we realize how difficult imitation is. When I see you move your arm, I simply make the same movements. Your arm movement produces a changing pattern of light on my retina that is interpreted by my brain. But how does my brain manage to translate a series of changing visual patterns into a series of muscle commands that will produce the same movement in my arm? For one thing, I can't see which muscles are involved. Furthermore, if I am imitating a child, I will have

---

[4] This is a disorder of the motor system in the brain, particularly associated with tics: purposeless repetitive movements and shouts. The disorder was first described by the French doctor Giles de la Tourette. This is his surname. His full name is Georges Albert Edouard Brutus Giles de la Tourette.

to send different commands to my muscles to get the same movement, because my arm is much longer.

We have exactly this problem when we design a computer. In a voice-activated word processing system, how does the machine translate the pattern of acoustic vibrations made by my voice into the marks on paper produced by the printer? The solution is to make internal models that bridge the gap. In the example of the voice-activated computer these internal models would be words. Once the input – the acoustic vibrations (or visual stimuli or key presses) – has been translated into words, then these can be output (as strings of letters or patterns of dots) into any printer.

In the case of movements, these internal models are the goals of the action. Now, in themselves movements are ambiguous. As John Searle has pointed out, if we meet someone walking toward the west, we don't know if he is going to the bakery across the street or walking to Patagonia. But we are all Bayesians now. We can remove this ambiguity because we know in advance which is his most likely goal.

We can demonstrate the importance of goals by studying the "errors" made by children in imitation games. In one such game, I tell the toddler sitting across the table from me to imitate everything I do. I lift my right hand. She lifts her left hand. Is this an error? She isn't moving the same hand. But she is behaving like a mirror. I touch my left ear with my left hand. She touches her right ear with her right hand, once again imitating mirror fashion. Now I reach across myself and touch my right ear with my left hand. She doesn't reach across herself. She touches her left ear with her left hand. Is this an error? She hasn't copied the movement, reaching across herself. She has copied the goal, touching her left ear. She has achieved this goal in the most sensible way – by reaching with the nearest hand.

But now I really tax her. There is a big button in the middle of the table. I bend down and press it with my forehead. What will she do now? Why should I be pressing the button with my head? What she does depends on my hands. If my hands are obviously restricted because I have decided it was cold and I am holding a blanket round my shoulders, then she will press the button with her hand. She assumes that my goal is to press the button and that I would have used my hands if I hadn't already been using them for something else. If my hands are clearly free for performing actions since they are resting on each side of the button, then she will press the button with her head. She assumes that my goal must be to press the button with my head.

Experimenter
"Do what I do"

Infant
"OK"

Figure 6.5 Infants imitate goals, not movements: left hand or right hand?
Children imitate the goal, touching the left ear, but not the movement, using the right
hand. They use the easier movement, touching the left ear with the left hand.

Source: Figure 1 from: Bekkering, H., Wohlschlager, A., & Gattis, M. (2000). Imitation of
gestures in children is goal-directed. *Quarterly Journal of Experimental Psychology, section A,
53*(1), 153–164.

Figure 6.6 Infants imitate goals, not movements: head or hand?
The child has to imitate the model, who presses the button with her head.
Top picture: When the model's hands are wrapped in the shawl, the child presses the button
with her hand.
Bottom picture: When the model's hands are free, the child presses the button with her head.

Source: Figure 1 from: Gergely G., Bekkering, H., & Kiraly, I. (2002). Rational imitation in
preverbal infants. *Nature, 415*(6873), 755. Reprinted by permission of Macmillan Publishers
Ltd: *Nature*, © 2006.

To imitate someone, we watch their movements closely, but we don't copy these movements. We use the movements to discover something in the mind of the person we are watching: the goal of their movement. Then we imitate them by making a movement that achieves the same goal.

Humans and Robots

As soon as we perceive movements in terms of goals, they become special. Anything can simply "move": rocks can roll in the stream; branches can thrash in the wind. But only certain creatures move of their own accord in order to attain their goals. I will call these goal-directed movements *actions*. And it is only the actions of creatures with goals (which I will call *agents*) that our brains will automatically imitate.

We don't need to measure activity in the brain to show that our brains automatically imitate the actions of other people. If I am just watching another person move, I can't tell that my brain is imitating the movement. The brain activity occurs, but there are no outward signs of this in my behavior. But what if I am trying to make a movement while watching someone else? If I am making the same action as the person I am watching, then I can perform my action more easily. This is the basis of mass gymnastics. But if I am trying to make a different movement, it will be more difficult to perform.

James Kilner performed a neat experiment in which people were asked simply to move their arms up and down rhythmically while watching someone else moving their arms from side to side. Careful measurement showed that watching these different movements made the observer's own movements become more variable. This was a sign of the brain's automatic tendency to imitate the actions of others. But if a robot arm was making the movements, then this did not interfere with the observer's movements. The brain does not automatically imitate a robot arm, because the movements of this arm are subtly wrong; we see them as mechanical rather than biological. The robot arm is not perceived as an agent with goals and intentions. When a robot arm moves, my brain sees only movements, not actions.[5]

---

[5] But of course in special circumstances movements themselves can become goals. The ballet dancer has the goal of producing a perfect *grand jeté*.

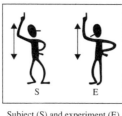 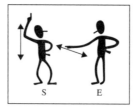

Subject (S) and experiment (E)
make the same movements

Subject (S) and experimenter (E)
make different movements

Recordings of the movements made by the subjects which
were repeated vertical or horizontal sweeps. These movements
are more variable (right-hand panel) when watching someone
else making different movements

Figure 6.7 Watching someone else move can interfere with our own movements

Source: Figures 1 and 2 in: Kilner, J.M., Paulignan, Y., & Blakemore, S.J. (2003). An interference effect of observed biological movement on action. *Current Biology*, *13*(6), 522–525.

Empathy

But imitation also gives us access to the private mental worlds of others. We don't just imitate gross movements of the arms and legs. We also automatically imitate the subtle movements of faces. And this imitation of faces makes us feel different. If I see a smiling face, I smile a little too, and I feel happier.[6] If I see a face filled with disgust, I will feel disgusted too. So even these private feelings are automatically shared through the ability of our brain to translate between perceptions and actions.

---

[6] There is an easy way to feel happier even if you don't see a smiling face. Hold a pencil between your teeth (withdrawing your lips). This forces your face into a smile and you feel happier. If you want to feel miserable, hold the pencil between your lips.

We often think of pain as the most private experience of all. I know if I am in pain, but how can I ever know anything about your pain? Philosophers like Wittgenstein have worried intensively about this problem, reaching conclusions that I find very hard to follow. We can know something about other people's pain by watching their behavior and listening to what they say. Using brain imaging we have discovered a network of areas, *the pain matrix*, that become active when someone experiences pain. So the physiological correlates of this experience are not private.

But the subjective experience of pain is not directly coupled to the physical nature of the stimulus that causes it. A hot rod feels less painful if you are distracted, even though the temperature of the rod has not changed. The subjective experience of pain can also be altered by hypnosis or by taking a harmless pill that you have been told is a pain killer. Activity in some parts of the brain matches with the physical temperature of the rod. Activity in other parts matches with the subjective feeling of the pain. We might contrast these as the physical aspect of pain and the mental experience of pain.

So what happens when we see someone else in pain? The same brain areas become active as when we experience pain ourselves. Is this the basis of empathy, our ability to share the inner feelings of others? Certainly people who are more empathic[7] show greater brain activation when they see another in pain.

How is this possible? How can I experience what you are feeling? We can answer this question by looking at precisely which areas that light up in the brain during empathy. As we have seen, activity in some brain areas relate to the physical aspects of the pain: how hot the rod is, or where it is touching you. These areas *don't* light up when you know that someone else is in pain.[8] Activity in other areas relates to your mental experience of the pain.[9] These areas *do* light up in response to someone

---

[7]   This is assessed by asking people to endorse statements like: "Unhappy movie endings haunt me for hours afterward." Or to reject statements like: "I cannot feel much sorrow for those who are responsible for their own misery."

[8]   But if you see a needle being stuck into someone else's hand, you will flinch, and there are corresponding changes of neural activity that responds when a needle is stuck into your hand.

[9]   The mental experience of pain is associated with activity in the anterior cingulate cortex. People who suffer from severe chronic pain were sometimes treated by cutting out this area of the brain (cingulotomy). After surgery these people still felt the pain, but they no longer had an emotional response to it.

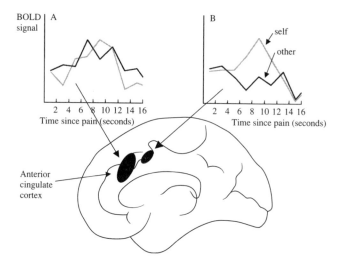

Figure 6.8 Experiencing the pain of others
The anterior cingulate cortex lies on the medial surface at the front of the brain. This region becomes more active when we feel pain.
What happens in the anterior cingulate cortex when we know that a loved one is getting a painful shock? At the back of the region (B) our brain only responds to our own pain. But, further forward, there is a brain region which responds to the pain of another as much to our own pain.

Source: From Figures 2 and 3 in: Singer, T., Seymour, B., O'Doherty, J., Kaube, H., Dolan, R.J., & Frith, C.D. (2004). Empathy for pain involves the affective but not sensory components of pain. *Science, 303*(5661), 1157–1162.

else's pain. So what we can share is the mental experience of the pain, not its physical aspect. These brain areas also become active when you anticipate pain, if you know that 5 seconds after hearing a tone you will be touched by the hot rod. If you can anticipate the pain that you will feel, is it so difficult to anticipate the pain that someone else will feel? Of course we can't experience the physical sensations that impinge on others. But we can construct the mental models based on these stimuli. It is because we make mental models of the physical world that we can share our experiences in the mental world.

The Experience of Agency

There is another experience, more ubiquitous than pain, but equally private. This is the experience of being in control, of deciding to do something and then doing it. Of being an agent in control of our destiny. We are all agents. But there is much more to our sense of agency than performing actions to achieve goals. We make choices. We decide which goals to aim for. We decide when to perform actions. We are not just agents. We are free agents. At least for the small things in life, we all believe that we are in control and can cause things to happen. My hand is resting on the table and I am staring at my finger, waiting for it to move. Nothing happens. And yet, whenever I want to, I can lift my finger. This is the mystery of mind over matter: the way thought can make things happen in the physical world.

"What mystery?" says the Professor of English. She has been watching me staring at my hand and confirming her prejudice that I am very peculiar. "Of course I can lift my finger when I want to. Are you one of those neuroscientists that say free will doesn't exist?"

It isn't just scientists who wonder how we can control our actions

She raised one hand and flexed its fingers and wondered, as she had sometimes before, how this thing, this machine for gripping, this fleshy spider on the end of her arm, came to be hers, entirely at her command. Or did it have some little life of its own? She bent her finger and straightened it. The mystery was in the instance before it moved, the dividing moment between not moving and moving, when her intention took effect. It was like a wave breaking. If she could only find herself at the crest, she thought, she might find the secret of herself, that part of her that was really in charge. She brought her forefinger closer to her face and stared at it, urging it to move. It remained still because she was pretending, she was not entirely serious, and because willing it to move, or being about to move it, was not the same as actually moving it. And when she did crook it finally, the action seemed to start in the finger itself, not in some part of her mind. When did it know to move, when did she know to move it?

Ian McEwan, *Atonement*

I don't really want to answer the Professor's question since my beliefs on free will are very ambivalent. What I do know is that I have a very strong *experience* of free will. I feel that I am in control of my actions.

However strong the pressure upon me to do something might be, I still feel that I have the ultimate choice. Some of us will choose to die rather than lose this freedom. But, most of the time, it is the small things in life that give us the sense of being free agents; of being in control.

I can make the doorbell ring by pressing the button. I am a little surprised by the chimes, but what the bell sounds like is not the point. The ringing will cause the Professor of English to come and open her door. This is the goal of my action. This is what makes me an agent. Agents make things happen. Being an agent is all about cause and effect.

Now, our brains are very good at linking cause and effect. It is all a matter of prediction and timing. The effect follows the cause. Having observed the cause, we can predict what the effect will be and when it will occur. This what the brain does. It makes predictions about the world and then checks how well these predictions work. Through this process of prediction the brain discovers which causes go with which effects. These causes and effects are then *bound* together to form units which, in this case, are actions performed by agents.[10] (Just as color, shape, and motion are bound together to form objects.)

This binding together of causes and effects in actions is revealed if we ask people to tell us about the time at which the various components of the action occur. For example, I can ask you to perform a very simple action, like pressing a button that causes a bell to ring. Using a special computerized clock-face, I can ask you to report the exact time when you press the button and also the exact time when the bell begins to ring (as in Benjamin Libet's experiment described in Chapter 3). We can call these the *mental* times. These are the times that the events happen in your mind. I can also measure the times that these events occur in the physical world. A computer records the exact time that you press the button and the exact time that the bell starts to ring. We can call these the physical times. These mental times and physical times are not the same. In your mind the button press occurs slightly later and the bell starts to ring slightly earlier. For you the cause and effect of your action seem closer together. In mental time the components of your actions are bound together.

Now we repeat the experiment, but this time change the agency. What happens if you don't press the button by yourself, but I make your finger move by applying a strong magnetic pulse to the top of your head, over

---

[10]   This binding together of causes and effects to create actions was demonstrated in a serious of ingenious experiments by Patrick Haggard.

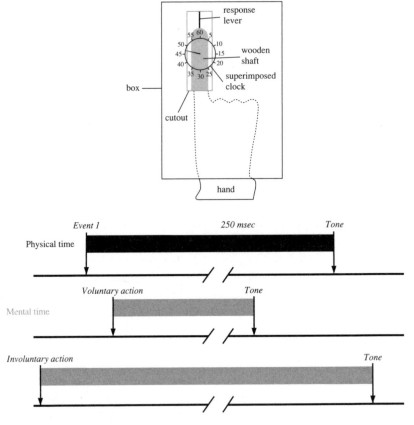

Figure 6.9 The brain binds together the causes and effects of actions
In this experiment, participants press a button with their finger which causes a tone 250 msec later. Using the virtual clock projected on top of their finger, participants report the time at which these two events occur.

When participants press the button and cause the tone, the two events are closer together in mental time than they are in physical time. The brain has bound together in time the cause and its effect. When participants make an involuntary movement (because the experimenter has stimulated their brain with a strong magnetic pulse), the movement and the tone are further apart in mental time.

Source: Illustration from data in: Haggard, P., Clark, S., & Kalogeras, J. (2002). Voluntary action and conscious awareness. *Nature Neuroscience*, 5(4), 382–385.

the motor cortex? When I do this you don't feel that you are causing the twitch of your finger. The movement happens without you intending it to happen. When the bell rings after I make your finger move, you don't feel that you have caused the bell to ring. The finger twitch is not an action. In this example, when your finger moves, but you are not performing an action, your brain no longer binds together the finger movement and the bell ring in your mental time. In this, case the mental times of the two events are pushed apart so that the mental interval between the events is now greater that the physical interval. Your brain recognizes that you are not being an agent, and so does not recognize you as causing an effect. It therefore reduces the binding of the events in time.

But what happens when I see someone else pressing a button and causing a bell to ring? Can I experience the sense of agency in someone else?

The Problem with Privileged Access

There are things that I know about myself that I can never know about you. When I perform an action, I have all sorts of sensations that I cannot share with you. The effort I put into the press. The feel of the button I am pressing. These signals, to which I have privileged access, enable me to have an experience of my own agency that I can never have about someone else's sense of agency. This is an experience that is private. I cannot share this experience of my own movements with you. And I cannot share your experience of your movements. Does this mean that my experience of my own agency must be quite different from my experience of your agency? Does this mean that I can know that I am an agent, but can never know that you are one? Our everyday experience is against this idea.

The brain creates my experience of agency by binding together the causes and effects of the actions I perform. So what happens if, instead of reporting the times of my own actions, I watch you pressing a button to make a bell ring and report the exact times of these two events? In this case I don't have your experience of pressing the button. But in spite of this lack, I still experience the two events as closer together in mental time than they are in physical time. I bind together the causes and effects of actions even when you are the agent, rather than me.

So it seems that even for my sense of my own agency I do not have to rely upon the private sensations that accompany my acts. The sense of agency simply relies on linking cause and effect through prediction. And so I can sense my agency in the same way that I sense yours.

"I am getting confused," says the Professor of English. "These private sensations you are talking about, these are the feelings I have when I move my finger. But you already told me at great length when you were trying to tickle me that these feelings are suppressed when we perform actions. So we cannot use these private sensations."

"Of course," I say, not wishing to reveal that I hadn't thought of this myself.

The implications of her insight are most profound. It is precisely when we are not being agents, when someone else is moving our arm, that we are most aware of these internal signals. When we are being agents, these private signals are suppressed. And this means that we perceive ourselves as being agents in the same way that we perceive others as being agents: we note the relations between actions and the effects they cause. We take into account what we know about prior intentions. But we don't take account of the physical sensations experiences by agents. It is precisely because we don't have any direct connections with the physical world, even the world of our own bodies, that we are able to enter the mental worlds of others. The mechanisms that evolved within our brains to understand the physical world also enable us to enter the mental worlds of others.

Illusions of Agency

But our ability to create models of the mental world also creates problems. Just as our picture of the physical world is a fantasy constrained by sensory signals, so our picture of the mental world, of our own or of others, is a fantasy constrained by sensory signals about what we, and they, are doing and saying. When these constraints fail, then we can have illusions about our actions.

Sometimes I can think that I have caused something to happen when I have actually done nothing. I described in Chapter 3 how Daniel Wegner can make his subjects think they have moved a computer mouse by putting the thought of making a movement into their minds just before the movement occurs. Experiencing the thought of making a movement just before the movement occurs is sufficient to make us think we have caused the movement. But the opposite effect can also occur in which we attribute our own actions to another person. We move, but we believe that the movement was made by someone else.

There is technique called "facilitated communication" that was developed as an alternative means of expression for people who cannot speak, or whose speech is highly limited. The idea is to enable a person with this disability to communicate by using a keyboard. The facilitator places her hands over the hands of the disabled person on the keyboard. The facilitator detects what the person wants to do and helps him to make the necessary movements. Strong claims have been made for this technique. It is possible that, in some cases, these claims are justified. But it is also clear that in many other cases the communication comes from the facilitator and not from the disabled person. For example, an examiner might present a series of questions for the disabled person to answer. But he secretly arranges for the facilitator to see different questions from the disabled person. From such experiments it is clear that it is the facilitator who is answering the questions, not the person she is supposed to be helping. But, until shown this evidence, the facilitator is convinced that it is the disabled person who is answering the questions. The facilitator has a strong illusion of agency. There is nothing special or odd about these facilitators. These illusions of agency happen to anyone put in the appropriate situation. They are like visual illusions.

Hallucinating Other Agents

For some unfortunate people the brain's fantasies about the mental world seem to become entirely unconstrained. Such people are typically diagnosed as suffering from schizophrenia.

Schizophrenia is one of the most misunderstood of all mental disorders. Firstly, schizophrenia is *not* split personality in which two minds inhabit one body. The split is between one part of the mind and another: between emotion and knowledge; between will and action. Secondly, schizophrenia is neither rare nor dangerous. One in a hundred of us are at risk for succumbing to this disorder.[11] Perhaps most misrepresented of all, while the disorder can cause terrible unhappiness for sufferers and their families, it is rarely associated with violence.

There are no objective physical signs of schizophrenia. The diagnosis is based on what the patient tells the doctor. Patients say that they hear voices when no one is there (false perceptions – hallucinations). Patients describe how they are persecuted by their colleagues at work when there is no evidence that this is the case (false beliefs – delusions). Patients with hallucinations and delusions are sometimes described as being out of touch with reality. But it is the mental world, rather than the physical

---

[11]   About the same as the risk of developing rheumatoid arthritis.

world, that they have lost touch with. In Chapter 1 I introduced you to George Trosse and L. Percy King. They heard voices when no one was there. But these were not just voices they heard. They were the voices of agents giving commands and commenting on the hearer's actions. Sometimes these agents take over. In Chapter 4 we met people who believe that their actions were being caused by alien forces. I showed how these people were aware of the sensations associated with movements that the rest of us suppress. But rather than saying, "My arm feels funny when I move it," these people believe that the movement is being caused by someone else. They are hallucinating about agents.

Peter sees agents everywhere. Even a leaf blowing in the wind has intentions and is trying to tell him something.

Mani feels agents creating unwanted emotions in her. She shares other people's emotional experiences against her will.

> It tries to put jealousy within me. I don't feel jealous about the person. There's a particular girl that he [the evil spirit] tries to make me jealous of. He tries to make her look striking. . . . I'm not jealous of that person, but he tries to make me jealous.

Most mysterious of all are the agents that interfere with thoughts. This is the experience described by Mary: her thoughts are not her own.

> I look out the window and I think that the garden looks nice and the grass looks cool, but the thoughts of Eamonn Andrews[12] come into my mind. . . . He treats my mind like a screen and flashes his thoughts onto it like you flash a picture.

What does it mean to have thoughts in your mind that are not your own? The French philosopher René Descartes is famous for his statement, "I think, therefore I am." Descartes was trying to discover if there is anything in our experience that we can be sure about. We can't be sure of our senses, because these sights and sounds might be hallucinations or dreams created by our brains.[13] We can't be sure of our memories of the past, because they might have been created a few seconds ago. Descartes concluded that all we can be sure about are our thoughts. Contemporary

---

[12]   Eamonn Andrews was the leading television personality in Britain from the 1950s to the 1980s.
[13]   Descartes imagined that they could be created by a malicious demon.

philosophers refer to this idea as "immunity to error through misidentification." If a person has a toothache, then it makes no sense, philosophers claim, to ask her, "Are you sure it is you that is having the toothache?" The experience must be hers. It cannot be anyone else's.

But when people with a diagnosis of schizophrenia report that thoughts that are not their own are being inserted into their minds, this seems to submerge our last remaining island of certainty about our experiences.

Where do thoughts come from? How do we know that our thoughts are our own? These are the mysteries that we confront, not just when thinking about schizophrenia, but whenever we worry about the mind. My answer is that we have to worry about the brain as well. It is the brain that makes the mental world of the mind, whether this is a normal mind or one that has lost touch with reality.

One of my motivations to be a neuroscientist has been to understand the problem of schizophrenia. I believe the key to the problem lies in the mechanisms in the brain that enable us to build models of the mental world and to use these models to predict what people are going to do. But I still have no idea precisely what has gone wrong in schizophrenia.

"That's not very surprising," says the Professor of English. "You don't know very much about what's going on in a normal brain either."

I think that I have direct contact with the physical world, but this is an illusion created by my brain. My brain creates models of the physical world by combining signals from my senses and prior expectations, and it is these models that I am aware of. I acquire my knowledge of the mental world – the minds of others – in the same way. However it may seem to me, my contact with the mental world is neither more nor less direct than my contact with the physical world. Using cues acquired from my senses and prior knowledge acquired from my experience, my brain creates models of the minds of others.

Part III

Culture and the Brain

Chapter 7

Sharing Minds – How the Brain Creates Culture

The Problem with Translation

We spend most of our time living in a mental world created by our brains – even when we are assaulted by the real world around us. Every morning, I, along with thousands of others, travel to work on the London Underground. But for most of this time I am oblivious of the physical world around me. I am not day-dreaming in a private world of my own. I am reading books and newspapers. I have entered someone else's mental world.

Without doubt our brain's most remarkable achievement is to permit communication between minds. The purpose of writing this book is to transfer ideas from my mind into yours. The Professor of English is devoting her life to the study of how we use words to create and communicate imaginary worlds. For the more practically minded there is much money to be made by developing and manufacturing products for communicating ideas. Not just books, but mobile phones and the internet. Sending ideas from one mind to another seems vital, almost a compulsion, for us. But if each mind is a private place, then this process of communication is impossible – isn't it?

Consider the problem of translation. Figure 7.1 shows a famously obscure Chinese poem by Li Shang-Yin (812?–858) that has been translated into English in many different versions. Even the titles of the poem have different translations: "The Patterned Lute," "The Inlaid Harp," "The Ornamented Zither." Here are three versions of the ending of this poem:

Did it wait, this mood to mature with hindsight?
In a trance from the beginning, then as now.

李 商 隐
Li Shang yin

锦 瑟
Inlaid harp

锦 瑟 无 端 五 十 弦,
Inlaid harp, no reason,   fifty   strings

一 弦 一 柱 思 华 年。
one string, one peg, thinking splendid years

庄 生   晓 梦   迷 蝴蝶,
sage Zhuang,   dawn dreaming, confused butterfly

望 帝 春 心 托 杜 鹃。
king Wang spring heart consigned cuckoo

沧 海 月 明 珠 有 泪,
blue sea, moon bright, pearls like tears

蓝 田 日 暖 玉 生 烟。
indigo field, sun warm, jade gives out smoke

此 情 可 待 成 追 忆,
this affection should last, become sought memory

只 是 当 时 已 惘 然。
only   at that time already   lost

Figure 7.1   The problem of translation
"The Patterned Lute": Li Shang-Yin (812?–858)

And a moment that ought to have lasted for ever
has come and gone before I knew.

This feeling might have become a thing to be remembered,
Only, at the time you were already bewildered and lost.

How do we decide which English version best reproduces the meaning
underlying the original Chinese? The problem is that we have no direct

access to this hidden meaning. We know about the meaning only through the Chinese characters that represent this meaning. There will be many English translations that are equally compatible with the original Chinese characters and there is no basis for deciding that one version is "better" than another. Therefore, the philosopher concludes, the notion that there is an underlying meaning to be discovered is misguided.[1]

"Quite right," says the Professor of English. "All we have is the text."

But this argument applies equally well to a conversation between two people.

I have in my mind some idea I want to communicate to you. I do this by turning my meaning into spoken words. You hear my words and turn them back into an idea in your mind. But how can you ever know that the idea in your mind is the same as the idea in my mind? There is no way you can get into my mind and compare the ideas directly. Communication is impossible.

And yet even at this moment we are having this vigorous interchange about the problem of meaning. Our brains have solved this impossible problem of communication.

Meanings and Goals

The problem of words and meanings is a more complex version of the problem of movements and goals. When I see a movement, I read the intention behind it. The Professor of English waves her hand and I see that she is beckoning me or wants me to go away. I see her hand movement as a goal-directed action. But movements are ambiguous. Many different goals can lead to the same movement. As I noted in the previous chapter, if we meet someone walking towards the west we don't know if he is going to the bakery or walking to Patagonia. Words are just as ambiguous in their relationship with meanings. The same words can mean different things. "Peter's very well read" sounds like an innocent remark describing Peter. But the next sentence, "He's even heard of Shakespeare," makes us realize that the Professor of English is using irony. She is telling us that Peter is *not* well read.[2]

---

[1] This is the idea of the indeterminacy of translation proposed by Willard Van Orman Quine.

[2] The problem of how we understand figures of speech, like this example of irony, has been analyzed in great detail by Dan Sperber and Deidrie Wilson.

Solving the Inverse Problem

Engineers refer to this ambiguity as the inverse problem. My arm is a simple mechanical device of a kind well understood by engineers. It is made of rigid rods (the bones) connected by joints. I move my arm by applying forces to the rods via my muscles. What will happen when I apply particular forces to this system? Finding an answer to this question is called the *forward problem*. The forward problem can be solved. Given a mechanical device like my arm, there is a direct relationship between the cause (the forces I apply to the muscles) and the effect (where my arm moves to). If an engineer knows about the forces, then he can predict exactly where the arm will go.

But there is also an *inverse problem*. If I want my arm to finish up in some particular position, then what forces should I apply? There is no exact solution to this problem. I can follow a different path and go at different speeds, yet still finish up in the same position. Many – indeed an infinite number of – different force applications will cause the arm to reach the final position I want. So how do I choose which forces to apply? Luckily I am not aware of this problem when I move my arm. My brain has solved the problem. Some solutions are better than others and, from past experience, my brain is pretty good at choosing the best one.[3]

It is the same inverse problem that has to be solved when we listen to words. Many different meanings can lead to the same words. So how do we choose the best meaning?

The key point is that this is the same problem that our brains have solved long ago in order to perceive the physical world. The meaning (in this case, the cause) of the signals that strike our senses is ambiguous in the same way. Many different objects in the world can lead to the same sensory signals. What looks like a complex pattern of lines in two dimensions could be a simple cube in three dimensions (see Figure 5.10). As we have seen, our brain solves this problem by using guesses about the world to predict what will happen next as we act upon the world. The errors in our predictions enable us to refine our guesses until we have a good model of what is out there in the world. In the same way we (or rather our brains) guess what someone's goals may be and then predict

---

[3] We don't yet know precisely how the brain defines best for movements. The best movement might be the one that uses least energy or it might be the one that is least variable.

what they will do next. We guess what someone is trying to communicate to us and then predict what she will say next.

Prior Knowledge and Prejudice

So how do we start with our guessing? Making guesses about what people are like before we have any information about them is prejudging them. It is prejudice. Prejudice might be a dirty word these days, but it is in fact crucial for our brains to function.[4] Prejudice enables us to start our guessing – and it doesn't matter how accurate the guess is, as long as we adjust our next guess in response to the error. To use an innocuous example from Chapter 5, when we perceive objects in the physical world our brain always expects the light to come from above (see Figure 5.7). This is a prejudice that has been built in by evolution. When our brain watches people moving, it expects them to achieve their goals with a minimum of effort (remember the studies of imitation I described in Chapter 6). This too is an innate prejudice. These prejudices enable us to start the cycle of guesses and predictions through which our model of the world becomes more and more accurate.

We are innately predisposed to be prejudiced. All our social interactions begin with prejudice. The content of these prejudices has been acquired through our interactions with friends and acquaintances and through hearsay. I talk quite differently with my work colleagues than with the non-scientists at the party. There are so many things I expect my brain imaging colleagues to know already, so much shared knowledge. I can use all that jargon about stimulation, and BOLD[5] signals and response suppression. But the Professor of English understands BOLD and suppression in quite a different way. I must be careful what I say – she undoubtedly thinks that all psychologists are Freudians.[6]

Our prejudices begin with stereotypes. The first clue I can get about the likely knowledge and behavior of someone I know nothing about is

---

[4] Long before neuroscientists became Bayesians, prejudice had already been rehabilitated by Hans-Georg Gadamer in his development of hermeneutics (the theory of understanding). Rather than closing us off, he suggests, our prejudices (or prior knowledge) open us up to what is to be understood.

[5] Blood oxygen level dependent signal: what we measure with functional magnetic resonance imaging.

[6] A regrettable sign of prejudice in our narrator.

Measuring prejudice in children

Here are two children. This is Jack and this is Chloë. One of these children has four trucks with which they play. Which child plays with trucks?

Here are two children. This is Emily and this is Owen. One of these children will become a nurse when they grow up. Which child will be a nurse?

Here are two people. This is Ella and this is Jonathan. One of these people makes all the food for dinner and then cleans the kitchen. Which person makes the food and cleans the kitchen?

from their gender. Even children as young as 3 have already acquired this prejudice. They expect boys to play with trucks and girls to become nurses.

Social stereotypes provide the starting point for our interactions with people we don't know. They enable us to make our initial guesses about the person's intentions. But we know that these stereotypes are very crude. The guesses and predictions we make from this limited knowledge will not be very good. Once we notice that someone is different in some way from our friends and acquaintances, then our brain expects that communication will be more difficult. We will have less in common. Our brain is less certain about what knowledge we share. So it is more difficult to predict what the other person will do and say. Of necessity, the way we communicate will be subtly altered when we try to communicate with someone different from us.

What Will He Do Next?

This is the problem with prediction. I predict what you are going to do on the basis of what I would do if I were in the same situation. So if you are different from me, my prediction may be wrong.

We are very good at recognizing our own actions, because we can predict what will happen next. Pianists can recognize themselves playing a keyboard in videos showing only the hands and keys made several

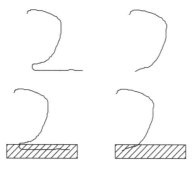

Figure 7.2 We can predict our own movements better than those of other people
This figure shows the number 2 and semi-circle in the author's appalling handwriting.
If you watched the movements of the pen, would you be able to predict whether the stroke
was going to finish as a 2 or a semi-circle? You can predict very well, but only if what you
are watching is a recording of your own handwriting movements.
Source: Redrawn after: Knoblich, G., Seigerschmidt, E., Flach, R., & Prinz, W. (2002).
Authorship effects in the prediction of handwriting strokes: Evidence for action simulation
during action perception. *Quarterly Journal of Experimental Psychology, Section A, 55*(3),
1027–1046.

months earlier, even if there is no sound and differences in the tempo of
the playing are removed. If we see the beginning of a movement, we can
predict what is going to happen next. We can predict where the dart will
land if we only see the beginning of the throw. But we do this much
better if we are watching a video of our own throws. My predictions
work best for people who are exactly like me.

I see the Emeritus Professor of Physics at the party and I guess that he
wants a drink. I predict what he will do next. My brain runs a virtual
imitation. "If I wanted a drink, this is what I would do. I would reach for
the glass. My fingers would close around it in exactly 950 milliseconds
from now." This is fine for my own actions, but someone else will make
a movement that is slightly different. If they are old and tired, then my
prediction may be very inaccurate.

Other People Are Contagious

Another of the many illusions that my brain creates is my sense of self. I
experience myself as an island of stability in an ever-changing world. The
Professor of English is hopelessly volatile, so sympathetic one minute, so

critical the next. I am very different from her, but I can't help reflecting her changes in mood. She is contagious. I can't help imitating her.

But it's not just her. It's everyone. We have already talked about empathy in Chapter 6, how I automatically share the emotion that you are experiencing. This makes me more like you. I have also told you about how your brain automatically imitates the actions that you see other people performing. Watch two people having an engrossing conversation and you see them gradually synchronizing their actions. Crossing and uncrossing their legs simultaneously. Leaning towards each other at just the same moment. When we interact with someone, we imitate them. We become more like them.

We don't even need to see people for this contagion to occur. A student comes into the social psychology lab and is tested for his "language ability." He has to turn random word lists into sentences. He is not told is that most of the words relate to stereotypes of elderly people: *worried, Florida, old, lonely, gray*, etc. The experimenter isn't really interesting in measuring language ability. He measures how quickly the student moves when he leaves the lab and walks back to the lift. Students who have been primed with the *elderly* words walk more slowly. They behave like an older person. They don't even know that they are doing it.

Other people are very contagious, even if you just think about them. Your prejudices and your observations of their behavior automatically make you become, for a moment, more like the person you are interacting with. This makes it easier for you to predict what they will do or say next.

Communication Is More Than Just Speaking

But how does predicting what someone will do next solve the problem of communication? However good my guesses and my predictions, however similar I become to you, I can never directly compare the meaning in my mind against the meaning in your mind. So how can I check if they are the same or not?

Remember, there is nothing special about the problem of minds. When I look at a tree in the garden, I don't have the tree in my mind. What I have in my mind is a model (or representation) of the tree constructed by my brain. This model is built up through a series of guesses and predictions. In the same way, when I am trying to tell you something, I can't have your idea in my mind, but my brain, again through guesses and predictions, can construct a model (a representation) of your idea in my mind. Now I have two things in my mind: (1) my idea and (2) my model of your idea. I can compare them directly. If they are similar, then I have probably communicated my idea to you successfully. If they are different, then I certainly haven't.

I can know that my communication has been unsuccessful when my prediction about what you will do next is not quite right. But the process does not stop there. If I know that my communication has not been successful, I can then change the way I communicate. I should also have a clue as to how I should change the way I communicate. I compare my idea and my model of your idea and I see that they are different. This is the prediction error. But I can also look at the nature of the error. Where precisely are the differences between my idea and my model of your idea? The nature of the prediction error tells me how to change my communication: which points I should emphasize and which points are not important. I don't just choose my words because of what they mean; I choose my words to suite the person I am talking to. The more I talk to someone, the better an idea I get of what words will suit – just as I get a better idea of how to perceive the world around me the more I look at it.

Teaching Is Not Just a Demonstration To Be Imitated

By modeling the mind of the person we are talking to we are able to alter the way we communicate with them. We can take account of what they know and what they are capable of understanding. Because people have different knowledge and capabilities, we don't communicate with everyone in the same way. This might seem obvious, but there are some surprising and subtle ways that this happens without our realizing it.

When a mother talks to her baby she uses a special kind of voice. She uses *baby talk* or *motherese*.[7] A mother will also use a special voice for talking to her pet cat. But there is a subtle difference between these two kinds of voice. To both her pet cat and her baby a mother will speak at a higher pitch. This special voice is more similar to the voices of the baby and the cat since they are smaller than her and smaller creatures have high-pitched voices. But only to her baby does the mother exaggerate

[7] "Fatherese" seems to be different from motherese, but is much less researched.

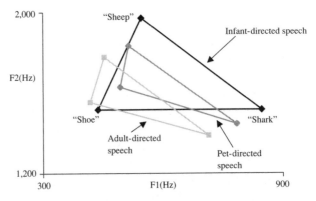

Figure 7.3 How mothers teach their infants, but not their pets, to speak

Vowel sounds, like the "ee" in sheep, the "ah" in shark, and the "oo" in shoe are defined by two frequencies (F1 & F2). The different vowel sounds can be placed in a vowel space defined by F1 and F2. When mothers talk to their infants, they use a special language called "motherese." They exaggerate the vowel sounds so that they are further apart in the vowel space. This helps the infants to recognize the differences between vowels in their native language. Mothers also use a special voice for talking to their cats, but here they don't exaggerate the vowels; they simply speak at a higher pitch than normal.

Source: Figure 1c from: Burnham, D., Kitamura, C., & Vollmer-Conna, U. (2002). What's new pussy cat? On talking to babies and animals. *Science, 296*(5572), 1435.

the differences in the sounds of her vowels. She makes the *ee* and the *oo* and the *aa* of *sheep, shoe,* and *shark* sound more different from one another. This "stretching of the vowel space" produces a caricature of speech, which exaggerates the distinctive features of the particular language spoken by the mother.

The baby learns the sounds of her native language by imitating her mother. By producing this caricature of speech, the mother makes it easier for her baby to learn her native language. When she talks to her cat, the mother does not caricature the language. She knows that the cat is not going to learn language.

Learning by imitation is not unique to humans. Mountain gorillas like to eat nettles. These plants are very nutritious, but unpleasant to eat because of the stings. Mountain gorillas have developed a complex technique for avoiding the worst stings by stripping the leaves from the stem of the nettle and then folding the leaves so that worst stings are inside the bundle that is popped into the mouth, avoiding the sensitive lips. Infant gorillas learn this skill by watching their mothers. But there is a critical difference from human mothers. The gorilla mothers show no interest in encouraging the infants to learn. They make no attempt to help the infant learn by altering their nettle-stripping procedure when the infant is watching.[8]

When human mothers and babies interact, the communication loop is fully closed. It is not just that the human mother is interested in what her baby is doing. The baby knows when her mother is interested. Babies prefer listening to *motherese* than to adult talk. They know the *motherese* is directed at them. When a baby sees her mother drop a saucepan on the floor and hears her say "*bother*," the baby doesn't learn that the word for a saucepan is "bother."[9] The baby knows when her mother is teaching her the names of things.

Closing the Loop

As you read this book, you respond to what I am saying, but your response has no impact on me. This communication is a one-way process. Face-to-face communication is a two-way process. You listen to what I say and respond to it. But, in turn, I respond to your response. I call this "closing the loop."

The amazing thing about face-to-face communication is how well it works most of the time. As a result, failing communications can be very funny and are the mainstay of comedy double acts. Think of all those bizarre interchanges between Groucho and Chico Marx.

Groucho: Now, here is a peninsula, and here is a viaduct leading over to the mainland.
Chico: Why a duck?
Groucho: I'm all right. How are you?

British comedy in the 1970s was dominated by Ronnie Barker and Ronnie Corbett. Their TV sketch show *The Two Ronnies* ran for 15 years.

[8] Dick Byrne has carried out beautiful work on the procedures by which gorillas prepare nettles for eating and shown how this skill can be imitated. He does not comment on the lack of teaching. I have inferred this from other studies suggesting that while infant gorillas show great interest in what their mothers are doing, the mothers show little interest in what the infants are doing. (See also Chapter 4, fn. 4 above.)
[9] But this can happen in children with autism, such as Paul. One day Paul's mother was reciting the nursery rhyme "Peter, Peter pumpkin eater" while she was working in the kitchen, when she suddenly dropped a saucepan. From that day on, Peter chanted "Peter eater" whenever he saw anything resembling a saucepan.

In 1999, ten years after the show had finished, "Fork Handles" was voted as the all-time best sketch from the show.[10] This interchange beautifully illustrates the ambiguities of communications and how they can be resolved by closing the loop.

Fork Handles: The Two Ronnies Close the Loop (Eventually)

In a hardware shop. Ronnie Corbett is behind the counter, wearing a warehouse jacket. He has just finished serving a customer.
Corbett (muttering): There you are. Mind how you go.
(*Ronnie Barker enters the shop, wearing a scruffy tank-top and beanie*)
Barker: Fork 'andles!
Corbett: Four candles?
Barker: Fork 'andles.
(*Ronnie Corbett makes for a box, and gets out four candles. He places them on the counter*)
Barker: No, fork 'andles!
Corbett (confused): Well there you are, four candles!
Barker: No, fork 'andles! 'Andles for forks!
(*Ronnie Corbett puts the candles away, and goes to get a fork handle. He places it onto the counter*)
Corbett (muttering): Fork handles. Thought you said "four candles!"
Barker: Got any plugs?
Corbett: Plugs. What kind of plugs?
Barker: A rubber one, bathroom.
(*Ronnie Corbett gets out a box of bath plugs, and places it on the counter*)
Corbett (pulling out two different-sized plugs): What size?
Barker: Thirteen amp!
(*and so on and so on*)

Ronnie B is trying to communicate his desire for fork handles, "Fork 'andles." To check he has the right idea, Ronnie C repeats his request, "Four candles?" Ronnie B hears "Fork 'andles." Everything seems to be all right. Ronnie C brings four candles. Ronnie B sees that his prediction about what Ronnie C would do next (bring fork handles) was wrong. He has not communicated his desire. He alters his communication, " 'Andles for forks." Success! Ronnie C behaves as predicted.

---

[10]   In 2005 it was voted in the UK as the third funniest sketch of all time.

Fully Closing the Loop

Communication, when we confront each other face-to-face, is not a one-way process from me to you. The way you respond to me alters the way I respond to you. This is a communication loop. But in addition it is not just me who is trying to predict what you will say next on the basis of my model of your idea. You also have a model of my idea in your mind. You also are trying to predict what I will say next. You also will alter what you say to indicate that your model of my meaning is not quite working to predict what I am going to say.

This is the big difference from my interactions with the physical world. The physical world is utterly indifferent to my attempts to interpret it. But when two people interact face-to-face, their exchange of meaning is a cooperative venture. The flow is never just one-way. Even when my aim is to communicate an idea to you, inevitably the idea that is finally communicated will have been colored by you. Meaning is like a gravitational field. The moon goes round the earth, but the movement of the earth is also altered by the presence of the moon.

In a successful communication the point is reached where my model of your meaning matches my own meaning, and I no longer need to show you that there is a problem. And, critically, at the same time, you too have reached that point where there is no discrepancy between your model of my meaning and your own meaning. At this point of mutual agreement communication has been achieved.[11] By building models of the mental world, our brains have solved the problem of how to get inside the minds of others. And it is this ability to make models of the mental world that has created the great gap between humans and all other species. Without the ability to build and share mental models of the world, there would be no such thing as language and culture.

Knowledge Can Be Shared

Our ability to make models of the mental world opens up an entirely new way of changing the behavior of others. In the physical world, behavior is changed by rewards and punishments. We stop doing things that cause us pain. We repeat actions that lead to pleasure. We can alter

---

[11] We are not aware of all these processes during most of our interactions. Is this because people are so predictable, or because we are not aware of the complexity of understanding?

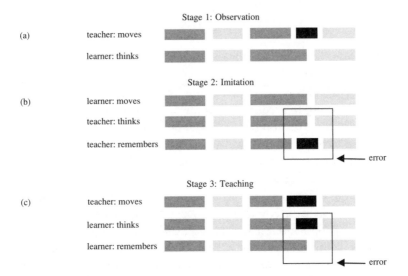

Stage 1: Observation

(a)   teacher: moves

learner: thinks

Stage 2: Imitation

(b)   learner: moves

teacher: thinks

teacher: remembers

← error

Stage 3: Teaching

(c)   teacher: moves

learner: thinks

learner: remembers

← error

Figure 7.4 How we might learn about the hidden states of another person's mind?
(a) The teacher makes a complex movement using a sequence of five different control states. The learner watches and tries to "read" the control states from the movement. He misses number four.
(b) The learner imitates the movement using only four different control states. The teacher watches and "reads" the control states from the movement. She sees only four control states. She remembers that she used five control states. She identifies the difference between what she thinks is the learner's intention and her own intention.
(c) The teacher moves and exaggerates the missing control state. The learner now correctly reads the five control states. He remembers that he used only four control states. He identifies the differences between what he thinks is the teacher's intention and his own intention. When he moves next time he will correct the error.

the behavior of others using pain and pleasure – this is how we train animals. But in the mental world behavior is changed by knowledge. I will take an umbrella with me, not because it is raining now, but because I believe it is going to rain later this afternoon. And we can use knowledge to change the behavior of others. Imagine a remote beach in Australia where the sea is infested with box jellyfish. You could learn by trial and error and much pain to avoid swimming in the sea there. But once you have learned this, you can put up sign saying "Beware of box jellyfish." Other visitors would not swim in the sea there. They have benefited from the experience that you are able to share with them by passing on your knowledge.

This sharing of experience is not just words. When I tell you of my experience, your brain will change as if you had had that same experience. We can show this using Pavlov's technique of conditioning. One such paradigm is fear conditioning. Whenever you receive a painful shock there will be an increase in activity in many brain regions. In Pavlov's terms, the shock is the unconditioned stimulus and brain activity is the unconditioned response. No learning is involved. A painful shock causes these changes in brain and body the very first time we experience it. In the fear-conditioning paradigm a visual cue (a red square, the conditioned stimulus) is presented on a screen just before the shock. After the experience of several such parings between the red square and the shock, the subject, whether a rat or a human volunteer, will start responding to the red square with fear. One aspect of this fear response is increased activity in the amygdala.[12] The fear associated with the shock has become attached to this arbitrary visual cue.

But there is another way of attaching fear to the red square. This method works only in human volunteers. I *tell* new, inexperienced volunteers that the red square will be followed by a shock. Before being told this, they show no fear responses to the red square. After being told, they immediately show fear responses to the red square, including activity in the amygdala. My experience that the red square will be followed by a painful shock has created fear in another person's brain.

Knowledge Is Power

"There's just one thing wrong with that experiment," say the Professor of English. "I don't believe you actually experienced the shock yourself. You only shock your volunteers, not yourself. You weren't sharing your experience. You were just telling them they would be shocked."

In one way she's wrong. I always want to find out what it's like for my volunteers, by trying out my experiments as a subject. But of course she is right in a much more important way. What we tell people doesn't need to be the result of experience. It doesn't even need to be true.

We can control people's behavior by giving them false knowledge. I can find a nice, quiet Australian beach that is perfectly safe. I can put up a sign saying "Beware of box jellyfish." This sign gives false knowledge. But it can be useful to me because it will keep other visitors away.

---

[12] As you will remember, this is a small, complex brain region inside the front of the temporal lobe. It has key role in attaching value (niceness or nastiness) to objects (see Figure 2.4).

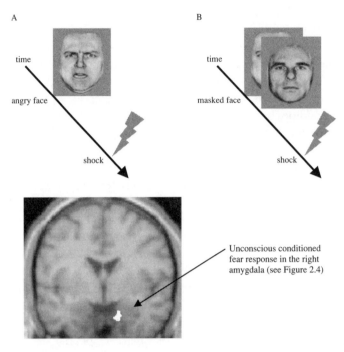

Figure 7.5   Unconscious fear conditioning
If the face is repeatedly followed by a shock, you will start making a fear response to the face (a conditioned response). This happens even if you are not aware of seeing the face because it has been masked.

Sources: From Figure 1 and Figure 2a in: Morris, J.S., Ohman, A., & Dolan, R.J. (1998). Conscious and unconscious emotional learning in the human amygdala. *Nature, 393*(6684), 467–470. Reprinted by permission of Macmillan Publishers Ltd: *Nature*, © 2006. Faces from: Ekman, P., & Friesen, W.V. (1976). *Pictures of facial affect*. Palo Alto, CA: Consulting Psychologists.

We understand that people's behavior is controlled by beliefs even if these beliefs are false. And we soon learn that we can control people's behavior by giving them false beliefs. This is the dark side of communication.

Without this awareness that behavior can be controlled by beliefs, even when these are false, deliberate deception and lying are impossible. In autism this awareness seems to be lacking, and people with autism can be incapable of deception. At first thought the inability of the autistic person to lie seems to be a charming and desirable trait. But this trait is part of a wider failure to communicate, which also makes people with autism seem rude and difficult. It can often make them lonely and friendless. In practice, friendly interactions are maintained by frequent little deceptions and circumlocutions that sometimes hide our true feelings.

At the other extreme from autism lies the person with paranoid schizophrenia who is aware of intentions that are invisible to rest of us. For the person with paranoia every statement can be a deception or a hidden message that has to be interpreted. Hostile statements can be interpreted as friendly. Friendly statements can be interpreted as hostile. One person heard voices saying "Kill yourself" and "He's a fool." He described these voices as two benevolent spirits who wanted him to go to a better world. Another person heard voices saying "Be careful" and "Try harder." These were "powerful witches who used to be my neighbours . . . punishing me."

This hyperawareness of the intentions and feelings of other people can be so intense as to be overwhelming.

> The walk of a stranger in the street could be a "sign" to me that I must interpret. Every face in the windows of a passing street car would be engraved on my mind, all of them concentrating on me and trying to pass me some kind of message. . . . The significance of the real or imagined feelings of people was very painful. To feel that s stranger passing on the street knows your innermost soul is disconcerting. I was sure that the girl in the office on my right was jealous of me. I felt that the girl in the office on my left wanted to be my friend but I made her feel depressed. . . . The intensity with which I felt [these impressions] made the air fairly crackle when the typists in question came into my office. Work in a situation like that is too difficult to be endured at all. I withdrew farther and farther.

In such a state the possibility of meeting other minds has been temporarily lost. This vivid experience of the minds of others no longer corresponds to reality. Like the person with autism, the person with paranoia is alone.

The Truth

In the very distant past our ancestors too were alone, constructing their models of the physical world, but unable to share them with others. At that time truth had no relevance for these models. It did not matter whether the model was a true reflection of the physical world. All that mattered was that the model worked by predicting what would happen next. But once we can share our models of the physical world, then we discover that other people's models are slightly different from our

There are many experiments exploring which brain regions are involved in reading minds. Volunteers go into the scanner and read stories about people who have false beliefs or they watch animations in which characters are teased or deceived. Two brain areas are consistently activated by these tasks: the posterior superior temporal sulcus and medial prefrontal cortex. But we have very little idea what these brain regions are actually doing.

Julie Grèzes developed a simple and striking method for studying mind reading. She made videos of people lifting up boxes of different weights. When you watch these videos it is quite easy to work out how heavy the box is that is being lifted. You do it by watching the way the person moves. This doesn t involve any mind reading. On some occasions the people in the video were told that the box was heavy, when it was actually light. It is not quite so easy, but you can also tell from their movements when the person in the video has a *false belief* about the weight of the box. The box comes up more quickly if it is lighter than they expect and they have to adjust their posture. Now you, the viewer, are using the movements to do mind reading – to discover what the person in the video believed about the weight of the box.

On other occasions the people in the video were told to *pretend* that the box was heavy when it was really light. In this case they are using their movements to communicate something to the person watching the video. They are trying to make you, the viewer, think that the box is heavier than it really is. Again it is not easy, but, since the people Dr. Grèzes recruited to make the video were neuroscientists rather than mime artists, you can detect when they are trying to deceive you. This is a true interaction between minds. You are trying to read the mind of someone who is trying to put a false belief into your mind.

Volunteers were scanned while they watched these videos and tried to detect when the people in the video had a false about the weight of the box or when they were trying to deceive the viewer about the weight of the box. The posterior superior temporal sulcus was more active when the volunteers saw the unusually movements that occurred when the box was lighter than expected or when there was an attempt to deceive. This area may be concerned with subtle analysis of the movements that give us clues about others' intentions.

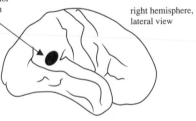

right hemisphere, lateral view

left hemisphere, medial view

Activity was greater in the medial prefrontal cortex when the observers believed that the actor had been misled or was trying to deceive. But this activity was in different places.

When the actor was believed to be making *unintended* movements the activity was further back.

When the actor was believed to be *deceptive* the activity was further forward.

Figure 7.6 Where our brain reads hidden intentions

Source: Figure 1 from: Grèzes, J., Frith, C.D., & Passingham, R.E. (2004a). Inferring false beliefs from the actions of oneself and others: An fMRI study. *Neuroimage, 21*(2), 744–750; plots of data by author from: ibid. and Grèzes, Frith, C.D., & Passingham, R.E. (2004b). Brain mechanisms for inferring deceit in the actions of others. *Journal of Neuroscience, 24*(24), 5500–5505.

own. Some people are experts who clearly have better models of some aspects of the world. By putting together the models of many people, we can construct a new model that is better than any model produced by a single individual. And our knowledge of the world is no longer derived from a single lifetime – knowledge passes from one generation to the next.

Can false models also be shared? A disordered brain can make a false model of the physical or mental world. Such a brain can create visions or the sound of voices when no one is speaking. But false models of the physical world are not so easy to share. I am not going to hear the voices created inside your brain. If I have a strange experience, I may check it out by sharing. "Do you hear a strange ringing noise, or is it just me?"

False models of the mental world are not easily so checked. And sometimes these false models are successfully shared with others. In cases of *folie à deux*, two or more people share the same psychotic delusions.

> A 43-year-old housewife-writer was admitted to the hospital in a severely agitated state. Her history revealed a delusional state of 10 years duration regarding a conspiracy in the literary world. Her husband and three adolescent children shared these beliefs. Her primary diagnosis was paranoid state with a schizophreniform psychosis. The patient responded quickly to drug treatment. The children and husband agreed after two visits that they had mistakenly gone along with the patient's "over intense imagination."

As long as this false model of literary world stayed within the family, the "normal" members believed it to be true. But once they discussed their beliefs outside the family, the lack of truth became immediately apparent.

But when false beliefs are shared by larger groups, truth becomes more fragile. This seems to have been the case in the tragic "Jonestown massacre."

> On November 18, 1978, in a cleared-out patch of Guyanese jungle, the Reverend Jim Jones ordered the 911 members of his flock to kill themselves by drinking a cyanide potion, and they did.

Jim Jones was the charismatic leader of a religious cult. He was almost certainly psychotic. He suffered from mysterious fainting spells, heeded advice from extraterrestrials, practiced faith healing, and experienced visions of a nuclear holocaust. He led his followers to a remote part of the Guyanese jungle, where they set up a community isolated from the rest of society. The community lived in fear of an unnamed enemy and destroyer. This enemy would descend upon them and kill them mercilessly. The mass suicide occurred after the visit of a US Congressman investigating claims that people were being held in the community against their will.

After the mass suicide a tape was found that is believed to record the final speech given by Jim Jones. Here is a fragment of that speech.

Jones: It's all over. The congressman has been murdered. Well, it's all over, all over. What a legacy, what a legacy. What the Red Brigade doin' that once ever made any sense anyway? They invaded our privacy. They came into our home. They followed us six thousand miles away. Red Brigade showed them justice. The congressman's dead.

  Please get us some medication. It's simple. It's simple. There's no convulsions with it. It's just simple. Just, please get it. Before it's too late. The GDF20[13] will be here, I tell you. Get movin', get movin', get movin'.

Woman: Now. Do it now!

Jones: Don't be afraid to die. You'll see, there'll be a few people land out here. They'll torture some of our children here. They'll torture our people. They'll torture our seniors. We cannot have this.

Our brains' ability to communicate ideas from one mind to another can bring horror as well as benefit. We all know how is easy it is, at least briefly, to be deceived by false beliefs.[14] Our mental currency consists of beliefs created by our brains. But I am optimistic. Whole communities rarely embrace false beliefs so whole-heartedly as the people in Jonestown. And beliefs are not as arbitrary as something like money. Our beliefs are models of the world, and the real world out there is a gold standard for our models. In the end false beliefs can always be discarded because they make bad predictions.

I believe that the truth is out there. As long as we have ways of showing that one model of the physical world works better than another, then we can aspire to developing a series of better and better models.

---

13   The Guyanese Defense Force.

14   The chance of winning the UK National Lottery is about 1 in 14 million, which is much lower than the risk of dying before the week's lottery is drawn. How close to the draw would you need to buy a ticket for the chance of winning to be greater than the risk of dying? The answer is apparently about three and a half minutes (given in John Lanchester's novel *Mr Philips*). But still many of us still think it is worth buying lottery tickets.

At the end of this series, although it is infinite in the mathematical sense, lies the truth – the truth of how the world really is. Reaching this truth is the program of science. Science progresses by making models of the world, making predictions on the basis of these models, and using the errors in these predictions to construct better models. Now science is revealing that our brains use the same principles to acquire knowledge about the world. We are also beginning to understand how our brains can make models of the mental world. It is by sharing these mental models that the program of science becomes possible.

"I might have guessed," says the Professor of English, "that you would conclude with *Science* as the pinnacle of human achievements."

It's true. I love science. But there are other pinnacles.

There is something even more remarkable than our ability to share our mental models of the world and create composite and better models. This is the ability of a few extraordinary individuals to transmit their experiences to us across time. To transmit their experiences even though we can never meet them face-to-face and close the communication loop.

We may never find the "right" translation for Li Shang-Yin's poem about the patterned lute, but we feel his melancholy for a lost or impossible love.

We may never have experienced a storm at sea, but we know what the experience is like when we look at the painting by J.M.W. Turner *Snow Storm – Steam-Boat off a Harbour's Mouth Making Signals in Shallow Water, and Going by the Lead* (see Figure CP7, color plate section). In order to paint this scene, Turner "got the sailors to lash me to the mast to observe it; I was lashed for four hours, and I did not expect to escape, but I felt bound to record it if I did." Turner had no doubt that he could paint his experience and that we could share it.

"You'll never get inside my mind," says the Professor of English.

"Too late," I reply.

"Go back to sleep," she says.

By making models of the minds of others (in the same way that it makes models of the physical world), my brain enables me to enter a shared mental world. By sharing my mental world with others, I can also learn from their experiences and adopt the models of others that are better than my own. From this process, truth and progress can emerge, but so can deception and mass delusions.

Epilogue:
Me and My Brain

We are embedded in the mental world of others just as we are embedded in the physical world. What we are currently doing and thinking is molded by whomever we are interacting with. But this is not how we experience ourselves. We experience ourselves as agents with minds of our own. This is the final illusion created by our brains.

Chris Frith and I

When I started writing this book, I did not expect to have companions for my journey through the evidence. I found my companions at that academic party in the Prologue and they stayed with me through the rest of the chapters. Now those companions are gone. With my book completed, the Professor of English and the Professor of Physics, with their very different ideas about science, dissolve back into nothing. They and their world do not exist outside these pages. And neither does the narrator, whose attitude to the Professor of English changed so radically during the course of the journey. The question "What happens next?" does not arise. For them all, this is the end.

But the "I" who narrates this book and then vanishes on the final page is no different from that other "I," Chris Frith, who wakes from nothing every morning at about 7 a.m. and vanishes again every night. I am not sure which of us is writing these final pages, but in both cases this "I" is created by my brain.

Throughout this book I have adopted the convention of distinguishing between me and my brain. So when objects are perceived and actions are performed without thought or awareness, then I say that my brain does it. But for conscious experience and conscious actions and decisions, then I say that "I" do it. But I am not a dualist. This "I" that deliberately does things is also created by my brain.

Searching for the Will in the Brain

So is there an area in my brain that corresponds to this "I"? This would be the area of the brain that decides what to do and then tells the rest of the brain how to do it. If there is such a place,[1] then it is the source of the top-down control signals that can, amongst many other things, activate the face area of the brain so that I can imagine seeing a face when there is no face actually there.

The first experiment I did when I got access to a brain scanner was an attempt to locate will in the brain. It had to be a very simple experiment because our research budget had all been spent on the scanner. In most experiments participants simply do what they are told: "Lift your finger each time it is touched." We can call this a *stimulus-driven* action. The stimulus (the touch) activates the tactile system. The association system converts the tactile signal into an action (lifting the finger that was touched). Finally, the motor system performs the action. In the scanner we can then see which areas of the brain are involved in stimulus recognition and response.

In my experiment, however, I wanted the participants to exert their own free will. They had to decide for themselves what to do, rather than being told. We can call this a *willed* action. At the same time they had to make their responses within the strict limits of a well-controlled experiment. So the instruction for the experiment on willed action was, "When your finger is touched, lift whichever finger you like."[2] To perform this task the brain must take an extra step. It is not sufficient to activate the tactile system, the association system, and the motor system. Now some part of the brain has to decide which finger to lift. The idea behind this simple experiment was as follows. When I compare willed action with stimulus-driven action, I should be able to find the parts of the brain where free choices are made. Amazingly, this experiment revealed one

[1]   Semir Zeki, who is an anatomist of the brain, has pointed out to me that there can be no area in the brain devoted solely to "top-down" control. He says this because there is no area where the neurons send only output signals and receive no input signals.
[2]   Only the first and second fingers of the right hand were involved in this experiment.

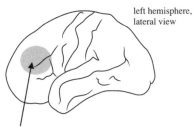

left hemisphere,
lateral view

When volunteers have to decide for themselves
what to do, then activity is seen in the
dorsolateral prefrontal cortex.

Figure e.1   Is this where free will is found in the brain?

Source: Drawn from data in: Frith, C.D., Friston, K., Liddle, P.F., & Frackowiak, R.S.J. (1991). Willed action and the prefrontal cortex in man – a study with PET. *Proceedings of the Royal Society of London, Series B – Biological Sciences, 244*(1311), 241–246.

part of the brain, the dorsolateral prefrontal cortex, that was more active when participants had to select responses for themselves, rather than simply making a prescribed response.

So is this where free will resides? Many other experiments suggest that this region at the front of the brain is important for choosing what to do. People with damage to their frontal lobes often become apathetic and do little or nothing. Or they may become impulsive and give in to every temptation. In both cases there is one basic problem. They can no longer choose actions for themselves. They either do nothing or respond to the next stimulus that comes along.

But there is something a bit paradoxical in my experiment. I am instructing the volunteer in my scanner to demonstrate free will. The participant has no choice in the matter but to make a freely selected response. What sort of freedom is this?

Where Is the Top in Top-Down Control?

In Chapter 3, I described the experiment by Benjamin Libet in which participants had to lift their finger whenever they felt the urge to do so. In this case the participants choose *when* to lift a finger, rather than *which* finger to lift, but the choice of the time is free. Here again we find the paradox of a *command* to behave freely. This freedom is to some extent illusory. The experimenter does not say so, but there are constraints on what the participant may do. Each participant would have intuitively known that Dr. Libet would not have been pleased if after half an hour or so they had not lifted their finger even once "because the urge never came."[3] So what are the implications of the instruction to "Lift your finger whenever you feel the urge to do so"? To do what Dr. Libet really wants, the participants need to severely curtail their free choice. They need to instruct themselves to behave something like this: "I shall make the interval between one finger lift and the next one different each time (but not too different) in such a way that the experimenter cannot easily predict when I will next lift my finger."[4] The participants are not actually making free choices about action. They are playing a complex game with the experimenter.

So where does the top-down signal come from that chooses the actions in these experiments on will? Does it come from the frontal cortex, the site of will in the brain? Or does it surreptitiously come from the experimenter through the constraints placed on the participant?

It all depends upon our point of view. If we look at a person and a brain in isolation, then the frontal cortex is the ultimate source of control. But people and their brains are rarely found in isolation. Isolation is bad for them. The human brain is exquisitely tuned for interactions with other people. Concepts like will, responsibility, and even meaning arise from these interactions. I showed in Chapter 7 how conveying meaning from one mind to another depends upon interaction. We each predict what the other will say and adjust our predictions until we reach mutual agreement. As a result the final meaning agreed upon depends on both people and therefore will be slightly different depending on whom we are talking to. Meaning arises from the interactions between minds.

If we want to understand the neural basis of these interactions, it is no good looking at just one brain. We need to study two brains as they interact. This program of research is only just beginning. We don't even know yet how we are going to put together measurements taken from two brains.

---

[3] It is alleged that that the composer Karlheinz Stockhausen once wrote a piece for orchestra in which the players are instructed to "do whatever they like" for two bars. During the first rehearsal the composer interrupted at this point, saying, "That's not what I meant at all."

[4] In one of a series of experiments on will, my colleague Marjan Jahanshahi gave such instructions explicitly – "Lift your finger once every 2–7 seconds" – and observed activation in the same brain areas as in experiments where participants are told to select actions "for themselves."

Figure e.2 The two-brain experiment
If we want to understand the neural basis of social interactions, we need to record activity
in both brains as two people interact. Read Montague and his colleagues linked scanners in
Pasadena and Houston while volunteers played a game of trust.
Source: Supporting Online Material Figure 1 from: King-Casas, B., Tomlin, D., Anen, C.,
Camerer, C.F., Quartz, S.R., & Montague, P.R. (2005). Getting to know you: Reputation and
trust in a two-person economic exchange. *Science*, *308*(5718), 78–83.

The Homunculus

When we think about how our brain works, we often fall into the trap of
creating another smaller brain inside the brain we are trying to explain.
In my experiment on willed action, I suggested that a special part of the
brain, the prefrontal cortex, was involved in making free selections. Rather
then me making free selections, it was this part of the brain that made
the free selections for me. But this is just a little "me" inside my brain
that makes free selections. This little me is often referred to as the
homunculus. And inside this little me is there an even smaller region, an
even more remote me, that really makes the free selections?

Psychologists have done much hard thinking to try to get rid of this
homunculus inside the brain. Rather than a single area that makes choices,
perhaps there is a network of areas that apply constraints in order to
determine the final choice. These constraints come from many sources:
our bodies – there are some actions that are physically impossible to
perform; our emotions – there are actions that we may regret. Above all
there are constraints from the social world – there are actions that are
"not done" in front of a Professor of English.

But I am hardly aware of these constraints. For me it seems as if I
am fully in control of my actions. This is why it is so hard to get rid
of the idea of a homunculus. It is the dominant part of my experience
that I am in control. There is a physical world in which I act and in this
physical world there are other agents like me who are also in control of
themselves.

Figure e.3   The homunculus
The little alien inside Rosenberg's head from the film *Men in Black*.

This is my brain's final illusion: to hide all those ties to the physical and social world and create an autonomous self.

This Book Is Not About Consciousness

When friends asked me what I was writing this book about, I told them it was not about consciousness. After the age of about 50, many neuroscientists feel that they have sufficient wisdom and expertise to set about solving the problem of consciousness.[5] Being neuroscientists, they are concerned with the problem of identifying the neural correlates of consciousness and to show how subjective experience can arise from activity in a physical brain. Many solutions have been proposed, none of which have proved very satisfying. I knew that I could do no better. That is why this book is not about consciousness.

Indeed, rather than writing about consciousness, I have emphasized how much my brain knows and does without me being aware of it. My brain makes me afraid of things I am not aware of seeing and can control complex limb movements without my knowing what I am doing. There

[5]   Whether or not they have ever done any experimental work on the topic.

seems very little left for consciousness to do. So, rather than asking how subjective experience can arise from activity in neurons, I ask the question, "What is consciousness for?" Or more particularly, "Why does my brain make me experience myself as a free agent?" My assumption is that we get some advantage from experiencing ourselves as free agents. So the question is: "What is this advantage?" My answer is, for the moment, pure speculation.

Why Are People So Nice
(as Long as They Are Treated Fairly)?

In comparison to other animals, people do many strange things. We speak. We use tools. We sometimes behave altruistically. And, most strangely of all, we sometimes behave altruistically to strangers.[6] Economists study this behavior by getting people to play simple games with money. One such game is called the Dictator Game: one player is given $100 and can choose to give as little or as much of this as he chooses to another player; he doesn't know the other player and will never meet him again. There is nothing to stop the player (the Dictator) keeping all the money for himself. But players typically give away about $30. Why? There is another, very similar game, called the Ultimatum Game. Once again one player is given $100 and can give some of this to the other player. But now the other player can influence the outcome. If he rejects the offer, then neither player gets any money. Here again the players don't know each other and will never meet again. If the second player rejects the offer, he gets no money. But nevertheless players typically reject offers of less than about $30. Why?

One explanation is that we all have a strong sense of fairness. It feels unfair to offer the other player no money, but our self-interest ensures that we keep a bit more than half. Likewise it seems unfair if we receive much less than half. Therefore, in the Ultimatum Game, we punish the

---

[6]   The explanation of altruism is one of the major problems for evolutionary biology. Natural selection leads us to expect animals to behave in ways that increase their *own* chances of survival and reproduction, not those of others. The explanation of altruism in terms of kin selection was a major advance in 20th-century biology. If we look after our relatives, our genes may survive even if we don't. As Haldane put it, "I'd lay down my life for two brothers or eight cousins." But why should we help strangers?

other player by rejecting his offer even though we lose out ourselves. We are effectively paying money so that we can punish him. This is called altruistic punishment.

What advantage is it to us to have this sense of fairness and this willingness to punish people who behave unfairly? Ernst Fehr has studied more complex economic games – called Common Good Games – in which many people play together. If everyone cooperates by putting their own money into the system, then everyone gains. But there are always a few people who behave unfairly. These are the *free riders*, players who realize that they can benefit from the fair behavior of other people without needing to donate any of their own money. Once free riders appear in the group, people gradually stop cooperating. Even the most generous player doesn't see why she should go on supporting someone who is putting nothing into the system. As a result the group finishes up with less money than they could have gained with full cooperation.

This is where altruistic punishment comes in. Ernst Fehr and Simon Gächter allowed players to punish the free riders. This was altruistic punishment since it cost $1 to punish another player, but that other player lost $3. When this punishment of the free riders is possible,[7] then cooperation in the group steadily increases and everyone gains.

But when we punish free riders, we are not deliberately trying to increase cooperation or thinking about how the group will benefit in the long term. We get immediate satisfaction from punishing people who have behaved unfairly. We do not feel any empathy for the suffering of these undesirable people. We have learned to dislike them. Our brain even gives us pleasure from the punishment of free riders.

Even an Illusion Has Responsibilities

But what has all this got to do with the homunculus and my feeling that I am a free agent? One important result of our experience of being free agents is that we recognize that other people are free agents just like us. And we believe that free agents are responsible for their actions. Already by the age of 3, children make a strong distinction between deliberate acts and events in which the outcome occurs by accident.

---

[7]   The punishment option introduces a further complication – *the second-order free rider*. These are players who rely on other players to do the punishing and never do it themselves.

Each of the four players gets £10. If a player invests this in the group, the £10 is increased to £16 and shared equally between the group.

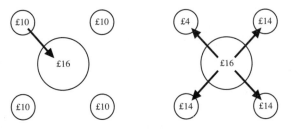

One player invests. She loses a little, but the group, as a whole, gains.

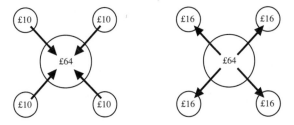

All players invest. Everyone gains.

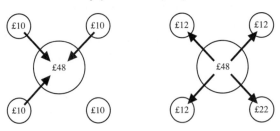

One player, a free rider, does not invest. The free rider gains a lot, but only because other players invest.

Figure e.4 A Common Good Game

Source: Drawing to illustrate: Fehr, E., & Gächter, S. (2002). Altruistic punishment in humans. *Nature*, *415*(6868), 137–140.

When people do something by accident, we do not consider that they are behaving badly. When people are forced to do something against their will, we do not consider that they are behaving unfairly. Only deliberately undertaken, freely chosen acts can be unfair. Free riders don't just behave unfairly. They deliberately behave unfairly. And it is only the deliberately wicked whom we wish to punish.

Tania Singer has shown how rapidly we come to dislike someone we have never met before if they behave unfairly. After just four unfair interactions we will show an emotional response just to the sight of their face. But we don't learn to dislike someone if we are told that they are only following instructions.[8]

There is an intimate relationship between our experience that we are free agents and our willingness to be altruistic, feeling pleased when we are behaving fairly ourselves and feeling upset by the unfairness of others. For these feelings to arise it is crucial that we experience ourselves and others are free agents. We believe that all of us make deliberate choices. Otherwise our willingness to cooperate would fall apart. This final illusion created by our brain – that we are detached from the social world and are free agents – enables us to create together a society and a culture that is so much more than any individual.

At the party with which this book began, our narrator had many annoying interactions. But he was most embarrassed by the accusation that, since he was a psychologist, he could read people's minds. By the end of the book we have discovered that mind reading is possible for all of us. It is possible because our creative brains will use any and all signals available to make models of what is out there in the physical world and also what is out there in the minds of others. Our creative brains use these models to predict what will happen next when we act upon the world and when we interact with others. If our predictions about other people are right, then we have successfully read their minds. But all this complex activity is hidden from us. So there is no need to be embarrassed. Just go back to the party and have fun.

[8]   Ironically, in these various experiments the unfair players, if they existed at all, were also stooges of the experimenter who had been told to behave unfairly. It is what we believe that counts. It's all in the mind.

The Evidence

Prologue

A statistical inference

Box, G.E.P., & Cox, D.R. (1964). An analysis of transformations. *Journal of the Royal Statistical Society*, Series B, *26*(2), 211–243.

The capacity of working memory

Miller, G.A. (1956). The magic number seven, plus or minus two: Some limits on our capacity for processing information. *Psychological Review*, *63*, 81–97.

Working memory in Welsh

Murray. A., & Jones, D.M. (2002). Articulatory complexity at item boundaries in serial recall: The case of Welsh and English digit span. *Journal of Experimental Psychology: Learning, Memory & Cognition*, *28*(3), 594–598.

Waterfall illusion

Mather, G., Verstraten, F., & Anstis, S. (1998). *The motion aftereffect: A modern perspective*. Cambridge, MA: MIT Press. (Also: *http://www.lifesci.sussex.ac.uk/home/George_Mather/Motion/MAE.html*.)

The pain of rejection

Eisenberger, N.I., Lieberman, M.D., & Williams, K.D. (2003). Does rejection hurt? An fMRI study of social exclusion. *Science*, *302*(5643), 290–292.

The value of mental practice

Yue, G., & Cole, K.J. (1992). Strength increases from the motor program: Comparison of training with maximal voluntary and imagined muscle contractions. *Journal of Neurophysiology, 67*(5), 1114–1123.

A damaged brain

Engelien, A., Huber, W., Silbersweig, D., Stern, E., Frith, C.D., Doring, W., Thron, A., & Frackowiak, R.S. (2000). The neural correlates of "deaf-hearing" in man: Conscious sensory awareness enabled by attentional modulation. *Brain, 123*(Pt. 3), 532–545.

Hearing changes in blood flow

Fulton, J.F. (1928). Observations upon the vascularity of the human occipital lobe during visual acuity. *Brain, 51*(Pt. 3), 310–320.

Measuring blood flow

Lassen, N.A., Ingvar, D.H., & Skinhoj, E. (1978). Brain function and blood flow. *Scientific American, 239*(4), 62–71.

Imagining walking along the street

Roland, P.E., & Friberg, L. (1985). Localization of cortical areas activated by thinking, *Journal of Neurophysiology, 53*(5), 1219–1243.

Imagining movement

Stephan, K.M., Fink, G.R., Passingham, R.E., Silbersweig, D., Ceballos-Baumann, A.O., Frith, C.D., & Frackowiak, R.S. (1995). Functional anatomy of the mental representation of upper extremity movements in healthy subjects. *Journal of Neurophysiology, 73*(1), 373–386.

The face area in the brain

Puce, A., Allison, T., Gore, J.C., & McCarthy, G. (1995). Face-sensitive regions in human extrastriate cortex studied by functional MRI. *Journal of Neurophysiology, 74*(3), 1192–1199.

Kanwisher, N., McDermott, J., & Chun, M.M. (1997). The fusiform face area: A module of extrastriate cortex specialized for face perception. *Journal of Neuroscience, 17*, 4302–4311.

The place (house) area in the brain

Epstein, R., & Kanwisher, N. (1998). A cortical representation of the local visual environment. *Nature, 392*(6676), 598–601.

Imagining faces and houses

O'Craven, K.M., & Kanwisher, N. (2000). Mental imagery of faces and places activates corresponding stiimulus-specific brain regions. *Journal of Cognitive Neuroscience*, *12*(6), 1013–1023.

An effect of culture on the brain

Paulesu, E., McCrory, E., Fazio, F., Menoncello, L., Brunswick, N., Cappa, S.F., Cotelli, M., Cossu, G., Corte, F., Lorusso, M., Pesenti, S., Gallagher, A., Perani, D., Price, C., Frith, C.D., & Frith, U. (2000). A cultural effect on brain function. *Nature Neuroscience*, *3*(1), 91–96.

Chapter 1

Neurons that represent to-be-attended information

Miller, E.K. (2000). The neural basis of the top-down control of visual attention in the prefrontal cortex. In S. Monsell & J. Driver (Eds.), *Control of cognitive processes: Attention and Performance 18*(pp. 511–534). Cambridge, MA: MIT Press.

Visual changes associated with migraine

Lashley, K. (1941). Patterns of cerebral integration indicated by scotomas of migraine. *Archives of Neurology and Psychiatry*, *46*, 331–339. (Also reprinted in: Kapur, N. (Ed.). (1997). *Injured brains of medical minds: Views from within* (pp. 121–127). Oxford: Oxford University Press.)

Vision in the brain

Zeki, S. (1993). *A vision of the brain*. Oxford; Boston, MA: Blackwell Scientific Publications.

Loss of color experience

Zeki, S. (1990). A century of cerebral achromatopsia. *Brain*, *113*(Pt. 6), 1721–1777.

Loss of motion experience

Zeki, S. (1991). Cerebral akinetopsia (visual motion blindness): A review. *Brain*, *114*(Pt. 2), 811–824.

Neuropsychology: The effects of brain damage on the mind

Broks, P. (2003). *Into the silent land: Travels in neuropsychology*. New York: Grove Press.

Learning a motor skill without any memory of doing so

Brooks, D.N., & Baddeley, A.D. (1976). What can amnesic patients learn? *Neuropsychologia, 14*, 111–122.

Patient DF

Goodale, M.A., & Milner, A.D. (2004). *Sight unseen*. Oxford: Oxford University Press.

Blindsight

Weiskrantz, L. (1990). *Blindsight: A case study and implications*. Oxford: Clarendon Press.

Musical hallucinations

Hammeke, T.A., McQuillen, M.P., & Cohen, B.A. (1983). Musical hallucinations associated with acquired deafness. *Journrnal of Neurology, Neurosurgery & Psychiatry, 46*(6), 570–572.

Charles Bonnet syndrome

ffytche, D.H. (2005). Visual hallucinations and the Charles Bonnet syndrome. *Current Psychiatry Reports, 7*(3), 168–179.

Scanning visual hallucinations

ffytche, D.H., Howard, R.J., Brammer, M.J., David, A., Woodruff, P., & Williams, S. (1998). The anatomy of conscious vision: An fMRI study of visual hallucinations. *Nature Neuroscience, 1*(8), 738–742.

Visual hallucinations in epilepsy

Panayiotololous, C.P. (1999). Elementary visual hallucinations, blindness, and headache in idiopathic occipital epilepsy: Differentiation from migraine. *Journal of Neurology, Neurosurgery & Psychiatry, 66*, 536–540.

Mize, K. (1980). Visual hallucinations following viral encephalitis: A self report. *Neuropsychologia, 18*(2), 193–202. ("Upon closing my eyes . . ." (pp. 31–32) from p. 194.) (Also reprinted in: Kapur, N. (Ed.). (1997). *Injured brains of medical minds: Views from within* (pp. 129–137). Oxford: Oxford University Press.)

Auditory hallucinations and epilepsy

Winawer, M.R., Ottman, R., Hauser, A., & Pedley, T.A. (2000). Autosomal dominant partial epilepsy with auditory features: Defining the phenotype. *Neurology, 54*, 2173–2176. ("Singing, music, voices . . ." (p. 32) from p. 2174.)

Hallucinations elicited by stimulating the brain

Penfield, W., & Perot, P. (1963). The brain's record of auditory and visual experience. *Brain*, *86*(Pt. 4), 595–696. ("[A] girl began . . ." (p. 32) from p. 629, Case 15; Case 21 (p. 33) from p. 634; Case 13 (p. 33) from pp. 627–628; Case 15 (p. 33) from p. 630.)

Hallucinogens

Huxley, A. (1959). *The doors of perception & Heaven and hell.* Harmondsworth: Penguin Books. ("This is how . . ." (p. 34) from p. 30; "brightly coloured . . ." (p. 34) from p. 38; Weir Mitchell (p. 34) from pp. 81–82.)

Hoffman, A. (1983). *LSD – My problem child* (J. Ott, Trans.) Los Angeles: J.P. Tarcher. ("Now, little by little . . ." and "My surroundings . . ." (p. 35) from Section 1.5, "Self-Experiments," available at: *http://www.flashback.se/archive/my_problem_child/chapter1.html#5.*)

The similarity of visual hallucinations from different sources

ffytche, D.H., & Howard, R.J. (1999). The perceptual consequences of visual loss: "Positive" pathologies of vision. *Brain*, *122*(Pt. 7), 1247–1260.

Hedgehogs on the ceiling

Manford, M., & Andermann, F. (1999). Complex visual hallucinations. *Brain*, *121*(Pt. 10), 1818–1840.

Deafness and ideas of persecution

Cooper, A.F. (1976). Deafness and psychiatric illness. *British Journal of Psychiatry*, *129*, 216–226.

Hallucinations in schizophrenia

Trosse, G. (1982). The Life of the Reverend Mr. George Trosse, Late Minister of the Gospel in the City of Exon, Who died January 11th, 1712/13. In the Eighty Second Year of His Age, Written by Himself and Publish'd According to His Order. Exon: Richard White, 1714. In D. Petersen (Ed.), *A mad people's history of madness* (pp. 26–38). Pittsburgh, PA: University of Pittsburgh Press. (Original work 1714.) ("I was haunted . . ." (p. 37) from p. 32; "I heard a Voice . . ." (p. 37) from pp. 29–30.)

King, L.P. (pseud.). (1964). Criminal complaints with probable causes (a true account). Bound, circular letter, ca. 1940. In B. Kaplan (Ed.), *The inner world of mental illness*. New York: Harper & Row. (Original work 1940.) ("I could see them nowhere . . ." (p. 38) from p. 134; "Were they ghosts? . . ." (p. 38) from pp. 134–136.)

Revising one's conception of reality

Chadwick, P.K. (1993). The stepladder to the impossible: A first hand pheno-menological account of a schizo-affective psychotic crisis. *Journal of Mental Health*, *2*(3), 239–250. ("I had to make sense . . ." (fn. 23) from p. 245.)

Chapter 2

Unconscious inferences

Helmholtz, H. von. (1866). *Handbuch der Physiologischen Optik*. Leipzig: Voss.
  Helmholtz, H. von. (1971). The facts of perception. In R. Kahl (Ed.), *Selected writings of Hermann von Helmholtz* (pp. 366–381). Middletown, CT: Wesleyan University Press. (Original work published 1878.) ("in order to avoid confusion . . ." (fn. 2) from p. 381.)

Change blindness

Rensink, R.A., O'Regan, J.K., & Clark, J.J. (1997). To see or not to see: The need for attention to perceive changes in scenes. *Psychological Science*, *8*(5), 368–373.
  Noë, A. (Ed.). (2002). Is the visual world a grand illusion? *Journal of Consciousness Studies*, special issue, *9*(5–6).

Subliminal perception

Marcel, A.J. (1983). Conscious and unconscious perception: An approach to the relations between phenomenal experience and perceptual processes. *Cognitive Psychology*, *15*(2), 238–300.
  Kunst-Wilson, W.R., & Zajonc, R.B. (1980). Affective discrimination of stimuli that cannot be recognized. *Science*, *207*(4430), 557–558.

Responding to fearful faces without awareness

Whalen, P.J., Rauch, S.L., Etcoff, N.L., McInerney, S.C., Lee, M.B., & Jenike, M.A. (1998). Masked presentations of emotional facial expressions modulate amygdala activity without explicit knowledge. *Journal of Neuroscience*, *18*(1), 411–418.

The amygdala responds to fearful faces

Morris, J.S, Frith, C.D., Perrett, D.I., Rowland, D., Young, A.W., Calder, A.J., & Dolan, R.J. (1996). A differential neural response in the human amygdala to fearful and happy facial expressions. *Nature*, *383*(6603), 812–815.

Unconscious detection of changes

Beck, D.M., Rees, G., Frith, C.D., & Lavie, N. (2001). Neural correlates of change detection and change blindness. *Nature Neuroscience*, 4(6), 645–650.

Synesthesia

Baron-Cohen, S., & Harrison, J.E. (Eds.). (1997). *Synaesthesia: Classical and contemporary readings*. Oxford: Blackwell. ("As a synaesthete . . ." (p. 51) from p. 269; "Listening to him . . ." (p. 51) from p. 103; "Of my two daughters . . ." (fn. 8) from p. 47; "Occasionally . . ." (p. 52) from p. 45.)

Mills, C.B., Boteler, E.H., & Oliver, G.K. (1999) Digit synaesthesia: A case study using a Stroop-type test. *Cognitive Neuropsychology*, 16(2), 181–191.

Examples of dreams

Jones, R.M. (1969). An epigenetic analysis of dreams. In M. Kramer (Ed.). *Dream psychology and the new biology of dreaming* (pp. 265–283). Springfield, IL: Charles C. Thomas. ("I dreamed I was coming into the room . . ." (p. 52) from p. 268.)

The physiology of dreaming

Hobson, J.A. (1988). *The dreaming brain*. New York: Basic Books.

REM sleep

Aserinsky, E., & Kleitman, N. (1953). Regularly occurring periods of eye motility, and concomitant phenomena, during sleep. *Science*, 118(3062), 273–274.

Recapitulation in dreams

Stickgold, R., Malia, A., Maguire, D., Roddenberry, D., & O'Connor, M. (2000). Replaying the game: Hypnagogic images in normals and amnesics. *Science*, 290(5490), 350–353. ("I see images . . ." (fn. 12) from p. 353.)

Chuang Tzu's dream as a butterfly

Borges, J.L. (1966). *Other inquisitions* (R.L.C. Simms, Trans.). New York: Washington Square Press. ("I dreamt I was a butterfly . . ." (p. 54) from p. 119.)

Descartes worries about dreams

Descartes, R. (1996). Meditations on First Philosophy – in which are demonstrated the existence of God and the distinction between the human soul and the body. First Meditation – what can be called into doubt. In J. Cottingham (Ed. and Trans.), *Descartes: Selected philosophical writings* (p. 13). Cambridge:

Cambridge University Press. (Original work published 1641.) ("I see plainly . . ."
(fn. 13) from p. 13.)

The bizarre content of dreams

Schwartz, S., & Maquet, P. (2002). Sleep imaging and the neuro-psychological
assessment of dreams. *Trends in Cognitive Sciences*, 6(1), 23–30. ("I had a talk . . ."
(p. 54) from p. 26.)

Fear in dreams

Revonsuo, A. (2003). The reinterpretation of dreams. In E.F. Pace-Schott, M.
Solms, M. Blagrove, & S. Harnad (Eds.), *Sleep and dreaming* (pp. 85–109).
Cambridge: Cambridge University Press.

Census of Hallucinations

Sidgwick, H. (with Johnson, A., Myers, F.W.H., Podmore, F., & Sidgwick,
E.M.). (1894). Report on the Census of Hallucinations. *Proceedings of the Society
for Psychical Research*, 10, 25–422. ("On October 5th, 1863 . . ." (p. 55) from
p. 256; "Have you ever . . ." (p. 56) from p. 33; "Among hallucinations of insane
persons . . ." (fn. 14) from p. 130; "I felt, more than I saw . . ." (p. 56) from
p. 161; "The hallucinations consisted of . . ." (p. 56) from p. 88; "Some years
ago . . ." (p. 57) from p. 178; "One evening at dusk . . ." (pp. 57–58) from
p. 95.)

Gladstone praises psychical research

Gauld, A. (1968). *The founders of psychical research*. London: Routledge & Kegan
Paul. ("It is the most important work . . ." (fn. 16) from p. 140.)

A hallucination of cats

Manford, M., & Andermann, F. (1999). Complex visual hallucinations. *Brain*,
121, 1818–1840. ("There seemed to be numerous cats . . ." (fn. 18) from p. 1823,
Case 3.)

Chapter 3

The rubber arm illusion

Botvinick, M., & Cohen, J. (1998). Rubber hands "feel" touch that eyes see.
Nature, 391(6669), 756.

The monkey and the rake

Iriki, A., Tanaka, M., & Iwamura, Y. (1996). Coding of modified body schema during tool use by macaque postcentral neurones. *Neuroreport*, 7(14), 2325–2230.

Lack of awareness of hand movements

Fourneret, P., & Jeannerod, M. (1998). Limited conscious monitoring of motor performance in normal subjects. *Neuropsychologia, 36*(11), 1133–1140.

Nielsen, T.I. (1963). Volition – a new experimental approach. *Scandinavian Journal of Psychology, 4*(4), 225–230.

Brain activity before will

Libet, B., Gleason, C.A., Wright, E.W., & Pearl, D.K. (1983). Time of conscious intention to act in relation to onset of cerebral activity (readiness-potential): The unconscious initiation of a freely voluntary act. *Brain, 106*(Pt. 3), 623–642.

Haggard, P., Newman, C., & Magno, E. (1999). On the perceived time of voluntary actions. *British Journal of Psychology, 90*(Pt. 2), 291–303.

Movement without awareness

Hallett, P.E., & Lightstone, A.D. (1976). Saccadic eye movements to flashed targets, *Vision Research, 16*(1), 107–114.

Pisella, L., Grea, H., Tilikete, C., Vighetto, A., Desmurget, M., Rode, G., Boisson, D., & Rossetti, Y. (2000). An "automatic pilot" for the hand in human posterior parietal cortex: Toward reinterpreting optic ataxia. *Nature Neuroscience, 3*(7), 729–736.

Roelofs illusion

Roelofs, C. (1935). Optische Localisation. *Archiv für Augenheilkunde, 109*, 395–415.

Bridgeman, B., Peery, S., & Anand, S. (1997). Interaction of cognitive and sensorimotor maps of visual space. *Perception and Psychophysics, 59*(3), 456–469.

Brain changes in songbirds

Nottebohm, F. (1981). A brain for all seasons: Cyclical anatomical changes in song control nuclei of the canary brain. *Science, 214*(4527), 1368–1370.

The phantom limb in the face

Ramachandran, V.S., Stewart, M., Rogers-Ramachandran, D.C. (1992). Perceptual correlates of massive cortical reorganization. *Neuroreport, 3*(7), 583–586.

Halligan, P.W., Marshall, J.C., Wade, D.T., Davey, J., & Morrison, D. (1993). Thumb in cheek? Sensory reorganization and perceptual plasticity after limb amputation. *Neuroreport, 4*(3), 233–236.

The woman with three arms

McGonigle, D.J., Hanninen, R., Salenius, S., Hari, R., Frackowiak, R.S., & Frith, C.D. (2002). Whose arm is it anyway? An fMRI case study of supernumerary phantom limb. *Brain, 125*(Pt. 6), 1265–74.

Denying disability (anosognosia)

Ramachandran, V.S. (1996). What neurological syndromes can tell us about human nature: Some lessons from phantom limbs, capgras syndrome, and anosognosia. *Cold Spring Harbor Symposia on Quantitative Biology*, *61*, 115–134. (Dialogue extracts (p. 75) from pp. 124–125.)

The anarchic hand

Marchetti, C., & Della Salla, S. (1998). Disentangling the alien and anarchic hand. *Cognitive Neuropsychiatry*, *3*, 191–208.

Is will an illusion?

Wegner, D.M. (2002). *The illusion of conscious will*. Cambridge, MA: Bradford Books.

Implementing arbitrary instructions without awareness

Varraine, E., Bonnard, M., & Pailhous, J. (2002). The top down and bottom up mechanisms involved in the sudden awareness of low level sensorimotor behavior. *Cognitive Brain Research*, *13*(3), 357–361.

Hypnotic amnesia

Estabrooks, G.H. (1957). *Hypnotism*. New York: E.P. Dutton & Co. ("We sit down . . ." (pp. 78–79) from p. 189.)
   Kopelman, M., & Morton, J. (2001). Psychogenic amnesias – functional memory loss. In G. Davies & T. Dalgleish (Eds.), *Recovered memories: The middle ground* (pp. 219–246). Chichester: John Wiley.

Word priming in amnesia

Shimamura, A.P. (1986). Priming effects of amnesia: Evidence for a dissociable memory function. *Quarterly Journal of Experimental Psychology*, A, *38*(4), 619–644.

Chapter 4

American infants learn Chinese by mere exposure

Kuhl, P.K., Tsao, F.M., & Liu, H.M. (2003). Foreign-language experience in infancy: Effects of short-term exposure and social interaction on phonetic learning. *Proceedings of the National Academy of Sciences USA*, *100*(15), 9096–9101.

Everything you could possibly want to know about the laboratory rat

Krinke, G.J. (Ed.). (2000). *The laboratory rat* (Handbook of Experimental Animals). London: Academic Press.

Pavlov's experiments

Pavlov, I.P. (1927). Lecture II. In *Conditioned reflexes* (G.V. Anrep, Trans.; pp. 17–32). London: Oxford University Press. (This can also be found in the very useful web resource Classics in the History of Psychology: *http://psychclassics.yorku.ca/Pavlov/lecture2.htm*.)

Color as a signal of fruit ripeness

Smith, A.C., Buchanan-Smith, H.M., Surridge, A.K., Osorio, D., & Mundy, N.I. (2003). The effect of colour vision status on the detection and selection of fruits by tamarins (*Saguinus spp.*). *Journal of Experimental Biology, 206*(18), 3159–3165.

Thorndike's experiments

Thorndike, E.L. (1911). An experimental study of associative processes in animals. In *Animal intelligence* (pp. 20–154). New York: Macmillan. (This can also be found in the very useful web resource Classics in the History of Psychology: *http://psychclassics.yorku.ca/Thorndike/Animal/chap2.htm*.)

How superstitions are learned

Skinner, B.F. (1948). "Superstition" in the pigeon. *Journal of Experimental Psychology, 38*(2), 168–172. (This can also be found in the very useful web resource Classics in the History of Psychology: *http://psychclassics.yorku.ca/Skinner/Pigeon/*.)

Learning can be better without awareness

Fletcher, P.C., Zafiris, O., Frith, C.D., Honey, R.A.E., Corlett, P.R., Zilles, K., & Fink, G.R. (2005). On the benefits of not trying: Brain activity and connectivity reflecting the interactions of explicit and implicit sequence learning, *Cerebral Cortex, 15*(7), 1002–1015.

Recording activity in single neurons

Hubel, D.H., & Wiesel, T.N. (1959). Receptive fields of single neurons in the cat's striate cortex. *Journal of Physiology, 148*(3), 574–591.

The synapse and more

LeDoux, J. (2002). *Synaptic self: How our brains become who we are*. New York: Viking.

Self-stimulation

Wise, R.A., & Rompre, P.P. (1989). Brain dopamine and reward. *Annual Review of Psychology, 40*, 191–225.

Reward prediction in the brain

Schultz, W. (2001). Reward signaling by dopamine neurons. *Neuroscientist, 7*(4), 293–302.

Barto, A.G. (1995). Adaptive critic and the basal ganglia. In J.C. Houk, J.L. Davis, & D.G. Beiser (Eds.), *Models of information processing in the basal ganglia* (pp. 215–232). Cambridge, MA: MIT Press.

Schultz, W., Dayan, P., & Montague, P.R. (1997). A neural substrate of prediction and reward. *Science, 275*(5306), 1593–1599.

Foraging in bees

Montague, P.R., Dayan, P., Person, C., & Sejnowski, T.J. (1995). Bee foraging in uncertain environments using predictive Hebbian learning. *Nature, 377*(6551), 725–728.

Playing backgammon

Tesuaro, G. (1994). TD-Gammon, a self-teaching backgammon program, achieves master-level play. *Neural Computation, 6*(2), 215–219.

Automatic preparation of action programs for grasping objects in the visual scene

Castiello U. (2005). The neuroscience of grasping. *Nature Reviews Neuroscience, 6*(9), 726–736.

Consciousness and the novel

Lodge, D. (2002). *Consciousness and the novel*. London: Secker & Warburg.

Learning about "unseen" stimuli

Morris, J.S., Öhman, A., & Dolan, R.J. (1998). Conscious and unconscious emotional learning in the human amygdala. *Nature, 393*(6684), 467–470.

The visual world stays still, despite eye movements

Helmholtz, H. von. (1866). *Handbuch der physiologischen Optik, Bd. 3.* Leipzig: Voss.
Bridgeman, B., Van der Hejiden, A.H.C., & Velichkovsky, B.M. (1994). A
theory of visual stability across saccadic eye movements. *Behavioral and Brain
Sciences, 17*(2), 247–292.

You can't tickle yourself

Weiskrantz, L., Elliott, J., & Darlington, C. (1971). Preliminary observations on
tickling oneself. *Nature, 230*(5296), 598–599.

Self-tickling doesn't activate the brain

Blakemore, S.J., Wolpert, D.M., & Frith, C.D. (1990). Central cancellation of
self-produced tickle sensation. *Nature Neuroscience, 1*(7), 635–640.

Active and passive movements

Weiller, C., Juptner, M., Fellows, S., Rijntjes, M., Leonhardt, G., Kiebel, S.,
Muller, S., Diener, H.C., & Thilmann, A.F. (1996). Brain representation of
active and passive movements. *Neuroimage, 4*(2), 105–110.

Learning through imagination

Yue, G., & Cole, K.J. (1992). Strength increases from the motor program:
Comparison of training with maximal voluntary and imagined muscle contractions. *Journal of Neurophysiology, 67*(5), 1114–1123.

Inverse and forward models

Wolpert, D.M., & Miall, R.C. (1996). Forward models for physiological motor
control. *Neural Networks, 9*(8), 1265–1279.

Helmholtz machines

Hinton, G.E., Dayan, P., Frey, B.J., & Neal, R.M. (1995). The "wake–sleep"
algorithm for unsupervised neural networks. *Science, 268*(5214), 1158–1161.

The story of IW

Cole, J. (1995). *Pride and a daily marathon.* Cambridge, MA: MIT Press.

Jaspers criticizes neuropsychology and psychoanalysis

Jaspers, K. (1956). On my philosophy. In W. Kaufman (Ed.), *Existentialism from
Dostoyevsky to Sartre* (pp. 131–158). New York: Penguin. (Original work published
1941.) ("brain mythology" and "mythology of psychoanalysis" (p. 109) from
p. 143.)

People with schizophrenia can tickle themselves

Blakemore, S.J., Smith, J., Steel, R., Johnstone, C.E., & Frith, C.D. (2000). The perception of self-produced sensory stimuli in patients with auditory hallucinations and passivity experiences: Evidence for a breakdown in self-monitoring. *Psychological Medicine*, *30*(5), 1131–1139.

Chapter 5

The neuron doctrine

Jones, E.G. (1994). The neuron doctrine 1891. *Journal of the History of the Neurosciences*, *3*(1), 3–20.

Cajal criticizes Golgi

Cajal, S.R. y. (1996). *Recollections of my life* (E.H. Craig, Trans., with the assistance of Juan Cano). Cambridge, MA: MIT Press. (Original work published 1937.) ("display of pride . . ." and "that was hermetically sealed . . ." (fn. 2) from p. 553.)

The development of information theory

Hartley, R.V.L. (1928). Transmission of information. *Bell System Technical Journal*, *7*, 535–563.
    Shannon, C.E. (1948). A mathematical theory of communication. *Bell System Technical Journal*, *27*, 379–423, 623–656.

Neurons as transmitters of information

McCulloch, W., & Pitts, W. (1943). A logical calculus of ideas immanent in nervous activity. *Bulletin of Mathematical Biophysics*, *5*, 115–133.

Bayes' theorem

Bayes, T. (1763). An essay towards solving a problem in the doctrine of chances. *Philosophical Transactions of the Royal Society of London*, *53*, 370–418.

Breast cancer screening controversy

Gotzsche, P.C., & Olsen, O. (2000). Is screening for breast cancer with mammography justifiable? *Lancet*, *355*(9198), 129–134.

When people behave irrationally

Sutherland, S. (1992). *Irrationality: The enemy within*. Harmondsworth: Penguin Books.

When being an ideal observer is not a good thing

Wolfe, J.M., Horowitz, T.S., & Kenner, N.M. (2005). Rare items often missed in visual searches. *Nature, 435*(7041), 439–440.

The brain as an ideal Bayesian observer

Ernst, M.O., & Banks, M.S. (2002). Humans integrate visual and haptic information in a statistically optimal fashion. *Nature, 415*(6870), 429–433.

Building models of the world

Kersten, D., Mamassian, P., & Yuille, A. (2004). Object perception as Bayesian inference. *Annual Review of Psychology, 55,* 271–304.

Evolution of color vision

Regan, B.C., Julliot, C., Simmen, B., Vienot, F., Charles-Dominique, P., & Mollon, J.D. (2001). Fruits, foliage and the evolution of primate colour vision. *Philosophical Transactions of the Royal Society of London, Series B – Biological Sciences, 356*(1407), 229–283.

Early visual experience hard-wires the brain

Hensch, T.K. (2005). Critical period plasticity in local cortical circuits. *Nature Reviews Neuroscience, 6*(11), 877–888.

What visual illusions tell us about perception

Gregory, R. (1997). *Eye and brain: The psychology of seeing* (5th ed.). Oxford: Oxford University Press. (1st ed. published 1966.)

Perceiving masks and hollow faces

Hill, H., & Bruce, V. (1993). Independent effects of lighting, orientation, and stereopsis on the hollow-face illusion. *Perception, 22*(8), 887–897.

Motion parallax (and other basic features of vision)

Gibson, J.J. (1950). *The perception of the visual world.* Boston, MA: Houghton Mifflin Co.

Illusions of color

Lotto, R.B., & Purves, D. (2002). The empirical basis of color perception. *Conscious Cognition, 11*(4), 609–629.

Filling in the blind spot

Ramachandran, V.S., & Gregory, R.L. (1991). Perceptual filling in of artificially induced scotomas in human vision. *Nature, 350*(6320), 699–702.

Seeing an A when it was really a B

Jack, A.I. (1998). Perceptual awareness in visual masking. Unpublished Psychology Ph.D., UCL. (shame, shame.)

The patient who cannot resist the sight of the turned-down bed-sheet

Lhermitte, F. (1986). Human autonomy and the frontal lobes. II. Patient behavior in complex and social situations: The "environmental dependency syndrome." *Annals of Neurology, 19*, 335–343. ("The patient . . . came to see me . . ." (p. 136) from p. 338.)

Attention activates sensory areas of the brain before the stimulus arrives

Kastner, S., & Ungerleider, L.G. (2001). The neural basis of biased competition in human visual cortex. *Neuropsychologia, 39*(12), 1263–1276.

An imagined Necker cube doesn't reverse

Chambers, D., & Reisberg, D. (1985). Can mental images be ambiguous? *Journal of Experimental Psychology: Human Perception and Performance, 11*(3), 317–328.

Chapter 6

Spoof paper

Sokal, A. (1996). Transgressing the boundaries: Toward a transformative hermeneutics of quantum gravity. *Social Text, 46/47*, 217–252.

Hermeneutics and cognitive science

Gallagher, S. (2004). Hermeneutics and the cognitive sciences. *Journal of Consciousness Studies, 11*(10–11), 162–174.

Biological motion

Johansson, G. (1973). Visual perception of biological motion and a model for its analysis. *Perception and Psychophysics, 14*(2), 201–211.

Pollick, F.E., Lestou, V., Ryu, J., & Cho, S.B. (2002). Estimating the efficiency of recognizing gender and affect from biological motion. *Vision Research*, *42*(20), 2345–2355.

Perception of biological motion in infants

Fox, R., & McDaniel, C. (1982). The perception of biological motion by human infants. *Science*, *218*(4571), 486–487.

Perception of biological motion in cats

Blake, R. (1993). Cats perceive biological motion. *Psychological Science*, *4*(1), 54–57.

Balls jumping over barriers

Gergely, G., Nadasdy, Z., Csibra, G., & Biro, S. (1995). Taking the intentional stance at 12 months of age. *Cognition*, *56*(2), 165–193.

The accuracy of detecting eye gaze direction

Anstis, S.M., Mayhew, J.W., & Morley, T. (1969). The perception of where a face or television "portrait" is looking. *American Journal of Psychology*, *82*(4), 474–489.

Using eye gaze direction to read minds

Lee, K., Eskritt, M., Symons, L.A., & Muir, D. (1998). Children's use of triadic eye gaze information for "mind reading." *Developmental Psychology*, *34*(3), 525–539.

Mirror neurons

Rizzolatti, G., & Craighero, L. (2004). The mirror-neuron system. *Annual Review of Neuroscience*, *27*, 169–192.

Giles de la Tourette's syndrome

Robertson, M.M. (2000). Tourette syndrome, associated conditions and the complexities of treatment. *Brain*, *123*(Pt. 3), 425–462.

Ambiguity of goal

Searle, J. (1984). *Minds, brains & science: The 1984 Reith Lectures*. British Broadcasting Corporation (published by Penguin Books in 1992).

Imitation of goals

Bekkering, H., Wohlschlager, A., & Gattis, M. (2000). Imitation of gestures in children is goal-directed. *Quarterly Journal of Experimental Psychology, Section A,* *53*(1), 153–164.

Gergely, G., Bekkering, H., & Kiraly, I. (2002). Rational imitation in preverbal infants. *Nature, 415*(6873), 755.

Interference from action observation

Kilner, J.M., Paulignan, Y., & Blakemore, S.J. (2003). An interference effect of observed biological movement on action. *Current Biology, 13*(6), 522–525.

Sharing disgust

Wicker, B., Keysers, C., Plailly, J., Royet, J.P., Gallese, V., & Rizzolatti, G. (2003). Both of us disgusted in My insula: The common neural basis of seeing and feeling disgust. *Neuron, 40*(3), 655–664.

The placebo effect in pain

Wager, T.D., Rilling, J.K., Smith, E.E., Sokolik, A., Casey, K.L., Davidson, R.J., Kosslyn, S.M., Rose, R.M., & Cohen, J.D. (2004). Placebo-induced changes in fMRI in the anticipation and experience of pain. *Science, 303*(5661), 1162–1167.

Empathy for pain

Singer, T., Seymour, B., O'Doherty, J., Kaube, H., Dolan, R.J., & Frith, C.D. (2004). Empathy for pain involves the affective but not sensory components of pain. *Science, 303*(5661), 1157–1162.

Flinching when you see a needle stuck into someone's hand

Avenanti, A., Bueti, D., Galati, G., & Aglioti, S.M. (2005). Transcranial magnetic stimulation highlights the sensorimotor side of empathy for pain. *Nature Neuroscience, 8*(7), 955–960.

Anticipation of pain

Ploghaus, A., Tracey, I., Gati, J., Clare, S., Menon, R., Matthews, P., & Rawlins, J. (1999). Dissociating pain from its anticipation in the human brain. *Science, 284*(5422), 1979–1981.

Cingulotomy reduces the unpleasantness of pain, but not the sensation

Folz, E.L., & White, L.E. (1962). Pain "relief" by frontal cingulotomy. *Journal of Neurosurgery, 19*, 89–100.

The brain binds causes to effects in action

Haggard, P., Clark, S., & Kalogeras, J. (2002). Voluntary action and conscious awareness. *Nature Neuroscience*, 5(4), 382–385.

Binding causes and effects in the actions of others

Wohlschlager, A., Haggard, P., Gesierich, B., & Prinz, W. (2003). The perceived onset time of self- and other-generated actions. *Psychological Science*, 14(6), 586–591.

Illusions of agency

Wegner, D.M., Fuller, V.A., & Sparrow, B. (2003). Clever hands: Uncontrolled intelligence in facilitated communication. *Journal of Personal Social Psychology*, 85(1), 5–19.

Green, G. (1994). Facilitated communication: Mental miracle or sleight of hand? *Skeptic*, 2(3), 68–76. (See also the resolution on facilitated communication from the American Psychological Association.)

Schizophrenia

Frith, C.D., & Johnstone, E.C. (2003). *Schizophrenia: A very short introduction.* Oxford: Oxford University Press.

Hallucinating a mental world

Cahill, C., & Frith, C.D. (1996). False perceptions or false beliefs? Hallucinations and delusions in schizophrenia. In P.W. Halligan & J.C. Marshall (Eds.), *Methods in madness* (pp. 267–291). Hove: Psychology Press. ("It tries to put jealousy within me . . ." (p. 158) from p. 281.)

Mellors, C.S. (1970). First-rank symptoms of schizophrenia. *British Journal of Psychiatry*, 117(536), 15–23. ("I look out the window . . ." (p. 158) from p. 17.)

The immunity principle

Gallagher, S. (2000). Self-reference and schizophrenia: A cognitive model of immunity to error through misidentification. In D. Zahavi (Ed.), *Exploring the self: Philosophical and psychopathological perspectives on self-experience* (pp. 203–239). Amsterdam/Philadelphia, PA: John Benjamins.

Chapter 7

Chinese poetry

Graham, A.C. (Ed.). (1977). *Poems of the late Tang.* Harmondsworth: Penguin.

The problem of translation

Quine, W.V.O. (1960). *Word and object*. Cambridge, MA: MIT Press.

How do we understand irony?

Sperber, D., & Wilson, D. (1995). *Relevance: Communication and cognition* (2nd ed.). Oxford: Blackwell. (1st ed. published 1986.)

The inverse problem in motor control

Flash, T., & Sejnowski, T.J. (2001). Computational approaches to motor control. *Current Opinions in Neurobiology, 11*(6), 655–662.

Harris, C.M., & Wolpert, D.M. (1998). Signal-dependent noise determines motor planning. *Nature, 394*(6695), 780–784.

The rehabilitation of prejudice

Gadamer H.-G. (1989). *Truth and method* (2nd rev. ed.; J. Weinsheimer & D.G. Marshall, Trans.). New York: Crossroad. (1st English ed. published 1975.)

Prejudice in children

Williams, J.E., Best, D.L., & Boswell, D.A. (1975). Children's racial attitudes in the early school years. *Child Development, 46*(2), 494–500.

Predicting what I will do next

Repp, B.H., & Knoblich, G. (2004). Perceiving action identity: How pianists recognize their own performances. *Psychological Science, 15*(9), 604–609.

Knoblich, G., & Flach, R. (2001). Predicting the effects of actions: Interactions of perception and action. *Psychological Science, 12*(6), 467–472.

Contagion: becoming like an older person

Bargh, J.A., Chen, M., & Burrows, L. (1996). Automaticity of social behavior: Direct effects of trait construct and stereotype-activation on action. *Journal of Personal Social Psychology, 71*(2), 230–244.

Motherese

Kuhl, P.K., Andruski, J.E., Chistovich, I.A., Chistovich, L.A., Kozhevnikova, E.V., Ryskina, V.L., Stolyarova, E.I., Sundberg, U., & Lacerda, F. (1997). Cross-language analysis of phonetic units in language addressed to infants. *Science, 277*(5326), 684–686.

Burnham, D., Kitamura, C., & Vollmer-Conna, U. (2002). What's new pussy cat? On talking to babies and animals. *Science, 296*(5572), 1435.

Imitation learning in mountain gorillas

Byrne, R.W., & Russon, A.E. (1998). Learning by imitation: A hierarchical approach. *Behavioral & Brain Sciences, 21*(5), 667–721.

Maestripieri, D., Ross, S.K., & Megna, N.L. (2002). Mother–infant interactions in western lowland gorillas (Gorilla gorilla gorilla). *Journal of Comparative Psychology, 116*(3), 219–227.

Babies know when their mothers are teaching them

Bloom, P. (2000). *How children learn the meanings of words.* Cambridge, MA: MIT Press.

Autistic children learn idiosyncratic words

Frith, U. (2003). *Autism: Explaining the enigma* (2nd ed.). Oxford: Blackwell.

Modeling the hidden states of other people

Wolpert, D.M., Doya, K., & Kawato, M. (2003). A unifying computational framework for motor control and social interaction. *Philosophical Transactions of the Royal Society of London, Series B – Biological Sciences, 358*(1431), 593–602.

Fear conditioning in the amygdala

LeDoux, J.E. (2000). Emotion circuits in the brain. *Annual Review of Neuroscience, 23*, 155–184.

Morris, J.S., Ohman, A., & Dolan, R.J. (1998). Conscious and unconscious emotional learning in the human amygdala. *Nature, 393*(6684), 467–470.

Fear conditioning by instruction

Phelps, E.A., O'Connor, K.J., Gatenby, J.C., Gore, J.C., Grillon, C., & Davis, M. (2001). Activation of the left amygdala to a cognitive representation of fear. *Nature Neuroscience, 4*(4), 437–441.

How brains read minds

Frith, C.D., & Frith, U. (1999). Interacting minds – a biological basis. *Science, 286*(5445), 1692–1695.

Grèzes, J., Frith, C.D., & Passingham, R.E. (2004a). Inferring false beliefs from the actions of oneself and others: An fMRI study. *Neuroimage, 21*(2), 744–750.

Grèzes, J., Frith, C.D., & Passingham, R.E. (2004b). Brain mechanisms for inferring deceit in the actions of others. *Journal of Neuroscience, 24*(24), 5500–5505.

The interpretation of voices in schizophrenia

Chadwick, P., & Birchwood, M. (1994). The omnipotence of voices: A cognitive approach to auditory hallucinations. *British Journal of Psychiatry, 164*(2), 190–201. ("Kill yourself . . ." (p. 179) from p. 194; "Be careful . . ." (p. 179) from p. 193.)

The overwhelming experience of schizophrenia

MacDonald, N. (1960). Living with schizophrenia. *Canadian Medical Association Journal, 82,* 218–221. ("The walk of a stranger . . ." (p. 179) from pp. 218–219.)

Sharing delusions (*folie à deux*)

Sacks, M.H. (1988). Folie à deux. *Comprehensive Psychiatry, 29*(3), 270–277. ("A 43-year-old housewife-writer . . ." (p. 181) from Case 1, pp. 275–276.)

The Jonestown massacre

Vankin, J., & Whalen, J. (1995). *The 60 Greatest Conspiracies of All Time.* Secaucus, NJ: Carol Publishing Group. ("On November 18, 1978 . . ." (p. 181) from p. 288; the transcript of Jim Jones' final speech is taken from "Alternative Considerations of Jonestown and Peoples Temple," sponsored by the Department of Religious Studies at San Diego State University: *http://Jonestown.sdsu.edu/.*)

Turner experiences a storm at sea

Clark, K. (1960). *Looking at pictures.* New York: Holt, Reinhart & Winston. ("got the sailors to lash me . . ." (p. 183) from p. 145.)

Epilogue

The narrator and I

Borges, J.L. (1964). Borges and I. In *Labyrinths: Selected stories and other writings* (pp. 246–247). New York: New Directions.

The will in the brain

Frith, C.D., Friston, K., Liddle, P.F., & Frackowiak, R.S.J. (1991). Willed action and the prefrontal cortex in man – a study with PET. *Proceedings of the Royal Society of London, Series B – Biological Sciences, 244*(1311), 241–246.

The effect of frontal lesions on willed action

Shallice, T. (1988). The allocation of processing resources: Higher-level control. In *From neuropsychology to mental structure* (pp. 328–352). Cambridge: Cambridge University Press.

Trying to please the experimenter by behaving unpredictably

Jahanshahi, M., Jenkins, I.H., Brown, R.G., Marsden, C.D., Passingham, R.E., & Brooks, D.J. (1995). Self-initiated versus externally triggered movements. I: An investigation using measurement of regional cerebral blood flow with PET and movement-related potentials in normal and Parkinson's disease subjects. *Brain, 118*(Pt. 4), 913–933.

Jenkins, I.H., Jahanshahi, M., Jueptner, M., Passingham, R.E., & Brooks, D.J. (2000). Self-initiated versus externally triggered movements. II: The effect of movement predictability on regional cerebral blood flow. *Brain, 123*(Pt. 6), 1216–1228.

The role of the experimenter in the participant's will

Roepstorff, A., & Frith, C. (2004). What's at the top in the top-down control of action? Script-sharing and "top-top" control of action in cognitive experiments, *Psychological Research, 68*(2–3), 189–198.

The first two-brain experiment

King-Casas, B., Tomlin, D., Anen, C., Camerer, C.F., Quartz, S.R., Montague, P.R. (2005). Getting to know you: Reputation and trust in a two-person economic exchange. *Science, 308*(5718), 78–83.

Getting rid of the homunculus

Monsell, S., & Driver, J. (2000). Banishing the control homunculus. In S. Monsell & J. Driver (Eds.), *Control of cognitive processes: Attention and Performance XVIII* (pp. 3–32). Cambridge, MA: MIT Press.

How can altruism evolve? Kin selection

Dawkins, R. (1976). *The selfish gene*. Oxford: Oxford University Press.

How can altruism evolve? Altruistic punishment

Boyd, R., Gintis, H., Bowles, S., & Richerson, P.J. (2003). The evolution of altruistic punishment. *Proceedings of the National Academy of Sciences USA, 100*(6), 3531–3535.

Haldane, J.B.S. (1999). Altruism. In K. Connolly & M. Margaret (Eds.), *Psychologically speaking: A book of quotations 10*. Leicester: BPS Books. ("I'd lay

---

down my life . . ." (fn. 6) from p. 10; originally *New Scientist*, September 8, 1974.)

The Dictator and Ultimatum Games

Henrich, J., Boyd, R., Bowles, S., Camerer, C., Fehr, E., & Gintis, H. (2004). *Foundations of human sociality: Economic experiments and ethnographic evidence from fifteen small-scale societies.* Oxford: Oxford University Press.

Altruistic punishment increases cooperation

Fehr, E., & Gächter, S. (2002). Altruistic punishment in humans. *Nature*, *415*(6868), 137–140.

We experience reward when we punish free riders

de Quervain, D.J., Fischbacher, U., Treyer, V., Schellhammer, M., Schnyder, U., Buck, A., & Fehr, E. (2004). The neural basis of altruistic punishment. *Science*, *305*(5688), 1254–1258.

We don't feel empathy for free riders

Singer, T., Seymour, B., O'Doherty, J.P., Stephan, K.E., Dolan, R.J., & Frith, C.D. (2006). Empathic neural responses are modulated by the perceived fairness of others. *Nature*, *439*(7075), 466–469.

Infants distinguish between accidents and deliberate acts

Shultz, T.R., Wells, D., & Sarda, M. (1980). Development of the ability to distinguish intended actions from mistakes, reflexes, and passive movements. *British Journal of Social and Clinical Psychology*, *19*(Pt. 4), 301–310.

We learn to dislike free riders

Singer, T., Kiebel, S.J., Winston, J.S., Dolan, R.J., & Frith, C.D. (2004). Brain responses to the acquired moral status of faces. *Neuron*, *41*(4), 653–662.

Illustrations and Text Credits

Illustrations

Color plate section

CP1: Thanks to Rosalind Ridley.

CP2: Thanks to Chiara Portas.

CP3: Panayiotopoulos, C.P. (1999). Elementary visual hallucinations, blindness, and headache in idiopathic occipital epilepsy: Differentiation from migraine. *Journal of Neurology, Neurosurgery and Psychiatry*, 66(4), 536–540. Reproduced with permission from the BMJ Publishing Group.

CP4: Figure 3 from: Schwartz, S., & Maquet, P. (2002). Sleep imaging and the neuro-psychological assessment of dreams. *Trends in Cognitive Science*, 6(1), 23–30. Copyright 2002, with permission from Elsevier.

CP5: Photo © 2004, Detroit Institute of Arts. Gift of Dexter M. Ferry, Jr. (46.309). Photo akg-images/Erich Lessing.

CP6: Colour illusion from R. Beau Lotto, Lottolab.

CP7: Tate Britain. Photo akg-images/Erich Lessing.

Figures

p.1: University of Wisconsin-Madison Brain Collection 69-314, *http://www.brainmuseum.org*. Images and specimens funded by the National Science Foundation, as well as by the National Institutes of Health.

p.2: Functional Imaging Laboratory; thanks to Chloe Hutton.

p.3: Figure 2 in: Engelien, A., Huber, W., Silbersweig, D., Stern, E., Frith, C.D., Doring, W., Thron, A., & Frackowiak, R.S. (2000). The neural correlates of "deaf-hearing" in man: Conscious sensory awareness enabled by attentional modulation. *Brain*, *123*(Pt. 3), 532–545. Used with permission.

p.4: Based on Figure 11.2 in: Zeki, S. (1993). A vision of the brain. Oxford: Blackwell. Reprinted by permission of Blackwell Publishing. Figure E1-3 in: Popper, K.R., & Eccles, J.C. (1977). *The self and its brain*. London: Routledge & Kegan Paul. Reprinted by kind permission of Lady Helena Eccles, on behalf of her late husband Sir John Eccles.

p.6: Functional Imaging Laboratory; thanks to David Bradbury.

p.7: Redrawn from Figures 1 and 3 in: Stephan, K.M., Fink, G.R., Passingham, R.E., Silbersweig, D., Ceballos-Baumann, A.O., Frith, C.D., Frackowiak, R.S. (1995). Functional anatomy of the mental representation of upper extremity movements in healthy subjects. *Journal of Neurophysiology*, *73*(1), 373–386. Used with permission.

p.8: Redrawn from Figure 3 in: O'Craven, K.M., & Kanwisher, N. (2000). Mental imagery of faces and places activates corresponding stiimulus-specific brain regions. *Journal of Cognitive Neuroscience*, *12*(6), 1013–1023.

1.1: Prof. W.S. Stark, Biology, St. Louis University, Missouri.

1.2: Figure 3.3 in: Zeki, S. (1993). *A vision of the brain*. Oxford, Boston: Blackwell Scientific Publications. Reprinted by permission of Blackwell Publishing.

1.3: Based on Figure 3.7 in: Zeki, S. (1993). *A vision of the brain*. Oxford, Boston: Blackwell Scientific Publications. Reprinted by permission of Blackwell Publishing.

1.4: Based on Lashley, K. (1941). Patterns of cerebral integration indicated by scotomas of migraine. *Archives of Neurological Psychiatry*, *46*, 331–339. Reprinted by permission of the American Medical Association, copyright © 1941, all rights reserved.

1.5: Lesion location: Plate 7; posting data: Figure 2.2 in Goodale, M.A., & Milner, A.D. (2004). *Sight unseen.* Oxford: Oxford University Press. Reprinted by permission of Oxford University Press – Journals.

1.6: Redrawn from data given in: ffytche, D.H., Howard, R.J., Brammer, M.J., David, A., Woodruff, P., & Williams, S. (1998). The anatomy of conscious vision: An fMRI study of visual hallucinations. *Natural Neuroscience, 1*(8), 738–742.

1.7: Case 2 (p. 613) from Penfield W., & Perot, P. (1963). The brain's record of auditory and visual experience. *Brain, 86*(Pt. 4), 595–696. By permission of Oxford University Press.

1.8: By permission of Comitè Jean Cocteau.

2.2: Ron Rensink: airplane: Department of Psychology, University of British Columbia.

2.3: Faces from: Ekman, P., & Friesen, W.V. (1976). *Pictures of facial affect.* Palo Alto, CA: Consulting Psychologists.

2.4: Figure 2 in: Whalen, P.J., Rauch, S.L., Etcoff, N.L., McInerney, S.C., Lee, M.B., & Jenike, M.A. (1998). Masked presentations of emotional facial expressions modulate amygdala activity without explicit knowledge. *Journal of Neuroscience, 18*(1), 411–418. Faces from: Ekman, P., & Friesen, W.V. (1976). *Pictures of facial affect.* Palo Alto, CA: Consulting Psychologists Press. Society for Neuroscience with the assistance of Stanford University's Highwire Press.

2.5: Drawn from data given in: Beck, D.M., Rees, G., Frith, C.D., & Lavie, N. (2001). Neural correlates of change detection and change blindness. *Nature Neuroscience, 4*(6), 645–656.

2.8: From p. 58 in: Wittreich, W.J. (1959). Visual perception and personality, *Scientific American, 200*(4), 56–60: photograph courtesy of William Vandivert. Used with permission of *Scientific American.*

2.9: Reprinted by permission of Eric H. Chudler, Ph.D.

3.2: Redrawn after Figure 1c: Obayashi, S., Suhara, T., Kawabe, K., Okauchi, T., Maeda, J., Akine, Y., Onoe, H., & Iriki, A. (2001). Functional brain mapping of monkey tool use. *Neuroimage, 14*(4), 853–861. Copyright 2001, with permission from Elsevier.

3.3: Redrawing of experiment in: Fourneret, P., & Jeannerod, M. (1998). Limited conscious monitoring of motor performance in normal subjects. *Neuropsychologia, 36*(11), 1133–1140.

3.4: Redrawing from data in: Libet, B., Gleason, C.A., Wright, E.W., & Pearl, D.K. (1983). Time of conscious intention to act in relation to onset of cerebral activity (readiness-potential): The unconscious initiation of a freely voluntary act. *Brain, 106*(Pt. 3), 623–642.

3.5: Redrawn after: Bridgeman, B., Peery, S., & Anand, S. (1997). Interaction of cognitive and sensorimotor maps of visual space. *Perception and Psychophysics, 59*(3), 456–469.

3.6: From Wright, Halligan and Kew, Wellcome Trust Sci Art Project, 1997. Used with permission.

3.7: Modified from: McGonigle, D.J., "The body in question: Phantom phenomena and the view from within."

3.8: Figure 2 in: Halligan, P.W., Marshall, J.C., Wade, D.T., Davey, J., & Morrison, D. (1993). Thumb in cheek? Sensory reorganization and perceptual plasticity after limb amputation. *Neuroreport, 4*(3), 233–236. Reprinted by permission of Lippincott, Williams and Wilkins.

3.9: Figure 2 in: Hari, R., Hanninen, R., Makinen, T., Jousmaki, V., Forss, N., Seppa, M., & Salonen, O. (1998). Three hands: Fragmentation of human bodily awareness. *Neuroscience Letters, 240*(3), 131–134. Copyright 1998, with permission from Elsevier.

3.10: Columbia Pictures, 1964.

4.1: RIA Novosti/Science Photo Library.

4.2: Robert M. Yerkes Papers. Manuscripts & Archives, Yale University Library.

4.4: Figure 3 in: Schultz, W. (2001). Reward signaling by dopamine neurons. *Neuroscientist, 7*(4), 293–302. Reprinted by permission of the publisher, Sage Publications.

4.5: Modified from: Bugmann, G. (1996, March 26–28). Value maps for planning and learning implemented in cellular automata. Proceedings of the 2nd International conference on adaptive computing in engineering design and control (ACEDC'96), Plymouth (pp. 307–309).

4.6: Redrawn after: Castiello, U. (2005). The neuroscience of grasping. *Nature Reviews Neuroscience*, *6*(9), 726–736.

4.7: From figures supplied by Sarah-Jayne Blakemore from data in: Blakemore, S.J., Wolpert, D.M., & Frith, C.D. (1990). Central cancellation of self-produced tickle sensation. *Nature Neuroscience*, *1*(7), 635–640.

4.8: M.C. Escher, *Hand with Reflecting Sphere*, 1935, lithograph. © 2006 The M.C. Escher Company–Holland. All rights reserved. *Http:// www.mcescher.com*.

5.1: Figure 117, Coupe tranversale du tubercule quadrijumeau antérieur; lapin âgé de 8 jours, Méthode de Golgi. In Cajal, S.R. y. (1901). *The great unraveled knot.* (From William C. Hall, Department of Neurobiology, Duke University Medical Center.)

5.2: From: Livingstone, M.S. (2000). Is it warm? Is it real? Or just low spatial frequency? *Science*, *290*(5495), 1299.

5.4: Kazimir Severinovich Malevich, *Black Square*, early 1920s (c.1923). St. Petersburg, State Russian Museum photo akg-images.

5.5: Photo taken by Professor Tony O'Hagan of Sheffield University.

5.6: From: Gesner, C. (1551). *Historia animalium libri I–IV. Cum iconibus. Lib. I. De quadrupedibus uiuiparis.* Zurich: C. Froschauer. Courtesy of the United States National Library of Medicine.

5.8: Professor Richard Gregory, Department of Experimental Psychology, University of Bristol. Reprinted by permission.

5.10: Necker cube: Necker, L.A. (1832). Observations on some remarkable optical phenomena seen in Switzerland; and on an optical phenomenon which occurs on viewing a figure of a crystal or geometrical solid. *The London and Edinburgh Philosophical Magazine and Journal of Science*, *1*(5), 329–337. Face/vase figure: Rubin, E. (1958). Figure and ground. In D. Beardslee & M. Wertheimer (Ed. and Trans.), *Readings in perception* (pp. 35–101). Princeton, NJ: Van Nostrand. (Original work published 1915.) Wife/mother-in-law figure: Boring, E.G. (1930). A new ambiguous figure. *American Journal of Psychology*, *42*(3), 444–445. (Originally drawn by the well-known cartoonist W.E. Hill, and reproduced in the issue of *Puck* for the week ending November 6, 1915.)

6.2: Redrawn from Figures 1 and 3 in: Gergely, G., Nadasdy, Z., Csibra, G., & Biro, S. (1995). Taking the intentional stance at 12 months of age. *Cognition*, *56*(2), 165–193. Copyright 1995, with permission from Elsevier.

6.3: Redrawn from Figure 1b, the Larry story, from: Lee, K., Eskritt, M., Symons, L.A., & Muir, D. (1998). Children's use of triadic eye gaze information for "mind reading." *Developmental Psychology*, *34*(3), 525–539. Reprinted by permission of the American Psychological Association and by permission of Kang Lee, Ph.D.

6.4: Part of Figure 2 from: Rizzolatti, G., Fadiga, L., Gallese, V., & Fogassi, L. (1996). Premotor cortex and the recognition of motor actions. *Cognitive Brain Research*, *3*(2), 131–141. Copyright 1996, with permission from Elsevier.

6.5: Figure 1 from: Bekkering, H., Wohlschlager, A., & Gattis, M. (2000). Imitation of gestures in children is goal-directed. *Quarterly Journal of Experimental Psychology, section A*, *53*(1), 153–164, by kind permission of the Experimental Psychology Society. Reprinted by permission of Professor Harold Bekkering and graph designer Christophe Lardschneider.

6.6: Figure 1 from: Gergely G., Bekkering, H., & Kiraly, I. (2002). Rational imitation in preverbal infants. *Nature*, *415*(6873), 755. Reprinted by permission of Macmillan Publishers Ltd: *Nature*, © 2006.

6.7: Figures 1 and 2 in: Kilner, J.M., Paulignan, Y., & Blakemore, S.J. (2003). An interference effect of observed biological movement on action. *Current Biology*, *13*(6), 522–525. Copyright 2003, with permission from Elsevier.

6.8: Reprinted with permission from Figures 2 and 3 in: Singer, T., Seymour, B., O'Doherty, J., Kaube, H., Dolan, R.J., & Frith, C.D. (2004). Empathy for pain involves the affective but not sensory components of pain. *Science*, *303*(5661), 1157–1162. Copyright 2004, AAAS.

6.9: Illustration from data in: Haggard, P., Clark, S., & Kalogeras, J. (2002). Voluntary action and conscious awareness. *Nature Neuroscience*, 5(4), 382–385.

7.2: Redrawn after: Knoblich, G., Seigerschmidt, E., Flach, R., & Prinz, W. (2002). Authorship effects in the prediction of handwriting strokes: Evidence for action simulation during action perception. *Quarterly Journal of Experimental Psychology, Section A*, 55(3), 1027–1046.

7.3: Reprinted with permission from Figure 1c from: Burnham, D., Kitamura, C., & Vollmer-Conna, U. (2002). What's new pussy cat? On talking to babies and animals. *Science*, *296*(5572), 1435. Copyright 2002, AAAS.

7.5: From Figure 1 and Figure 2a in: Morris, J.S., Ohman, A., & Dolan, R.J. (1998). Conscious and unconscious emotional learning in the human amygdala. *Nature*, *393*(6684), 467–470. Reprinted by permission of Macmillan Publishers Ltd: *Nature*, © 2006. Faces from: Ekman, P., & Friesen, W.V. (1976). *Pictures of facial affect*. Palo Alto, CA: Consulting Psychologists.

7.6: Figure 1 from: Grèzes, J., Frith, C.D., & Passingham, R.E. (2004a). Inferring false beliefs from the actions of oneself and others: An fMRI study. *Neuroimage*, *21*(2), 744–750; plots of data by author from: ibid. and Grèzes, Frith, C.D., & Passingham, R.E. (2004b). Brain mechanisms for inferring deceit in the actions of others. *Journal of Neuroscience*, *24*(24), 5500–5505.

e.1: Drawn from data in: Frith, C.D., Friston, K., Liddle, P.F., & Frackowiak, R.S.J. (1991). Willed action and the prefrontal cortex in man – a study with PET. *Proceedings of the Royal Society of London, Series B – Biological Sciences*, *244*(1311), 241–246.

e.2: Reprinted with permission from Supporting Online Material Figure 1 from: King-Casas, B., Tomlin, D., Anen, C., Camerer, C.F., Quartz,

S.R., & Montague, P.R. (2005). Getting to know you: Reputation and trust in a two-person economic exchange. *Science*, *308*(5718), 78–83. Copyright 2005, AAAS.

e.3: *Men in Black* © 1997 Columbia Pictures Industries, Inc. All Rights Reserved. Courtesy of Columbia Pictures.

e.4: Drawing to illustrate: Fehr, E., & Gächter, S. (2002). Altruistic punishment in humans. *Nature*, *415*(6868), 137–140.

Text

Extract from *Atonement* by Ian McEwan. Copyright © 2001 by Ian McEwan. Published by Jonathan Cape, and NanTalese/Doubleday. Used by permission of The Random House Group Limited, and Alfred A. Knopf, Canada.

Extract from "After Apple-Picking" from *The Poetry of Robert Frost* edited by Edward Connery Lathem. Copyright 1923, 1930, 1939, 1969 by Henry Holt and Company. Copyright 1958 by Robert Frost, copyright 1967 by Lesley Frost Ballantine. Reprinted in the US and Canada by permission of Henry Holt and Company, LLC and in the UK and Commonwealth (excluding Canada) by permission of The Random House Group Limited.

Every effort has been made to trace copyright holders and to obtain their permission for the use of copyright material. The publisher apologizes for any errors or omissions in the above list and would be grateful if notified of any corrections that should be incorporated in future reprints or editions of this book.

Index

7367 072

WITHDRAWN
OWENS LIBRARY
N.W.M.S.U